D1397426

DATE DUE			

WEST CAMPUS

CREATIVITY REVEALED

Discovering the
Source of Inspiration

Scott Jeffrey

CREATIVE CRAYON PUBLISHERS

Kingston, New York

Image of the "Accumulating deviation of results from chance expectations" on page 32 was recreated from the Global Consciousness Project. Printed with permission of Roger Nelson.

Image of "Lorenz's Butterfly" on page 87 was created by James P. Crutchfield. Printed with permission.

Dust jacket and interior illustrations by Jared McDaniel, Studio430.com

Creative Crayon Publishers
230 Kings Mall Court, Suite 142
Kingston, New York 12401

10-Digit ISBN: 0-9714815-5-5
13-Digit ISBN: 978-0-9714815-5-8
Library of Congress Control Number: 2008901056

Manufactured in the United States of America
Printed on recyled paper

To the Eternal Student
from whom creativity is
sure to flow

Contents

Foreword

Creativity is intrinsic to the evolution of life. It is the manifestation of the hidden substrate of all existence, termed "consciousness."

Upon examination, it becomes obvious that evolution and creation are actually one and the same phenomenon. The essence of life as creation is an expansion of the "Light" of Divinity. This creativity, which is a function of the Self, reflects the soul of mankind.

As explained further in this erudite book, creativity is an innate biological engine. It results in growth via the constant process of learning and assimilation of experience. Creativity is the result of the assimilation and progressive organization of information. Even a simple plant "knows" how to assimilate chemical or light energy for its survival. Creativity is the result of evolutionary learning that produces the linear from the ever-present energy field of the nonlinear.

Each human life is a result of a unique consequence of Creation. Through choices arise the probabilities of propensities classically termed "karma," or destiny. Thus, choice is a priority for the human condition.

Also innate to creativity is inspiration, which has historically been referred to as the "muse" whose influence is often primarily subliminal. Classically, the muse has been associated with the arts, but it is equally a critical factor in the sciences as represented, for instance, by Albert Einstein or the development of quantum physics.

Creativity is thus representative of the basic quality of "emergence" by which "becoming" is innate to the expression of intelligence. The mind of man is the energy field out of which arises the creation of a wide range of possibilities and solutions. Thus, whether to create that which is heavenly or hellish is the constant human option.

Creativity is thus the expression of freedom of the will and the arena of multitudinous options and choices. In the final consequence, the soul creates its own ultimate destiny. Thus arises the famous quotation from the *Rubaiyat of Omar Khayyam*:

> I sent my Soul through the Invisible
> Some letter of that After-life to spell:
> And by and by my Soul returned to me,
> And answered, "I Myself am Heaven and Hell."

David R. Hawkins, MD, PhD
Director, Institute of
Advanced Spiritual Research

Preface

Be prepared for anything. If I've learned anything on this journey, it's that the landscape keeps changing. Holding onto "what seems to be" only blocks a deeper understanding of *what is*. As Ralph Waldo Emerson aptly noted in his essay "Circles," "Everything looks permanent until its secret is known."

With the willingness to learn and grow, what we *think* we know often morphs into a higher realization. From this higher viewpoint, or what we'll call Higher Ground, everything you thought you knew looks completely different—your thoughts and beliefs hold new meaning within the profound re-contextualization of Higher Ground.

So all I can say is be prepared.

This book was originally a text on results planning and strategic thinking for executives. As the topic was pursued further, it became obvious that an explanation of the nature of thoughts and the act of thinking was needed. This led to the realization that an innate, but often hidden quality of creativity is a more pertinent topic to explore for today's highly-intelligent, ultra-busy professional. By understanding what makes up or determines our creative nature, we can more freely manifest our greatest human potential.

This book is not an academic look at creativity—there are far more qualified researchers to write such a book—nor is this designed to be a workshop on creativity. Instead, this book presents the concept of creativity from an expanded, philosophically-unique lens that incorporates advanced theoretical science, the so-called New Science, and a spiritual understanding of consciousness (or subjective awareness). To fully understand our creative nature, this unusual dialogue will require us to examine the nature of our perception, our thoughts, and even existence itself.

Thoughts, as we all know, are powerful. There's good reason why we say, "Be careful what you wish for." Our thoughts tend to manifest in the physical world—for better or for worse. We want to understand how this manifestation unfolds and the role we play in this manifestation. Understanding the nature of creativity will help us attract it more effortlessly into our lives, for the betterment of humanity.

Much of this information requires a foundational understanding to make it relevant and comprehensible. As a conesquence of a book's linear page-by-page nature, it's difficult to present the necessary context for each core idea without toggling back and forth between sections. To help you assimilate these concepts, the work has been divided into two parts or Books. *Book I: The Farthest Reaches of Thought* provides the framework for understanding your thoughts as they relate to perceiving both your inner world and the observable, physical domain. We'll discuss the old paradigm that pervaded our Western thinking for the past three centuries, as well as the new paradigm that has emerged over the last 80 years. The discussion on creativity in *Book I* is limited. Instead, we'll focus on understanding the mind, how thinking manifests, and the phenomenon of consciousness itself. *Book I* provides the necessary framework for comprehending the creative process as outlined in *Book II: Uncovering the Creative Impulse.* These two sections should be read sequentially. (My apologies to all you highly nonlinear creative types who hate following a predetermined order. Wading through the far-reaching content of *Book I* will be worth the payout of *Book II.*)

The appendices and additional notes are provided for advanced students or those interested in delving deeper into the information. Concise definitions of the terms used are provided in the glossary (appendix D).

Exploring the nature of thought is exhilarating for some, frightening for others. This journey requires us to lay aside our beliefs and assumptions—to suspend what we've presumed to be true. We've become accustomed to believing what others tell us and what we read. We all observe, however, the errors mankind continues to make through its evolutionary journey. The alternative approach to the hearsay of others is the inward search through the process of self-inquiry—an introspective stance that allows insights to arise from an inner knowingness as opposed to an intellectual connection of thoughts.

Self-knowledge guided by universal truths can help remove certain inner barriers that exist within our belief systems and reality distortions (beliefs we have about "how things are" based upon our experience) that hinder our growth and evolution. Techniques for creativity are useless if the blockades to the creative impulse aren't removed. We want a deeper understanding to clear our path.

How you apply this knowledge is up to you. I hope that it enriches your life experiences, and uplifts the lives of those around you.

To your Creative Journey,

Scott Jeffrey
Upstate New York

Introduction

A brief introduction of today's cultural climate and the emerging Creative Professionals

The Dawning of the Creative Age

Have you considered what differentiates Man from the rest of the animal kingdom? Appearances aside (we share over 98% of our genetic makeup with chimps[1]), the most noteworthy difference between Man and other animals is the intellect—the capacity for thinking and higher functioning—rooted in the prefrontal cortex.[2] This intelligence gives Man the prowess to "dominate" the rest of the animal kingdom, despite being surrounded by creatures of far greater strength, speed, stamina, and sensory acuity.

This capacity for thinking is more pronounced in today's hyper-advancing society than in any prior period in history. The currency we exchange is no longer tangible like produce, machines, or even technology. In the past, farmers learned how to farm from their ancestors, the "secrets of the land" passed down by family members for generations. Factory workers were trained step-by-step how to perform their jobs. Today, we exchange information—words, systems, abstract concepts, thoughts and ideas. (Consider the 21st-century value of a company like Google.com, which helps us search, find, catalog, and target information more efficiently.)

What of today's knowledge workers, whose jobs are primarily to gather information, interpret data in new ways and draw new conclusions? Basically, knowledge workers are paid to *think* and manifest new ideas, yet ironically, in the Age of Information, we aren't taught how to *create* the currency that dominates our lives, causing modern thinkers like Abraham Maslow and David Bohm to acknowledge our "crisis of creativity."[3]

The father of humanistic psychology, Abraham Maslow, was passionate about the exploration of creativity:

Only recently have we become aware, fully aware, from our studies of healthy people, of the creative process, of play, of aesthetic perception, of the meaning of healthy love, of healthy growing and becoming, of healthy education, that every human being is both poet and engineer, both rational and nonrational, both child and adult, both masculine and feminine, both in the psychic world and in the world of nature. Only slowly have we learned what we lose by trying daily to be only and purely rational, only "scientific," only logical, only sensible, only practical, only responsible. Only now are we becoming quite sure that the integrated person, the fully evolved human, the fully matured person, must be available to himself at both these levels, simultaneously.[4]

Maslow understood the need to let go of the intellect from time to time to allow what William Blake called "Poetic Genius" to flow through us. Creativity represents a profound quality of what it is to be human while also connecting us to that Source beyond humanness. As anyone who has ever experienced even a moment of true inspiration can attest, creativity is the gateway to the Divine.

Perhaps what lies beyond the Information Age is the Creative Age. With complete access to a virtually unlimited database of worldwide, cross-cultural information (thanks in large part to the Internet), isn't it only natural that we would continue to evolve, liberating the mind to dream, adapt, change, and pioneer?

Interestingly, creativeness, the quality of being creative, is one of the reasons why it's impossible to predict future events, especially in terms of the economy and overall marketplace. The definition often used for economics is *the allocation of scarce resources.* Economist Paul Zane Pilzer astutely debunks this definition, explaining that it doesn't take into account human ingenuity.[5] Human creativeness and ingenuity change the playing field from a finite list of possibilities to a new context of unlimited potentiality. For example, we turned whale blubber into a source of fuel before discovering oil, and we transformed sand into silicon chips that power our computers.

There may have been an era when creative thinking was unnecessary, when just "doing your job" as prescribed by convention was enough. Not today. This Creative Age is governed by new paradigms: with the information age charging ahead at an ever-increasing speed, we must become Masters of the Mind to navigate the demanding, turbulent current toward our chosen ports.

WHO IS TODAY'S CREATIVE PROFESSIONAL?

This book is written especially for the Creative Professional—today's knowledge worker who *thinks* for a living. Surprisingly, a great many of us fall into this category. Business executives, marketers, technologists, educators, designers, managers, small business owners, organizational leaders, psychologists, writers, speakers, coaches, consultants—the list of today's "thinkers" encompasses more than philosophers and scientists.

As Creative Professionals, we often have specialized knowledge in niche arenas. As the collective knowledge of mankind increases, the ability to master an entire field is becoming more difficult. As a consequence, we now have fields within fields of specialization. For example, thirty years ago, an alternative health-care practitioner may have utilized acupuncture, body work, energy medicine, herbology, and even psychotherapy. Now, an alternative healthcare practitioner likely specializes in one of these inter-disciplines because of the vast body of knowledge required for training and certifications, which generally restricts "mastery" of the entire alternative healthcare field. A "renaissance" person like Leonardo da Vinci, who studied topics as diverse as art, science, anatomy, botany, and engineering, is uncommon in our modern, information age.

In a chaotic, ever-changing society, many Creative Professionals are paid to combine their knowledge and creative intuition to help their clients, customers and team members achieve a desired result. The standard corporate hierarchy with specific roles and responsi-bilities for its employees is not the optimal model. Instead, smart businesses are now moving toward a highly flexible project team infrastructure where individual responsibilities rotate based on the needs of a particular project.[6] This development towards a "systems theory" approach to business—where the team operates in an organic fashion with less rigidity and fragmentation—is a natural corporate evolution to help keep up with an increasingly complex, dynamic world.[7]

Additionally, Creative Professionals aren't driven exclusively by personal gain. Instead, we receive great satisfaction from supporting the entire team. Anita Roddick, founder and president of the Body Shop International, exemplifies this shift: "I don't want our success to be measured only by financial yardsticks.

What I want to be celebrated for is how good we are to our employees and our community. It's a different bottom line."[8]

Beyond financial gain, Creative Professionals want to feel a sense of appreciation, connection, and belonging. When the team wins, everyone wins. Essentially, the corporate ladder is collapsing. Sure, there are still those driven solely by personal achievement and financial gain, but they represent a dying breed.

Creative Professionals are motivated to contribute and to serve others. As a consequence, organizations are governed less by control and delegation since Creative Professionals typically possess internal accountability for solving problems and completing projects.

Creatives also tend to gravitate toward a higher quality of life, with less stress and more freedom. The go-go-go days of the 80s and 90s seem to be morphing into an appreciate-the-beauty mentality. We once stood impatiently, waiting for our microwaves to defrost a frozen dinner. Now, our kitchens are becoming culinary laboratories to test and delight in exotic cuisine (the Food Network is distributed to over 90 million households in the United States[9]).

We once took pride in late hours at the office. Now, we're prone to leaving work early to pursue some form of personal exploration: yoga, dance, art, music, martial arts, foreign languages, cooking, wine tasting, sports, meditation, volunteering, or walks with our dogs. (Think about the wild proliferation of specialized classes at your local gym over the last decade. Also, distance-learning and continuing education programs at universities have become a multi-billion dollar industry.)

A profound shift in ecological awareness is guiding the Creative Professional. Feeling connected to the planet and having concern for future generations, we are turning away from the strictly profit-driven enterprise model, as testified by the proliferation of "green companies" that support the environment while still growing profitable businesses. The emergence of energy companies utilizing recycled material and global organizations dedicated to environmental preservation as well as the growing move away from pesticides to organic farming are all signs of this ecological shift in awareness.

As a collective, we've also embraced the notion of "spirituality," although we often don't label it as such (especially in business). Instead, we use terms like *integrity* and *trust*. Customers and investors alike are fed up with deceptive corporate maneuvers that lack integrity (think Enron, Worldcom, and Martha Stewart), and are choosing instead to conduct business only with companies they trust. This explains why corporations like Apple and Southwest Airlines continue to grow profitable businesses in highly competitive markets—they love their customers and continue to deliver their promises on a consistent basis.

The Creatives are responding to a higher calling that has been awakened in their collective soul: a return to simplicity, beauty, growth and nature, and a longing for a life filled with richness beyond monetary and material gain. A person's lifestyle is becoming increasingly more important than his or her status in the business community. Thanks to the connectedness provided by the Internet, over 20 million American business owners telecommute.[10]

Authors Sherry Anderson and Paul Ray have profiled a new category of people, termed the "Cultural Creatives," which, according to their study, represents roughly 50 million progressive men and women in the U.S. alone (approximately 26% of the population and growing) who are prioritizing a shift toward a more peaceful, spiritual life.[11] The Creative Professional is likely to resonate with this segment of the population.

The Creatives share a new frustration with society's intrinsic structure: our longing for freedom clashes with the boundless onslaught of information in the form of major projects, back-to-back meetings, conference calls, emails, instant messages (IMs), text messages, and telephone interruptions that relentlessly command our attention. We are required to achieve more significant objectives (often requiring greater creativity) on shorter deadlines, and we are completely swamped! As a consequence, we're overwhelmed, fighting against time, pushing deadlines, barely staying afloat. Further, as we'll learn in this treatise, our innate drive to "stay busy" conflicts with our desire for freedom. It's truly amazing we survive at all.

Our overall level of productivity is, in many ways, determined by our ability to achieve creative results in the wake of chaotic events involving family, work, politics, or world affairs. Those that have learned to attune to a higher degree of creativity can focus on their craft without becoming distracted by the infinite attention-demanding obstacles of daily life that never stop materializing. How does one attune to higher creativity? And what exactly does that mean? We'll explore these questions in what follows.

A deeper understanding of the creative impulse helps today's knowledge workers transcend distraction and tap into higher creativity. Let's begin …

AUTHOR'S NOTE

If we attempt to examine creativity under the dominant lens through which most of us view the world, this topic is likely to remain mysterious and confusing. So before we begin exploring the creative impulse, it's helpful to first understand our lens. To do this, we must set our beliefs and assumptions aside—at least momentarily. A great deal of what will be discussed throughout this text may directly contrast with what you firmly believe to be true. I don't expect you to take these words as truth simply based on my recommendation; rather, consider this perspective with an open mind and heart, only accepting new knowledge as provisionally true until you seek the answers from within.

BOOK I
The Farthest Reaches of Thought

We begin with an exploration of the ethereal nature of thought. Understanding the nature of perception and how we think helps reveal unconscious, limiting "programs" that control our worldview. Bringing these programs to light paves the way for an understanding of our conscious awareness, which is the precursor to discovering the anatomy of the creative impulse.

The subject of creativity covers a magnificently vast landscape. To attempt to understand this expansive field, we must first build a high tower with a strong foundation so we can climb up and view the entire landscape. Book I provides this necessary infrastructure, so the discussion about the creative impulse will be limited until we reach Book II. Then, we can survey the wondrous fields with reverence and marvel.

Chapter 1
Collective Mind

There is a theory which states that if ever anyone discovers exactly what the Universe is for and why it is here, it will instantly disappear and be replaced by something even more bizarre and inexplicable.

There is another which states that this has already happened.

—Douglas Adams, *The Restaurant at the End of the Universe*

BONDS OF PERCEPTION

At first glance, there appears to be two worlds: the external "out there" world and our internal "in here" experience. As human beings, we have a tendency of assuming these two worlds are one and the same even though they are not. The external world is translated for our internal experience via *perception*. Let's explore how perception works.

Consider the eyesight of the red-tailed hawk: his range is over ten times greater than our human range, allowing the hawk to identify mice and other prey where we would see only grass and fields. Peer over this book to your surrounding environment. Focus on a particular object like a glass of water or a tree you can see through a window. Now, imagine magnifying that image, doubling its size. What features would you notice? How would your peripheral vision change? How would your experience of the object and everything else in the room be altered? Obviously, the hawk's experience of the world as a consequence of this single difference (vision times ten) is difficult for us to comprehend.

A more startling comparison of perception is found between humans and our canine companions. Dogs have approximately 200 million sensory receptors in their noses, while we have only around five million.[1] Like the hawk's enhanced vision, it's difficult to imagine what our overall sensory experience would be like if our sense of smell doubled, let alone increased by 40 times. When a dog inhales an autumn breeze, he's taking in a world beyond our experiential reality. We can't accurately conceptualize how this sensory difference would affect our perception of something as simple as smelling an old couch.

What about the sensory experience of each human being? Do we each experience the same reality? Human perception requires an organ like the eye or nose to communicate information from the outside world for our internal interpretation. We tend to believe that our perception of things and events is what's *real*. We think we each observe the same events in the same way. From our mind's perspective, our perception represents an accurate reality.[2] Consider, however, that DNA testing has demonstrated that over 50 percent of eyewitness accounts have resulted in wrongful convictions.[3] Our individual perception is actually a weak interpretation of what can be called Reality (with a capital "R").

Professor of Psychiatry at Duke University Roy Mathew explains:

> Contrary to popular belief, perception is highly subjective. The brain attempts to make sense out of the crude sensory information decoded from the electrical impulses it receives. Expectancy, anticipation, mood, and so on determine

perception to a considerable degree. What the brain sees and what falls on the retina are often not identical. There is a whole lot more to seeing than simple image reconstruction.[4]

Sensory signals from our five senses interacting with environmental stimuli like the wind current, sunlight, or a unique aroma are sent to the brain via the nervous system. In a matter of milliseconds, the brain processes and translates this information from the outside world. The process of perception utilizes *space* to evaluate qualities like distance, direction, dimension, and size, as well as *time* to process the information it assimilates from the outside world. Both space and time, as Einstein noted, are *relative*, leading him to call our experience of reality "a kind of optical delusion."[5]

Through our perceptual filters, we are unable to see things as they truly are. For example, when you look at the book you're holding, what do you *really* see? When you look at this book, are you not instantly accessing past experiences that include sitting and reading books? Doesn't your mind spontaneously associate memories of other books you have read and the meanings you've linked to those books? How else would you know to call it a book, what its function is, or what to do with it? Consider how a baby would interact with this book: putting it on his head, trying to eat the pages, drooling on the cover, ripping it apart.

Memories of past experiences, assumptions, projected meanings, beliefs, stored information, and significant connections happen so quickly in our mind that we're generally unaware of the process. With all of these internal connections firing sub-consciously, how can we experience things "as they are"? As bizarre as this may sound, we're not experiencing Reality—rather, we're processing our perception of reality, a poor simulation at best.

The Buddhist story of the six blind men and the elephant demonstrates our experience of reality. Six blind men who had heard about the massive size and demeanor of an elephant wanted to experience one firsthand. Coming upon the great beast, one man reached out and touched the animal's leg. "The elephant is like a tree," he exclaimed.

A second blind man felt the breeze from the flapping of the elephant's ear. "An elephant is like a fan."

Another man bumped into the animal's flank, declaring, "It's solid as a wall!"

A fourth man related the squirming trunk to a snake. The fifth man grasped the elephant's swinging tail and likened the elephant to a rope. And the sixth man caught hold of the tusk and announced, "The elephant is like a spear."

All six blind men who experienced a very real part of the elephant assumed they knew *elephant*. Based on a very limited perspective, their minds made associations to other objects available in memory and then applied those connections to the new experience. *Elephant* was now cataloged into groups like tree or fan, which have their own projected meanings based on beliefs and past experiences.

It's easy to say, *Yeah, but I don't do that. I see the whole elephant.* The story illustrates a fundamental flaw in perception. Due to the nature of our thoughts, experienced through the lens of perception, we're restricted to experiencing only a fragment of reality.

Plato gave us another powerful illustration of the limiting qualities of perception with his famous cave allegory.[6] A group of human beings having their bodies and heads bound since birth face the back wall of a cave. They can't see each other or what's behind them. Growing up bound in the deep, dark cave, they've never experienced life outside. Far behind them, a fire rages and in front of the fire is a path where free people frequently pass. The light from the fire projects images of the passersby onto the cave wall that our restrained friends are able to see.

So what do our friends observe? Seeing the projection of these people onto the wall, wouldn't they perceive the images to be "real"? With no prior experience of three-dimensional people (because they were bound with their heads facing the cave wall, not toward each other), how could they distinguish between the projected, two-dimensional images on the wall and the actual, three-dimensional people walking behind them in the distance?[7]

Plato effectively illustrates the challenge we face with perception. Could we, as human beings, be the ones bound and tied, observing the projections on the wall and considering them reality? Certainly, *we* couldn't be that blind to our own ignorance. For millennia, sages from all the great traditions—those rare Self-realized souls—have been telling us the answer is YES!

You may be familiar with the optical illusion called "My Wife and My Mother-in-Law."[8] Take a moment to focus on the image on the following page. When you look at the image for the first time, you'll either see a young lady or an elderly woman. The young lady is turning her head away from you, wearing a hat with a feather and a necklace. Refocusing on the image, an old woman emerges, facing you. The young lady's chin morphs into the elderly woman's nose and the necklace changes into the older woman's mouth. Magic!

MY WIFE AND MY MOTHER-IN-LAW

With practice, you can consciously shift back and forth between the two women. Which perspective is "real"? Well, whichever one you're experiencing at the moment, of course. But does that negate the reality of the other image? Don't both images exist simultaneously?

Why is this discussion important? First, an understanding of the faulty nature of perception tends to foster humility, which is a prerequisite for understanding creativity. The mind secretly thinks it's infallible, but honest observation and logical inquiry reveal otherwise. Plato's teacher, Socrates, accurately noted that man is intrinsically innocent because he can only choose what he perceives to be good, unable to discern the true good from the false illusions of the world.[9] Ever consider how two seemingly intelligent people can hold diametrically opposing positions on controversial topics like politics or religion? Or consider how some people are able to justify acts of violence with rationalizations devoid of basic logic.

With humility, we are less likely to canonize our thoughts and experiences. We are less likely to say, "This is how it is. I'm right and you're wrong." Old perceptions fade into greater awareness with an expanded perspective—Higher Ground. We're even able to "see" or notice things we didn't see before. My mother is always amazed by my father's inability to see things right under his nose. If you don't want to see the saltshaker, it's very possible to make it disappear from perception through a lack of focus of what is present.

The fragmented experience of the mind can be transformed into an array of infinite colors and hues. Think of a purple wildflower growing on the side of the road. To a botanist or nature lover, this is a wondrous flower—a symbol of beauty, variety, and splendor. To a landscaper, it's a weed. With greater awareness, we are able to see and appreciate both perspectives, along with their various shades of reality in between.

By staying flexible in your perspective, you open yourself to discovering a vastly different world that's right under your nose. With humility, our perception can transform to accommodate a Reality of boundless beauty. As Blake envisioned, "If the doors of perception were cleansed, everything would appear to man as it is, infinite."[10]

For right now, keep in mind that perception can be tricky and often inaccurate, giving us a little less certainty that we're experiencing true Reality.

WHAT ARE THOUGHTS?

Thought is the primary tool employed by our perceptual faculties to interpret the world around us. Have you ever considered the structure or plethora of thought? Psychologists estimate we each have approximately 50,000 thoughts per day. (If this sounds inconceivable, close your eyes and try counting all the random thoughts that float through your awareness in 60 seconds.) When you consider this staggering number, it's amazing that we can defy distraction to communicate coherently or accomplish any task at all.

Asking *What are thoughts?* seems to present a kind of paradox or circular dialogue. To answer the question requires the very thing we're trying to define—thinking. *Thinking* is the act of using thought. Well, that's a nice distinction, but it brings us no closer to understanding what *thinking* or *thoughts* are. The question and the answer are comprised of thoughts as well. This dilemma is similar to one created when we try to define a word using the same word, like defining *sculpting* as the act of making a sculpture.

Thinking generally happens in the background. Thinking, like breathing, seems so innate to us that we rarely take time to understand or examine its subtle nature. We know we constantly have thoughts. We also have the sense that not all thoughts are equal. Higher quality thoughts are generally associated with intelligence; novel thoughts may be linked to creativity; and truly extraordinary thoughts are often associated with genius. Still other thoughts can be viewed as harmful to oneself and possibly others. In business, we might say that higher quality thoughts about better serving the customer can help a business grow, while exploitative or greedy thoughts can lead a company to bankruptcy. Society seems to value the utilitarian function of thoughts, but it doesn't occur to us to inspect the nature of our thoughts: *What are they? How do they arise? Do they have a true function? What is their meaning?*

In *Hamlet*, William Shakespeare proposed, "For there is nothing either good or bad but thinking makes it so."[11] Roman Emperor, Marcus Aurelius Antoninus said in *Meditations*, "The world is nothing but change. Our life is only perception."[12]

The world's great traditions seem to teach a similar concept. Buddha said, "Our life is shaped by our mind; we become what we think."[13] The Bible gives us the proverb, "For as he thinketh in his heart, so is he."[14]

Literature throughout the ages, from every religion and philosophy around the world, has preached this tenet: *thoughts are things, a kind of bridge from the invisible to the visible.*

Still, this doesn't seem to sufficiently answer the question, *What are thoughts?* Perhaps the only way to understand the nature of thought is experientially.

*   *   *

Experiment: Watch Your Thoughts

Finish reading this paragraph, put down this book, take a deep breath and close your eyes. For sixty seconds, simply watch your thoughts. Do your best not to participate with them. Just watch the thoughts arise and then move on to watching the next thought as if you were watching a movie theatre screen.

Begin now ...

*   *   *

So what did you learn? First, you probably noticed that thoughts flow continuously. You can't stare at the mental blank screen for too long before another thought pops up. If your mind is clever, it will trick you into thinking that you're not really thinking when, in fact, you're thinking about that movie screen.

What else? If you didn't get "hooked" by a particular thought, which leads to a series of related thoughts, you probably noticed the utter randomness of your thoughts. It's quite fascinating how many seemingly meaningless, irrelevant thoughts constantly pass through our awareness. Like fish jumping out of a lake, thoughts constantly rise and fall.

If you've never meditated before and you actually completed this experiment, congratulations! You just meditated. If you already meditate, you're most likely better acquainted with the nature of thought than you realize. Regardless, we're now ready to delve deeper into thought's peculiar terrain.

THE COLLECTIVE MIND

Where do thoughts come from? Most of us would find such a question silly. *Our mind, obviously*, we might say. The next logical question would be, *What is the mind?* Is the mind the same as our brain, the physical organ located in our skulls? Does the brain fuel the mind or vice versa?

Nobelist Eric Kandel defines *mind* as "a set of operations carried out by the brain, much as walking is a set of operations carried out by the legs, except dramatically more complex."[15] So where exactly is this "set of operations" located? The assumption we all subconsciously make is that we each have a personal mind located in or around our brains which creates personal thoughts, unknown to others unless we communicate them.

Yet, we also have evidence of a *collective mind*, a shared pool of thoughts, ideas, beliefs, and assumptions. We can observe the effects of this collective mind in various cultures, ethnicities, religions, social groups, and even the stock market. Consider that competing companies often launch similar products and services simultaneously. It is easy to assume that the secret was leaked or both companies caught onto the same trend through research, but the collective mind is likely the culprit.

It's not a coincidence that people of various races, ethnicities, and religions have their own unique customs. Jewish people, for example, seem to have similar characteristics whether you're in Israel, New York City, or Minnesota. One can observe consistent mannerisms, a love for food, a near addiction to worrying, and at least a loose adherence to basic traditions. Again, one may assume these customs are passed on through learned behavior, from generation to generation, as opposed to being transmitted through a collective mind.

Science probably has the most blatant examples of a collective mind. Charles Darwin and Alfred Russel Wallace independently postulated the theory of evolution (natural selection) within a short period of time of each other.[16] Sir Isaac Newton and Gottfried Wilhelm Leibniz independently invented calculus in two different parts of the world and had to defend themselves throughout their lifetimes as to who actually originated the concept. Physicists Erwin Schrödinger and Werner Heisenberg each wrote the wave equation for quantum mechanics without conferring with the other. Neurosurgeon Karl Pribram and physicist David Bohm formulated a holographic framework for the brain and the universe, respectively.[17]

Carl Jung encountered many "meaningful coincidences" which he termed *synchronicity* during his psychoanalytic work.[18] He postulated the existence of a collective field of human experiences—a communal pool to which everything is connected, existing beyond the physical dimensions of time and space. Myths, dreams, hallucinations, and religious visions, Jung believed, all spring from this source, shared by all conscious beings.

The meticulous work of the late mythology expert Joseph Campbell offers further support for a collective unconscious. Where most historians and comparative mythologists highlight the differences between cultures, religions, and myths, Campbell focused on the striking similarities throughout all of them. In *A Hero with a Thousand Faces*, Campbell demonstrates how the same "Hero's Journey" has been told throughout time, across all myths, legends, and religions.[19] Identifying the same archetypal patterns woven throughout classic and modern storytelling further reveals the existence of this collective mind.

COLLECTIVE MEMORY

Our beliefs, recurring questions, ideas, world and life views, references, and behaviors are all filters of perception, which collectively make up our unique, subjective experience. These "Thought Systems" include a set of social programs and bundles of concepts, little of which we consciously create. There are subsets of social programs and conditioning that are cultural, societal, and religious, and others that appear more "personal."

Social programming, consisting of beliefs and concepts propagated by a specific culture, varies in different parts of the world. In corporate America, we often take lunch at our desks to save time and keep working. In many warm-climate, Spanish-speaking countries and various other cultures, work comes to a dead halt in the middle of the day for a *siesta*. Each culture has rites, customs, and rituals that are propagated via social programming beyond the individual's conscious choice.[20]

One may assume that customs and beliefs are passed on through word-of-mouth and learned observation, from generation to generation. In fact, these ritualistic tendencies are actually encoded in the collective mind. These specific encodings are sometimes referred to as morphic fields, a concept developed by theoretical biologist Rupert Sheldrake. This concept provides an interesting model to demonstrate the collective behavior in nature.

According to Sheldrake's Hypothesis of Formative Causation, each species has its own morphogenetic field and within each organism is a composite of many fields.[21] The concept of morphogenetic (form-shaping) fields arose in 1920s biology to try to explain how form arises. How does an embryo develop from a fertilized egg, for example? The traditional notion was that a miniature version of the form was contained in the egg, so for example, a miniature oak tree was contained in the acorn. In this theory, everything that needed to create the oak tree was contained in the neat little package of the acorn.

In Sheldrake's view, morphogenetic fields both within and around all organisms explain their evolutionary development. Within the human body, for example, there's an all-encompassing morphogenetic field for the entire body, plus morphogenetic fields for each limb, muscle, organ, and cell, all the way down to the molecular levels. Each of these morphogenetic fields contain its own "memory," derived from former similar life forms. In this view, the *field* of the mighty oak tree is contained in a tiny acorn, just like the DNA of an entire human being is encoded in a single human cell.

The morphogenetic field of an oak tree is patterned after previous oak trees and is dormant, but present, in the acorn. The human body generates an entirely new stomach lining approximately every five days. The morphogenetic field of the stomach lining is patterned after the field of previous stomach linings. These fields resonate with each other via a process Sheldrake calls *morphic resonance*. While morphogenetic fields refer to physical attributes, *morphic fields* refer to nonphysical characteristics like memory, beliefs, cultures, traditions, and rituals.

For thousands of years, man tried to run a mile in under four minutes. Prior to May 6, 1954, this feat was considered impossible. On that day, Sir Roger Gilbert Bannister broke the four-minute barrier in a meet between British AAA and Oxford University. Forty-six days later, Bannister's rival, John Landy of Australia broke Bannister's record. Once Bannister broke the four-minute mile, a new morphic field was formed.[22] Every time a new runner broke the four-minute mile, the field became energized, paving the way for future runners. Now, over 50 years later, many high school and college athletes run a mile in under four minutes. What to perception appeared impossible is now viewed as a viable potentiality.

The etymology of *mind* reveals something interesting. "Mind" comes from Old English *gemynd*, which is akin to Old High German *gimunt*, meaning memory, Latin *monere* to remind, and Greek *mimneskesthai* to remember. So the origin of our word "mind" refers to memory and recall, with an emphasis on past "programming."

Morphic fields explain a kind of "collective memory" exhibited throughout the world in groups of animals and humans sharing similar characteristics. The concept of morphic fields helps demonstrate the nonpersonal, collective nature of our thoughts (a concept that will greatly advance our understanding of the creative condition discussed in Book II).[23]

ENTRAINMENT

Morphic resonance also helps explain another extraordinary phenomenon that occurs in nature. Have you ever seen a flock of geese flying in a perfect "V" formation? Or perhaps a flock of birds sporadically taking off and landing in the trees, or a school of fish darting in unison back and forth through the water?

A National Geographic special featured a type of dolphin that feasted on sardines. The dolphins positioned themselves along the perimeter of a school of over a million sardines. The sardines instinctively formed a blockade. The dolphins then took turns diving into the blockade to feast on the sardines. What was fascinating was how the sardines responded to the attack. As soon as a dolphin retreated from the mangled blockade, the sardines immediately and perfectly repositioned themselves within the wall.

It is easy to assume that the sardines were somehow communicating with each other through physical cues, implying an observable, local connection. The same assumption might be made regarding a flock of birds flying in "V" formation, making hairpin turns as a collective group. We assume the lead bird must somehow be signaling the other birds when it's time to shift directions. Biologist Wayne Potts, however, discovered that the conscious response time (via muscle movements) of flocking birds is too slow to account for the ultra-fast course corrections these birds can make.[24]

This phenomenon seen throughout nature is called *entrainment*. The flock of birds and the school of fish are entrained to a nonlocal (not in any one position in space), collective mind. Under the appropriate conditions, if you fill a room with pendulum-operated cuckoo clocks set to various times, eventually, the clocks will synchronize.[25] In a large concert hall, tumultuous, chaotic clapping at the end of opera and theatre performances often shifts to a harmonious, rhythmic applause at a slower tempo.[26]

Gazing at a field lit up by hundreds of fireflies is enchanting. For centuries, there were tales of the synchronous flashing of scores of fireflies, especially in Southeast Asia. All of these accounts were anecdotal until the research team of John and Elizabeth Buck studied the phenomenon at the great Chao Phraya (Meinam) River south of Bangkok. They observed this peculiar synchronous firefly flashing, which led to an inquiry into how fireflies adjust their rhythms in response to other flashing fireflies.[27] To test, they mimicked the flash of a firefly with an artificial light, and exposed it to a real firefly in a laboratory. The Bucks and their colleagues found that the individual firefly somehow shifted its flashing to sync up with the outside stimulus. Steven Strogatz, author of *Sync*, concludes, "Thus we are led to entertain an explanation that seemed unthinkable just a few decades ago—the fireflies organize themselves. No maestro is required, and it doesn't matter what the weather is like. Sync occurs through mutual cuing, in the same way that an orchestra can keep perfect time without a conductor."[28] Once again, we see the phenomenon of entrainment to a collective morphic field in nature.

The so-called *100ᵗʰ Monkey Phenomenon*, proposed in the 1950s, provides a fun metaphor to illustrate entrainment to morphic fields. On the island of Koshima off the coast of Japan, scientists observed the Macaca Fuscata monkey.[29] The scientists dropped sweet potatoes in the sand for the monkeys. The monkeys enjoyed the taste of the sweet potatoes, but didn't like the coarse texture of the sand. An 18-month-old female monkey discovered a solution: wash the sand off the sweet potato in a stream. She taught this trick to her mother and her peers who, in turn, taught their mothers.

Six years later, roughly 99 Macaca Fuscata monkeys were washing their sweet potatoes in the stream. Then, something peculiar occurred—almost ALL the monkeys on the island began washing their sweet potatoes. Even more bizarre is that colonies of monkeys on distant islands and the troop of monkeys at the main island of Takasakiyama began washing their sweet potatoes. Once a critical mass is entrained to a particular field, the field washes over the collective like a strong ocean current.

Entrainment through the collective mind isn't a phenomenon restricted to Mother Nature. It is also observable within the retail industry, whereby products like the Pet Rock, Beanie Babies, Tickle Me Elmo, Pokemon, and Webkinz become consumer obsessions overnight. The effect of this phenomenon is well documented in Malcolm Gladwell's *The Tipping Point*.

The phenomenon can also be detected at the ethereal level of thoughts and emotions. The Global Consciousness Project, for example, is attempting to demonstrate this phenomenon through the use of a synchronized network of random number generators. Led by Roger Nelson, former research coordinator of Princeton

Engineering Anomalies Research (PEAR) at Princeton University, the purpose of the project is "to examine subtle correlations that reflect the presence and activity of consciousness in the world."[30] Random number generators (RNGs) are connected to computers running specialized software at over 60 sites around the world including the United States, Canada, India, Fiji, New Zealand, Japan, China, and Russia. Each RNG continuously collects data at a rapid 200-bit trial per second. Each local system comprised of a RNG and a computer is connected to a network via the Internet, sending synchronized information to a central server in Princeton, New Jersey. There, the packets of data are archived and later analyzed.

The hypothesis is that the collective intentions and emotions of humans around the globe can affect the randomness of a RNG in a statistically-relevant way—essentially bringing a degree of organization to the seemingly random numbers. Imagine a straight, horizontal line going across a standard chart where the line represents pure randomness. Anything above or below this baseline signifies a leap beyond the realm of *chance*. The farther away you go from baseline, the less likely an event is random.

The results of this project, which began in 1998, are promising. During highly-emotional events like New Year's Eve at the turn of the 21st century, the funeral ceremony of Princess Diana, the first hour of NATO bombing in Yugoslavia, and 9/11, there's an observable shift out of randomness. These ongoing studies and others of a similar vein, help point to a unified, collective mind.[31]

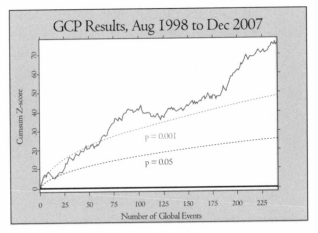

ACCUMULATING DEVIATION OF RESULTS FROM
CHANCE EXPECTATIONS

*The jagged line shows the accumulating excess of significant events relative to chance.
The Project estimates that the odds against chance are about a million to one.*

We unknowingly become entrained to belief systems all the time. A news report leads to hysteria in the public, and each person who adopts the belief energizes the belief's morphic field. Over 150 years ago, Charles Mackay documented a myriad of entertaining cases of mass hysteria in his classic, *Extraordinary Popular Delusions & the Madness of Crowds.*

Like the Macaca Fuscata monkeys, humans are constantly being entrained to positive and negative collectively-influential thought fields. With this basic awareness of perception, thoughts, and the collective nature of memory and beliefs, we now turn our attention to the *content* held within the collective field.

Chapter 2
Concepts of the Old World

For many confused scientists and philosophers, the equation, the concept, or the blueprint have become more real than the phenomenological reality itself.

—Abraham Maslow, *The Farther Reaches of Human Nature*

OLD PARADIGMS

Even though we might intuit the collective nature of our thoughts, we often feel suspicious of the notion, believing that our thoughts are private. *But wait a second,* you may be thinking, *I know I'm thinking my thoughts. I know my thoughts are mine.* When a bizarre, even violent or sadistic thought crosses our awareness, the assumption is that we originated the thought, leading to feelings of guilt or shame. In our narcissism, we believe we are the first person to conceive such a horrendous thought, even though rationally, we know this is not likely.

We'll delve into the mechanisms behind "personal" thinking in chapter 4. For now, it's only important to remain open to the idea that our perception is often misleading and there's a collective mind linked to collective memory. With this awareness, we can surmise the existence of different assumptions, beliefs, or *programs* in the collective mind beyond our conscious choice.

Examining some of these programs helps us remove hidden mental barriers to a larger worldview. Aware of potential limitation, we can explore our assumptions and beliefs, and choose whether or not they support our way of viewing the world. For example, if we believe that our religious affiliation is the "right" one and all others are "wrong," we create a wall of separation from the whole of humanity, exclude the possibility that errors exist within our religion, and deny the potentially-higher truths of other teachings. Scholar Joseph Campbell's life work demonstrated the obvious and remarkable parallels that exist throughout all religions and myths for thousands of years, bringing a sense of uniformity and appreciation for *all* the world's traditions.[1]

Our viewpoints often further fragment our experience by separating us from large segments of the world's population via nothing more than a belief system. In his classic study of scientific discovery, *The Structure of Scientific Revolutions*, Thomas Kuhn defined a paradigm as a set of common practices and assumptions that scientists (and others) share about a scientific discipline or the meaning of particular problems during a period of time.[2] For example, for decades, neurologists believed—or rather, *knew*—that no new neurons are created in a developed brain. Despite reports to the contrary, it wasn't until Princeton professor and neuroscientist Elizabeth Gould conclusively demonstrated that new brain cells are indeed created by the mature animal brain that the exciting field of neurogenesis emerged.[3]

A paradigm can be so dominant and pervasive that it falls below our awareness, while still influencing and limiting the way we think or perceive reality. This leads to what we might call "paradigm blindness" or "paradigm allegiance."[4] Examples of paradigm blindness are seen throughout history. We once *knew* the earth was the center of the galaxy; we once *knew* the earth was flat; we once *knew* the atom was the smallest building block of matter.

And today, science still *knows* the universe is explainable through the deterministic or reductionistic paradigm. As former president of the Institute of Noetic Sciences Willis Harmon, and human behaviorist Howard Rheingold wisely explain:

> Since we can easily observe that other cultures, past and present, have their hidden biases and blind spots—from societies that tolerate slavery or cannibalism, to those that worship cats or live in fear of eclipses—it is reasonable to assume that our culture probably has its own biases. But to anyone with years of scientific training, all through which the conviction was thoroughly drummed in that conventional science is our surest guide to truth, it can come as a shock to realize that science itself (or unreasoning belief in its unlimited power) might be seriously biased.[5]

Before we can transcend an old paradigm, we must uncover it, and this discovery process often leads to new insights. As Arthur Koestler aptly determined, "Discovery often means simply the uncovering of something which has always been there but was hidden from the eye by the blinkers of habit."[6]

*   *   *

Experiment: Uncovering Blindness

Contemplate on the following questions:

[1] What do you hold to be true? What do you *know* is true (as opposed to what you read or heard about from someone else)?

[2] What do you believe about the world? About your country? About your culture? About the fate of humanity?

[3] What are your beliefs about people in general?

[4] Are you aware of any destructive beliefs you may have about yourself, your community, your religious affiliation, or any other aspects of your identity?

Simply surveying or contemplating any of these questions reveals a host of positions and belief systems that may be limiting one's understanding of reality.

*   *   *

SCIENCE'S OLD WORLD

The word "science" comes from the Latin root *scire* meaning "know." Although science is now used mainly in the context of examining the physical world, a broader definition of science might be explained as *the systematic pursuit of knowledge or truth*.

Science plays a larger role in our lives than we realize. In addition to increasing our understanding of the physical world (which leads to breakthroughs in our understanding of nature and technological advances affecting our quality of life), science greatly impacts the collective thinking of our culture.

First, we're going to explore the dominant paradigm of the past three centuries: the *Old World* of classical physics. Then, in the following chapter, we'll contrast this paradigm with the *New World* view of advanced theoretical science.

The Old World was comforting. Scientists believed that everything in the world followed precise, observable laws. The right intellectual maneuvers coupled with mathematical computations would help us uncover how the entire universe started, how it all works, and with the same precision, how it will all end.

In the Old World, we believed if you couldn't see or measure something, it wasn't real.[7] This was actually a critical belief for Old World thinkers because if there *were* things beyond measurement, how could we ever hope to fully comprehend what things were and how they worked? There seemed to be a lot of data and experience to support this what-you-see-is-what-you-get perspective. You could use formulas to accurately predict where a ball would land based on its velocity, weight, and trajectory. Impressive, indeed.

Unexplainable anomalies lurked in the shadows, however. Unpredictable data that fell outside the understanding of this worldview were labeled as errors, chaos, or noise. Phenomena including psychic abilities like telepathy,[8] synchronistic occurrences,[9] spontaneous healings,[10] prodigies, and near-death experiences[11] all fell outside the model. The Old World dealt with the overwhelming evidence of these "anomalies" by sweeping them under the rug or simply rationalizing them away with remarks like, *It must have been a misdiagnosis or miscalculation,* or *Something else must have caused it.*[12]

Perhaps there were more obvious flaws in Old World thinking: *How can you measure your love for someone else? What is the meaning of a sunset? What is the meaning of a flower's beauty?* Or as we addressed in the previous chapter, *how does the mind work? Or where do thoughts form?* While the external, objective world of science is measurable, there appears to be another domain, an internal, subjective one, that science has trouble understanding. The belief of the Old World is that *everything*—which would include both the objective and subjective world—is definable, measurable, and knowable. As His Holiness the Dalai Lama explains:

> In addition to the objective world of matter, which science is masterful at exploring, there exists the subjective world of feelings, emotions, thoughts, and the values and spiritual aspirations based on them. If we treat this realm as though it had no constitutive role in our understanding of reality, we lose the richness of our own existence and our understanding cannot be comprehensive. Reality, including our own existence, is so much more complex than objective scientific materialism allows.[13]

Moreover, the varied-yet-unifying testaments regarding an experiential and subjectively verifiable Oneness of existence from mystics and sages across every culture and tradition worldwide for the last 5,000 years is difficult for even a scholar to deny.[14] These similarities were documented by William James in *The Varieties of Religious Experience*, Joseph Campbell in *The Hero with a Thousand Faces*, and Aldous Huxley in *The Perennial Philosophy*, among others.

DYNAMIC DUO OF THE OLD WORLD

Over a century ago, the father of modern psychology, William James, warned us of our ignorance: "[U]nderstand how great is the darkness in which we grope, and never forget that the natural-science assumptions with which we started are provisional and revisable things."[15]

Two brilliant minds of the 17th Century are generally given credit for the discovery of Old World: French philosopher and mathematician René Descartes and English physicist and mathematician Sir Isaac Newton.[16]

René Descartes (1596-1650)

A pioneering thinker of his time, René Descartes realized the need for establishing guidelines or rules for the study of truth. To that end, he crafted four rules for finding truth in his famous *Discourse on Method* in 1619: [17]

[1]   *Never accept anything as true that one does not clearly know to be such.*

As we observed in our discussion on perception, this rule poses numerous problems. What we think we know is based on a set of beliefs, experiences, thoughts, memories, and meanings. Anything that is processed through the mind—contained in the form of thought—is not *knowledge*, but rather theory and belief. As the Sages reveal, the mind cannot *know* anything—it can only *know about* something.[18] To *know* something requires you to *be* it as a consequence of subjective realization. For example, you can know everything there is to know *about* being a bird; however, a human being can never *know* what birdness is like.

[2]   *Divide each of the difficulties under examination into as many parts as possible.*

The underlying assumption here is the sum of the parts equals the whole. This law forms the foundation for a machine-like (mechanistic or deterministic) worldview.

By this "rule," if you dissect an ant into all of its individual parts, you can learn everything there is to know about an ant. Science's current understanding of complexity theory concedes that you cannot accurately comprehend a particular organism isolated from the environment and other contextual factors in which it exists.[19] Although the parts tell certain aspects about the "whole," they do not communicate the entire story.

[3] *Begin with the simplest and easiest, then work step-by-step to the more complex.*

Again, we see a linear, mechanistic thought process that assumes if we break something complicated into individual steps, we'll be able to understand the complex system as a whole. The development of nonlinear dynamics (the mathematical aspect of chaos theory) discussed later demonstrates a reality far more sophisticated than a "step-by-step" linear approach can reveal.

[4] *Make enumerations so complete and reviews so general to be assured nothing is omitted.*

If the world is governed strictly by mathematical laws, as the Descartes worldview held, it must be completely knowable, provable, and definable. A strictly physical world governed by strictly physical laws would negate the reality of inner subjective experience, which is nonlinear (in that it does not follow a cause-and-effect relationship as there is no beginning, middle or end), and generally unprovable, yet verifiable through conscious awareness.

Descartes realized thoughts and the elements of the mind didn't fit his rules. He viewed physical matter as a substance that occupies space, while the mind consisted of a "thinking substance" that does not occupy space. The nature of body (matter) and mind were so different that there was no basis for a relationship between them (even though experience tells us otherwise). This dilemma was explored in his inability to reconcile *res cognitas* (the cognitive, internal experience) from *res extensa* (the objective, external world as it is)[20]—which has come to be known as *Cartesian Dualism*. The nature of the mind and of the physical, material world was so different to Descartes that there was no basis for a relationship.[21]

As Bohm explains:

> Descartes solved the problem by assuming that God, who created both mind and matter, is able to relate them by putting into the minds of human beings the clear and distinct thoughts that are needed to deal with matter as extended substance. It was also implied by Descartes that the aims contained in thoughts had somehow to be carried out by the body, even though he asserted that thought and the body had no domain in common.[22]

To summarize, Descartes saw the world as a machine (or "the whole"), where the collective pieces equaled the sum of its parts. This material, mathematically-organized world is seen as limited, finite and definable. As such, this world is knowable, explainable, and understandable. This deterministic philosophy has become known as *Cartesian thinking* and is still highly-pervasive throughout the sciences (as well as in the collective thinking of mankind).

Sir Isaac Newton (1643-1727)

Another genius of that era who helped solidify the roots of Old World science was the English physicist Sir Isaac Newton. Newton is considered the founder of classical physics (also known as Newtonian physics), calculus, and a host of other foundational areas of science. In his pioneering *Philosophiae Naturalis Principia Mathematica* in 1687, Newton identified three laws of motion and a description of universal gravitation from which the physical world appeared to operate. Classical physics is based upon the notion that the material world is comprised of tiny bits of matter/energy interacting in definable, measurable ways, where every event is preceded by an observable cause.

Newton's three laws of motion formed the foundation of classical physics:

[1]   *Objects in motion tend to stay in motion, and objects at rest tend to stay at rest unless an outside force acts upon them.*

Force. Counter-force. Action. Reaction. This linear, cause-and-effect relationship in matter forms the basis for the reductionistic model of the Old World. As we'll demonstrate shortly, the belief that events have a direct "cause" is an error of perception. From an individual's perspective, cause and effect appears to be an actual phenomenon; however, quantum mechanics has demonstrated that this is not the case at the subatomic level.

[2]   *The rate of change of the momentum of a body is directly proportional to the net force acting on it, and the direction of the change in momentum takes place in the direction of the net force.*

Newton believed all motion is created by *force* initiated in the observable universe. This has been the predominant assumption of classical physics for the last three hundred years. Recently, physicist Efthimios Harokopos demonstrated that a *power* operating outside the physical domain (rather than *force* initiated in the physical universe) governs motion in the universe.[23]

[3] *To every action (force applied) there is an equal and opposite reaction (equal force applied in the opposite direction).*

Once again, we note the same deterministic, linear, cause-and-effect thinking still prevalent today. (See "Beyond Causality" below for an in-depth discussion on this topic.)

Using Newton's laws, physicists calculate events in the observable world with reasonable accuracy—a truly extraordinary achievement. The observations of Newtonian science are relatively consistent with our senses. We can visually *see* the response when a cue ball smacks into a rack of billiard balls—the balls scatter in predetermined patterns based on the trajectory and velocity of the cue ball and the positions of the other balls.

Newton, despite his accomplishments and advancements in scientific investigation, was humbly aware of the limitations of his worldview. "I do not know what I may appear to the world; but to myself I seem to have been only like a boy playing on the seashore, and diverting myself now and then finding a smoother pebble or a prettier shell than ordinary, whilst the great ocean of truth lay all undiscovered before me."[24]

SYMBOLS, WORDS & THEORIES

As we've stated, the mind is incapable of seeing Reality as it is. Bohm called this "fragmented thinking" one of mankind's greatest obstacles to solving the world's problems because it leads to a limited worldview.[25] The mind operates with fragmented abstractions, mistaking the concepts or symbols it uses for the real thing instead of what they represent.[26] The mind confuses *essence* with *appearance*, believing the description of something represents what a thing actually is or means.[27] We also noted the mind's inability to *know* anything; it can only *know about* things because to know something requires being it. The dog knows what dogness is as a consequence of being a dog, an experiential state beyond language and concepts. A human being can only *know about* what it is to be a dog.

A "theory" or "word" points to something, but in itself, the theory or word holds little meaning. For example, if someone asks why plants are green, the basic answer is chlorophyll. If we ask, *How do plants capture the energy of light, process it, and store it as energy?* the answer is photosynthesis, and we could go on to explain the process we've come to understand. Our minds then assume that photosynthesis is a "real" thing, objectively-defined by science, as opposed to a term representing a naturally-occurring phenomenon. Photosynthesis is a concept—a symbol we use in language. Reality requires no words.

Take a banana peel, an empty can of tuna, and a container of leftover food and place them on the kitchen counter. Each of these items may have their own meaning; however, if they are placed in a receptacle with a plastic bag, they merge into a fourth concept we call "garbage." Garbage holds different meaning than the individual objects it contains.

Scratch your arm when it's dry and you'll notice an accumulation of dead skin cells under your fingernails. Now, scratch your head and the same white, powdery substance will flake off your scalp as "dandruff," which, at least in American culture, means something different than, say, your standard household dust found in the corner of a room, largely comprised of the same dead skin cells. This dust, which floats around the room via tiny air currents, is breathed in through your nose where it is caught by tiny moist hair follicles. When enough of this dust (dead skin cells) accumulates, it forms another concept with a completely different meaning: snot or boogers!

Constellations offer a proficient way of highlighting the mind's ability to abstract based on information from the external world. Looking up at the night sky, we can observe patterns formed by the stars. We give these formations names like Andromeda, Orion, Pegasus, and Ursa Minor. These patterns, in reality, are arbitrary points of light and not actual forms observable from a spacecraft.[28]

Two foundational concepts are worth noting here because they form not only the basis for science, but also, our daily experience: time and space. Einstein's discovery of the relativity of time ushered in a new perspective for understanding the cosmos. *Time* is a necessary concept for perception with no independent existence in the physical world. As physicist Peter Lynds observes, "[A] 'flowing' time and progressive present moment are the products of our subjective perceptions and underlying neurobiology, without actual physical foundation in nature."[29] Time is merely a concept we project onto the world. *A Course in Miracles* cautions, "Time is a trick, a sleight of hand, a vast illusion in which figures come and go as if by magic."[30]

Mystical poets like William Blake intuited the illusionary nature of time:

> Till the Heavens & Earth are gone
> Still admired by Noble minds
> Followed by Envy on the winds
> Reengraved Time after Time
> Ever in their Youthful prime
> My Designs unchanged remain
> Time may rage but rage in vain
> High above Time's troubled Fountains
> On the Great Atlantic Mountains
> In my Golden House on high
> There they Shine Eternally[31]

Similarly, *space* is an illusionary concept with no independent existence used by the mind to facilitate perception and cognition.[32] *Causality*, the law of cause and effect, is also a concept, not an actuality. For our later discussion on creativity, it will be helpful to examine the concept of causality as well as the notion of opposites in order to better comprehend their innate limitations.

BEYOND CAUSALITY

The Old World of Newtonian science solidified the notion of causality: condition A *causes* condition B. For centuries, mankind believed Newton's laws of cause and effect to be irrefutable laws of nature.[33]

The concept of causality can be observed across the full range of disciplines. In medicine, we look for the *cause* of disease. In law, we look for the perpetrator or cause of the crime. In psychology, we look for what *causes* the mental illness, like socioeconomic conditions or childhood trauma. In natural science, we look for the *cause* of the universe, like the "Big Bang."[34]

Every action has a resulting consequence (Newton's Third Law of Motion) is the commonly-held belief. For example, it is assumed that if someone has a cold, you can "catch it" through the transmission of germs. Does this always happen? Of course not. Why not? There are innumerable additional factors, like the state of the person's immune system, their nutritional constitution, their white blood cell count, and their emotional and mental health. If the person is in prime physical condition and manages stress effectively, they are less likely to "catch a cold" regardless of how much direct contact they have with the ill individual. The germs don't *cause* the cold—the conditions for the cold to arise must first be present before the cold can manifest.

What causes a flower to grow and bloom? One might say the soil, sun and water cause the flower to bloom, but this is an error. Nothing *causes* the flower to bloom. It is the flower's nature to bloom when the right conditions are present: the right amount of light, sufficient nutrients in the soils, and adequate rain or water. When the proper conditions are present, the flower blooms as a consequence of its essence, but those conditions cannot be said to *cause* the flower's blooming.

The concept of causality is deeply rooted in our business thinking. Let's say a marketer runs a particular radio advertisement and sales spike over 10% during the period the ad runs. The marketer's mind assumes a cause-and-effect relationship: the ad caused the sales spike (the effect). Then, the marketer runs a similar ad, but this time, there's no correlating sales spike. What happened?

There are an infinite number of possibilities. The ad may represent a particular condition that helped lead to a sales increase, but it is not an *independent cause*. Deeper insight may reveal factors like the specific market the ad ran, the exact tone and energy of the ad, market timing, and its underlying strategy collectively produced the optimal conditions needed for customer acceptance or rejection of the company's products.

Now let's apply this notion to the topic we are going to explore: creativity. Creativity researchers generally approach their studies by trying to uncover the psychological, environmental, social, neurological, or relational *causes* of creativity. Just because a creative genius like Sigmund Freud may have had mentors or confidants in his early years of development and periods of isolation in the later years of his creative work should not imply a *cause* for his creativeness or even prerequisite factors.

Even if this pattern is consistent in ALL creative geniuses, this pattern could only imply two approximate conditions when genius manifests. Furthermore, if one is able to uncover all the apparent external, observable conditions of creativity, he still lacks the elusive, inner conditions needed for creativity to manifest. All the external traits may be present, but if the nonlinear, unmeasurable aspects of creativity are not, creativity will not manifest.[35] The challenge with academic approaches to the study of creativity is that within the Old World paradigm, you can't see the whole picture because there is no *cause* for creativity.[36]

As will become apparent in Book II, an examination of the inner conditions is infinitely more useful. When the subjective, inner conditions are appropriate, the creative impulse has a greater possibility of emerging. All the external "causes" for creativity like an individual's personality, their physical environment, and the overall culture can be present and creativity may not arise. Uncovering the inner conditions necessary to foster creativity is more useful in helping us to understand the mystery of creativity.[37]

Professor Emeritus of Physiology at the University of California, San Francisco Benjamin Libet's relevant discovery in neurobiology helps demonstrate the illusionary nature of causality. The brain needs a relatively long period of activation before an event can be registered in awareness, according to Libet's research. He and his colleagues have experimentally demonstrated that "awareness of a sensory event does not appear until up to 0.5 seconds after the initial response of the sensory cortex to the arrival of the fastest projection to the cerebral cortex."[38] When you tap your finger on a table, you believe you experience the event in real-time; however, you have conscious awareness of the finger tapping only *after* the brain has adequate time to process the event. Unconscious brain processes precede sensory awareness; the external world is not being experienced in real-time as we assume. This unperceived sensory delay leads us to believe we make a decision and then act, simulating a causal sequence that does not necessarily exist. Essentially, we are experiencing reality (via perception) through a time delay. We assume that we are controlling events as independent causal agents of our actions; however, Libet's research is suggesting otherwise.

Chaos theory has arrived at a similar conclusion as authors John Briggs and F. David Peat noted, "The scientists of change have learned that the evolution of complex systems can't be followed in causal detail because such systems are holistic: everything affects everything else."[39]

The mind sees an object moving through space. The mind projects motion onto the object, assuming the force of the prior moment is causing the position in the current moment. This illusion is similar to our experience with a picture flipbook. Although each image is self-contained on an individual page, when you flip through the book quickly, the ordering of the images gives the illusion of movement.

Why do we so readily see "causal" connections? The mind processes "events" linearly, from a starting point to an end point, assuming the prior point is the cause of the next point. This linear sequencing gives rise to a perceived causal relationship of events. What is actually happening is *emergence*—an unfolding of Creation from instant to instant.[40] In Reality, everything in this observable domain is happening of its own accord, when the conditions are appropriate.[41] Nothing is *causing* anything else to happen.[42]

A popular illustration from quantum mechanics, a common simplification of Bell's Theorem, derived by physicist John Bell, will underline this acausal understanding.[43] Imagine a small explosion of light in front of you, which emits two special kinds of particles called photons. These two particles are motionless when they emerge, meaning they aren't spinning at all. Now, imagine one particle stays where it is, say, somewhere in the United States, and the other finds its way to the coast of Australia. You decide to observe the particle in the United States. Amazingly, that particle begins to spin clockwise. More amazingly, the particle that remains in Australia simultaneously begins spinning counter-clockwise, even though there's no local connection between the two.

Observing the particle in the United States doesn't *cause* it to spin, nor does the spinning particle in the United States *cause* the particle in Australia to spin in the reverse direction. All of these events arise on their own and occur simultaneously or, to borrow the Jungian term, synchronistically. This illustration, which continues to baffle scientists, demonstrates how human observation in the form of consciousness affects the subatomic world.[44] This new understanding of the quantum reality, discussed further in the next two chapters, has led theoretical science to a revised perspective about causality.[45]

Observing conditions, instead of looking for "causes," can be a fruitful perspective in any field. For example, let's say you own a business and you want to have more loyal customers as opposed to constantly generating "new business." Can a business determine the characteristics of a brand on its own, or does it need the customer to embrace the desired brand experience? Although designing a logo and touting the benefits of your company are nice, the *experience* of the brand is mainly in the hands of the customer, not the company. Can the Disney Corporation make someone have fun at Disney World? Of course not. All they can do is present the right conditions: a clean park, rides that work, fresh cotton candy, friendly employees including Mickey and the gang to mingle with the visitors. These conditions increase the likelihood of a positive customer experience. Ultimately, building a brand is a "co-authored experience" with the customer.[46]

TRANSCENDING THE OPPOSITES

The mind is dualistic by design. The mind believes itself to be the subject and everything outside of itself is the object. Think about how perception operates, taking *in* information through the five senses from the *outside* environment. The mind's dualistic wiring, where a "this" is observing a "that," is the core obstruction in one's ability to move beyond the Old World perspective to a more expansive worldview.

In dualizing reality, the mind sees everything as separate from itself. A this-or-that, you-or-me, subject-or-object, either-or relationship is always perceived. The mind sees things as black or white, hot or cold, on or off. Think back to high school algebra: A+X=B. You're given two different variables and asked to solve for X. The mind tends to think in terms of concrete variables like A and B, good and bad, right and wrong.

From the Higher Ground perspective, however, there is only one variable, not two. For example, let's take light and dark. There's no such quality as darkness—just the absence of light. There is either light or no light, and there are infinite gradations of light like blinding light, bright light, strong light, subdued light, dim light, and dusk light. Even "darkness" contains various degrees of the absence of light like dark and pitch black.[47]

Similarly, there is no duality between black and white. There's only the color white and its infinite gradations. Each gradation is experienced by the mind as being separate from every other degree. When light hits a prism, the light breaks into a vibrant spectrum of color. A color is nothing but a concept or a label—a name you give something. Red, orange, yellow, green, blue, indigo, and violet are colors, but they are really just manifestations of an all-encompassing quality called light.

As another example, consider water. Water can take various forms: liquid, vapor, or ice. Although each of these forms appears different, they're simply qualities of H_2O.[48]

And electricity—when you turn a light switch on, electricity courses through the wire. What happens when you turn the light switch off? Does *no-electricity* flow through the wire? There's no such quality as no-electricity. Similarly, the switch is either on or not on—there's no quality called "offness."

Fritjof Capra, in his classic book paralleling the lessons for quantum physics with Eastern philosophy, *The Tao of Physics*, explains:

> Opposites are abstract concepts belonging to the realm of thought, and as such they are relative. By the very act of focusing our attention on any one concept, we create its opposite ... Mystics transcend this realm of intellectual concepts, and in transcending it become aware of the relativity and polar relationship of all opposites. They realize that good and bad, pleasure and pain, life and death, are not absolute experiences belonging to different categories, but are merely two sides of the same reality; extreme parts of a single whole.[49]

The challenge with opposites runs much deeper than mere linguistics. The black and white, dualistic thinking of the Old World presents a nearly insurmountable barrier to understanding the non-linear, subjective domain required for understanding creativity.[50]

You can catch the mind any time it tries to judge an event through its dualistic lens by saying, "This is good" or "This is bad." The mind assumes there are only two positions: the one it's holding and another of opposite value, with no possibilities in between.

Becoming aware of the mind's dualistic proclivity, we begin to transcend this illusion and notice a continuum of possibilities instead of an either-or scenario. An opposite is merely perceived as such from the position of the observer. The context of what is being perceived by the observer changes the meaning of that which is observed. The conditions of an event change the appearance of the event. What appears to be an opposite at one level is seen as *degrees* or *gradations* of possibilities from a higher level of understanding.

By turning inward to an awareness of one's subjective reality, one has the potential of transcending the duality of the opposites, revealing a new understanding of Reality.

*   *   *

Both Descartes and Newton were true geniuses of their time. Their contributions catapulted mankind into a new era of science, paving the way for the modern, technologically-driven society we enjoy today. Now, the collective knowledge and discoveries of the past century require us to let go of many Old World assumptions. Operating from a 300-year-old paradigm limits our understanding of the world around us. The Old-World view is now called the "mechanistic paradigm" (also called the Newtonian paradigm, scientific determinism or atomistic thinking). Those who still preach it are labeled "material reductionists" because they reduce everything down to the material, physical, observable world and deny or negate the potential truth inherent in an inner, subjective, "mathematically unprovable" experience. The Newtonian paradigm is not "wrong"; rather it is limited and contained within a larger, more expansive paradigm we'll now explore.

The Flat Earth Society, founded in 1547, still maintains the belief that the earth is flat, 500 years after Christopher Columbus's discovery. The organization still exists today and accepts new membership.[51] Indeed, old belief systems are often hard to release. Our need to better understand our creative nature, however, requires the surrendering of the Old World paradigm.

Chapter 3
The New World and Beyond

The kingdom of God cometh not with observation. Neither shall they say, Lo here, lo there! For the kingdom of heaven is within you.

—Luke 17:20-21

WELCOME TO THE NEW WORLD

Today, quantum mechanics and the New Science represent the emergence of a New World that began in the early 1900s, and required restructuring how we understand reality. One might think the Old World paradigm would have faded with the development of the New Science. A century later, however, the mechanistic paradigm of the Old World still grasps the collective mind in its weakening clutch.

When physicists broke down the atom into its basic form, they discovered that subatomic particles were actually *vast regions of empty space*. Take a book, table, rock, tree, or even a human cell, and when you break it down to its core substance, there's only empty space. The basic stuff of the entire universe—the building blocks of the physical world—has no dimension. (Yes, it's difficult to fathom and strange indeed.)

Things became more confusing when scientists made another unforeseen discovery: when they observed the subatomic particle (like an electron, for example), it was there, but when they weren't observing it, they couldn't definitively determine whether or not it was still present. They could only calculate the chance or *probability* of a subatomic particle existing at a given point in time and space. This led physicists to introduce a language of probabilities into discussions regarding physical matter. (A brief history of quantum mechanics can be found in appendix A.)

In Newtonian physics, it is presumed that a researcher conducts experiments as an outside observer and the observer (a human being) doesn't influence what is being observed (the experiment). This distinction cannot be made in quantum mechanics, where the human observer and that which is being observed are inextricably linked. The *Heisenberg Uncertainty Principle*, named after one of the founders of quantum mechanics, Werner Heisenberg, says at any given time only one of two complementary variables—position and momentum—can be measured with absolute certainty. If you observe the position of a quantum object, you can't ascertain its momentum; if you measure the momentum, you can't definitively know the position of the object in space-time. In fact, the more you know about a quantum object's position, the less you can know about its momentum and vice versa. The Heisenberg Uncertainty Principle was unacceptable to Newtonian thinkers who believed that *nothing* in the universe could be uncertain.[1] More importantly, this concept perplexed physicists because it means you can't eliminate the observer from the equation because the observer's *intention* on an event affects the event.

Our mere conscious act of observing a thing, Heisenberg noted, affects and changes it. Human consciousness in the form of the experimenter's intention affects what is being observed. For our purposes, *thoughtful intention increases the probability of affecting physical matter.* By holding a desired result in mind, we actually increase the probability that the result will manifest in the physical domain.

It's easy to underestimate the power of our thoughts. The mere act of focusing one's thoughts on achieving something, however, increases the probability it will manifest. Do our thoughts *cause* things to happen? As we've previously discussed, causality is a mental construction. Nothing causes anything to happen. The conditions must be appropriate for something to manifest. You can look at your intention as simply one of the conditions necessary for the manifestation of what you hold in mind.

The physical laws of the Old World are only "approximations" of a nonlinear, nonlocal, and nondual reality—meaning it is beyond the capacity of the linear, dualistic-based human mind to comprehend. This realization requires a profound level of humility: *can something really be beyond our intellectual understanding?*

The mind wrestles endlessly with this undefinable aspect of reality—it simply will not accept the fact that it cannot intellectually decipher an explanation with precise clarity. So first, we note our inability to accurately define a thought. Now, we come to realize that the universe we experience cannot be accurately conceptualized. These truths are difficult for the mind to accept.

To better comprehend the distinctions between the Old World and the New World, review the chart on the following page.

OLD WORLD	NEW WORLD
Logical	Incomprehensible
Predictable	Unpredictable
Orderly	Disorderly
Duality	Nonduality
Form	Formless
Local	Nonlocal / Diffuse
Temporal	Timeless
Measurable	Unmeasurable
Tangible	Intangible
Fact / Definition	Meaning
Separation	Oneness
Finite	Infinite
Object	Subject
Relative	Absolute
Visible	Invisible
Predictable	Unpredictable
Linear	Nonlinear

OLD WORLD VERSUS NEW WORLD

In contrasting the two different paradigms, we can appreciate the difficulty in transcending the Old-World view. The New-World view represents an enormous leap from the comfortable and tangible to an unknown realm devoid of the familiar. Advanced theoretical science is preparing us for a collective leap into a new paradigm. These advanced theories point us toward an entirely new landscape—a realm, quite literally, beyond our wildest imagination.

A SCIENCE OF CONSCIOUSNESS

Although the New Science points to a new context for understanding Reality, these theories are intrinsically limited. Science is beginning to accept that in order to understand the true nature of Reality, it must explore a "final" frontier: consciousness. The Heisenberg Uncertainty Principle demonstrates, as we noted, that observation in the form of human consciousness affects what is being observed. The nature of human consciousness, however, is shrouded in mystery. The topic of consciousness has perplexed the world's top philosophers since antiquity.

How are we aware that we exist? In the past, such a deep, pervasive question may have been exclusively relevant for the philosophers of old. Now, it has become relevant to the advancement of human thought. Physicist Amit Goswami cautions us against semantic confusion since *consciousness* is a relatively recent word in the English language and is often used synonymously with *mind*.[2] We've loosely defined the mind as the element or complex of elements that thinks and feels, but consciousness needs further contextualization, which it will receive in a moment.

The term 'consciousness' is becoming well-used lately with the popular grass roots film *What the #$*! Do We Know!?* as well as the scientific community's recent interest in the subject. Understanding *consciousness* from the linear framework of the Old World is, simply put, impossible. Attend any of the Science & Consciousness conferences like the ones held annually in Tucson, Arizona, or read a consciousness journal like the *Journal of Consciousness Studies*, and you'll notice a lot of confusion and disagreement within the scientific community on how to define consciousness.[3]

A true science of consciousness will, ironically, take science beyond itself, which explains why science fears this unknown abyss, often used analogously to Lewis Carroll's "rabbit hole" from *Alice in Wonderland*.[4] Today's science is trying to use its Old-World paradigm to formulate a science of consciousness, keeping one foot firmly on the ground while sticking the toe of the other foot into the rabbit hole.

Our mechanistic Old-World paradigm is often the root of our resistance, even for those of us who openly embrace the New Science.[5] To overcome our paradigm blindness, it is helpful to disconnect from our Western, Newtonian upbringing and to visit the ancient wisdom of the Eastern Sages. The value of the Sage is that he forgoes intellectual interpretation (that yields a web of complex concepts and interpretations of those concepts) and instead relies on the *knowingness* of experience—a direct, internal *Realization*. The realized Sage *knows* a direct experiential Reality— not the perceptual lens of the ego-identified individual. These Sages speak from an experiential, subjective reality, transcending the mind's concepts about reality.

Some notable Western visionaries in various fields of science have learned useful insights from Eastern spiritual teachers, helping them make pioneering discoveries in their fields. Eminent Swiss psychologist Carl Jung visited the sage Ramana Maharshi on Arunachala hill in India.[6] Pioneering physicist and philosopher David Bohm spent a great deal of time dialoguing with the Indian philosopher J. Krishnamurti.[7] (Incidentally, Bohm was also good friends with His Holiness, the Dalai Lama.[8])

OBJECTIVITY VERSUS SUBJECTIVITY

Why is a study of consciousness important to understanding creativity? The creative process is a highly subjective, inner experience. In order to comprehend the anatomy of creativity, we must acquaint ourselves with the quality from which subjective experience arises and the Source of life itself. This can be daunting to comprehend. As Maslow pointed out, we're generally ambivalent when it comes to knowing about ourselves—we want to know, yet we fear an inner knowing.[9]

To many, consciousness is equated with cognition, as exemplified by Descartes' famous, "I think, therefore, I am." The material reductionist of the Old World posits that consciousness is nothing more than a complex neural network located somewhere in the brain, like a so-called, "God Gene." Basically, they believe our conscious awareness is simply a by-product of neuronal activity, that life is the result of a magic formula of chemical interactions. Underlying this assumption is a belief in an objective reality beyond any kind of subjective experience. But what gives these reductionists the ability to conjure up such a belief? It's the very substrate of subjectivity—the sense of *presence* that one has throughout the day, the knowledge that they *are*, that they *exist*.

Without that underlying subjective awareness, these reductionists would not be able to put forth *any* theory, or even awaken in the morning.

Psychiatrist David R. Hawkins summarizes the material reductionist's challenge in understanding consciousness and provides the only possible solution:

> All mental approaches to a definition of truth are eventually confronted by the necessity of making a paradigm jump from the abstract to the experiential, and from the supposedly objective to the radically subjective. Thus, the statement "Only the objective is real" is a purely subjective premise. The mechanistic reductionist, therefore, actually lives in an intrapsychic, subjective reality, the same as everyone else. The resolution of the dilemma of a description and knowingness of absolute truth requires the leap into the field of research of consciousness itself, which makes it clear that the only actual, verifiable reality of knowingness is by the virtue of "being" (i.e., all intellectualizations are "about" something), which requires that the observer be extraneous in order to be the witness of the thing to be examined.[10]

Radical Subjectivity uncovers the substrate of existence itself, a universal quality that is impersonal and undifferentiated. Sages across the world, throughout time, have similarly professed an experience of Self-Realization as experiencing the Presence of Divinity within, which is impersonal and not unique to an individual.

The Indian sage Swami Muktananda said, "All the scriptures declare the same principle: The Absolute is *sacchidānanda*—Being, Consciousness, Bliss. The world, which is born from the

Absolute, is not different from it. All these appearances—'I,' 'you,' 'this'—are simply His play. Identity appearing in diversity, diversity appearing in identity—all this is the Lord."[11] The *Bhagavad-Gita* says, "They are forever free who renounce all selfish desires and break away from the ego-cage of 'I,' 'me,' and 'mine' to be united with the Lord. This is the supreme state. Attain to this, and pass from death to immortality."[12] Another well-known Indian sage, Sri Nisargadatta Maharaj said, "The Supreme Reality manifests itself in innumerable ways. Infinite in number are its names and shapes. All arise, all merge in the same ocean, the source of all is one. Looking for causes and results is but the pastime of the mind."[13]

That sense of presence—that subjective sense that you exist—is difficult to investigate from a scientific perspective because science utilizes external (objective) observation from the scientist's perspective as its primary tool. The physical world "out there" can be studied through perception, as the Old-World perspective has clearly demonstrated. But what about the world "in here"—the inner realm of subjective experience?

Science uses the mind to study the outside world, but in order to study the inner domain, the mind must be examined.[14] With what tool can this be accomplished? The field of neuroscience is called forth to explain this ethereal function, but it is still constrained by an objective study of neurons, not the experiential reality of our awareness. Herein lies the dilemma modern society faces in understanding consciousness. Professor Roy Mathew explains: "Objectivity is the basis for all science. However, consciousness is the quintessential basis of the subject, and it can never be displaced into the objective world since the objective world cannot exist without it. The object simply cannot exist without the subject."[15]

The 3,000-year-old *Upanishads* states the mind's limitation to know truth: "There is only one way to know the Self, and is to realize him yourself. The ignorant think the Self can be known by the intellect, but the illumined know he is beyond the duality of the knower and the known."[16]

We can use the mind's capacity for logic to help us on our journey to understand this challenging topic. Eventually, this pathway through the intellect, however, must give way to a subjective realization, meaning one must intuitively *experience* this innate consciousness as opposed to simply *thinking* about what it is.

RELATIVISM VERSUS ABSOLUTE TRUTH

The "Radical Subjectivity" of the Mystic must be differentiated from an ideology called "relativism" prevalent in our culture. Relativism is a philosophic position stating that *what is right for me is right for me* or *this is true for me, it doesn't have to be true for you.* This narcissistic viewpoint negates the existence of any Absolute Truth (Divinity) or even moral and ethical standards.[17] As Brad Macdonald, assistant managing editor for the *Philadelphia Trumpet*, wrote:

Moral relativism is the belief that defining right and wrong is an individual and personal choice. Denying the presence of absolute law, this ideology teaches that every decision is a matter of personal feeling. Moral relativism means that adultery, for example, is not objectively wrong. While I may believe that adultery is wrong and it destroys marriages, you are entitled to believe it is right and strengthens a marriage. The same reasoning applies for murder, stealing, pedophilia and every other facet of human life. With this ideology, there is no absolute definition of right and wrong—only what you perceive to be right and wrong. Moral relativism destroys the law that defines right and wrong, moral and immoral.[18]

A relativist who finds the word "God" offensive seeks to have the reference to Divinity removed from U.S. currency and our nation's courthouses.[19] From an extreme moral relativistic viewpoint, acts of mass murder or hate groups like the Ku Klux Klan can be rationalized as "free expression."[20]

The first formalized expression of relativism is arguably from ancient Greece where Protagoras believed *what appears to me is what exists for me and what appears to you is what exists for you.*[21] Thus, Protagoras believed there was no such thing as falsehood and since each of our subjective experiences was unique, there was no absolute truth. This notion leads to solipsism, which states only the self (with a small "s") is real and no reality exists beyond my internal subjective world.[22] In essence, perception is just perception; it is not necessarily representative of reality.

Relativism is arguably one of the greatest threats to our current society because it negates the reality of an Absolute Truth and, often, basic morals and ethics.[23] The relativist believes that everything has equal value and that a description of something equals its reality. For example, the media typically provides equal time to contradicting perspectives on a particular topic, even if one side clearly lacks any degree of integrity or truth. Of course, we can't fault the media for this sentiment since our inability to discern truth from falsehood has been a trademark quality of mankind since our emergence on the planet. Through relativistic positions truth is subverted thereby distorting reality.

In contrast, the internal Realization of the Sage is universal, and points to an Absolute Truth. James noted, "There is about mystical utterances an eternal unanimity which ought to make a critic stop and think."[24] The Sage seems to tap into the very substrate of existence itself to a nonlinear Reality beyond verbal description or linear comprehension. Reality (with a capital "R"), then, is what something *is*, not how a person might describe it, and is experienced by all Sages regardless of the time period. These enlightened Sages, including Jesus Christ, Buddha, Krishna, Huang Po, Bodhidharma, Meister Eckhart, Mother Teresa, Gandhi, Nisargadatta Maharaj, Ramana Maharshi, Swami Muktananda, and David R. Hawkins, all communicate the same subjective realization of the Self (Divinity) even though they use different language depending on the context and culture of their time. As the German philosopher G. W. F. Hegel noted, "For the Absolute is not supposed to be comprehended, it is to be felt and intuited; not the Notion (concept) of the Absolute, but the feeling and intuition of it, must govern what is said, and must be expressed by it."[25]

In pursuing a subjective understanding of consciousness, we're seeking a unified, infinite field and not a private, separate reality.

THE NATURE OF CONSCIOUSNESS

As you contemplate the nature of consciousness, keep in mind that it's not likely useful to consider the information herein with, "Yes, I agree," "No, I disagree," or "I'm not sure." This type of response means you're only *thinking* about consciousness; you're objectifying a subjective experience. The ancient Indian term *Vipassana* means to see things as they really are, to gain insight that unveils the essence behind appearance. Understanding the nature of consciousness comes only to those who *realize* it—either through contemplation or self-inquiry, a form of meditation, or what can be called "sudden enlightenment" (which is statistically very rare).

As human beings, we generally identify with our bodies and minds as the core of what we are. The Sages, however, tell us we are neither the body nor the mind, but that which gives the body-mind organism sentience. Below are some illustrations to help peel away some of the blocks to an understanding of consciousness.

Illustration 1

If your hand got cut off, would "you" still be you? What if your arm got cut off? All your limbs? Slice away all your body parts and as long as you're still conscious—as long as you have a sense of presence—will you still have the feeling that *you are?*

Illustration 2

You visit a friend and she is sleeping.

Someone asks if you saw your friend. What would you say? Probably, "No, she was sleeping."

Even though you may have visually seen your friend's physical body, that which you identify as being your friend was not present.

In the state of deep sleep, that aspect that gives us the sense that *we are* is dormant or nonexistent in both ourselves and in others.

It seems apparent, then, that we are not our bodies. *Acceptable*, you may agree, but in our current society, we actually have a higher degree of sophistication. We don't really believe we are our bodies; we assume we are our minds.

Illustration 3

If you are your mind and you tell your mind to stop thinking, will it stop? If you try this exercise yourself for sixty seconds, you'll notice the mind goes on thinking whether you want it to stop or not.

We assume control of our minds belongs to us; however, this very simple exercise demonstrates otherwise. With focused intention, we appear to be able to maneuver our thoughts, but as soon as focus dissipates, and often while attempting to focus, our mind goes off in the direction *it* wants to pursue.

Illustration 4

If you close your eyes and watch your thoughts, you will notice an aspect of awareness "watching" your mind's thought stream. Essentially, there's an aspect of *you* watching the mind; *you* are able to watch the mind. Simply put, that which watches the mind cannot be the mind.

If we're not the body-mind organism, then what are we? As Maharaj instructs, "First know your own mind and you will find that the question of other minds does not arise at all, for there are no other people. You are the common factor, the only link between the minds. Being is consciousness."[26] The Sages teach that we are consciousness itself. So what is consciousness?

Illustration 5

Upon awakening in the morning, there's an immediate sense of presence. You know you *are*. For a brief moment, there's no identification as male or female, of being a particular ethnicity, or experiencing emotions like happiness or sadness—there's just a feeling of existence. This core feeling is with you throughout the day, buried under life's endless distractions. Our minds tune into the continuous thought flow and the busyness around us, distracting us from this primary source of awareness that gives us the capacity to *experience*.[27]

This sense that you *are* is not present when you fall asleep at night, entering into oblivion. In deep sleep, there is no sense that you *are*; however, upon awakening, the sense of presence returns.[28] Throughout life, the body changes, as do your beliefs, thoughts, assumptions and memories. The person you think you are today is different in form and experience to the person you thought you were a decade ago, or two decades ago. That sense of presence you experience upon awakening, however, is a consistent quality that doesn't change throughout your life.

Consciousness—that sense of existence, that sense that you are, beyond all words, thoughts, memories, or emotions—is your primary asset; in fact, it is your only asset. The subtle quality of consciousness generally goes unnoticed since you don't have to do anything to experience consciousness. In fact, without consciousness, there would be no experiencing because there would be no *you* to experience anything. Maharaj often asked his visitors: *if you could have a million dollars or consciousness, which would you choose?*[29] The obvious point of the question is that without consciousness, the concept of a million dollars is meaningless, as there would be no one to use it.

As stated above, in exploring the nature of consciousness, it is helpful to forgo linear, intellectual processing in exchange for internal, subjective experience. The mind deals strictly in symbols and concepts, often mistaking the symbol for the real thing. To understand consciousness, you must look beyond the symbol to what the symbol represents. Contemplation, meditation, and self-inquiry are the basic pathways of this inward journey.

Illustration 6

Arthur Deikman, Clinical Professor of Psychiatry at the University of California, San Francisco, suggests you close your eyes and look within to try locating the core of your subjective experience:

When you introspect you will find that no matter what the contents of your mind, the most basic "I" is something different. Every time you try to observe the "I" it takes a jump back with you, remaining out of sight. At first you may say, "When I look inside as you suggest, all I find is content of one sort or the other."

I reply, "Who is looking? Is it not you? If that 'I' is a content can you describe it? Can you observe it?" The core 'I' of subjectivity is different from any content because it turns out to be that which witnesses—not that which is observed. The "I" can be experienced, but it cannot be "seen." "I" is the observer, the experiencer, prior to all conscious content.[30]

The "I" to which Deikman refers to is the core of our subjective experience, and this "I"—which is prior to any personal identifications—brings us closer to what we mean by the term *consciousness*.[31] Are we so sure that the source of all subjective awareness is personal, localized to each individual sentient being?

Physicist Erwin Schrödinger, one of the founders of quantum mechanics, echoes Deikman's realization. "The 'I' that observes the universe is the same 'I' that created it."[32]

The Sages of old and today have all shared a similar realization: the "I" that the individual assumes to be a private, personal self, is in reality the universal "I," or Universal Consciousness. The undifferentiated, universal consciousness mistakenly identifies itself with the body-mind organism through a mechanism we call the ego (discussed in detail in chapter 6).

As Westerners, in assuming we are our minds, what do we mean? We generally imagine a homunculus center in the brain as the core of our personal self—some master controller, like the great Oz hiding behind an elusive curtain.

Illustration 7

Who is the mysterious thinker behind your thoughts? Behind your actions? What exactly is making decisions from moment to moment? When you say, "I decide," who is that "I" of which you speak?

We assume there's a thinker behind our thoughts, a doer behind our actions, a speaker behind the speaking, and a listener behind the listening. But, where is the Wizard? The Sages say there is no Wizard hiding behind the curtain. Instead, the infinite field of consciousness (often called God or Divinity) is the source of all existence. Saint Francis of Assisi pointed out, "What we are looking for is what is looking."[33] Saint Catherine of Genoa said, "My Me is God, nor do I recognize any other Me except my God Himself."[34]

The Sage is restricted to explaining what we are by pointing out what we are not. For example, Indian sage Ramana Maharshi asked *Who am I?* and answered as follows:

> The gross body, which is composed of the seven humors, I am not; the five cognitive sense organs, i.e., the senses of hearing, touch, sight, taste, and smell, which apprehend their respective objectives, i.e., sound, touch, color, taste, and odor, I am not; the five conative sense organs, i.e. the organs of speech, locomotion, grasping, excretion, and procreation, which has as their respective functions speaking, moving, grasping, excreting, and enjoying, I am not; the five vital airs … which perform respectively the five functions of in-breathing, etc., I am not; even the mind which thinks, I am not.[35]

After negating all of these basic functions and qualities of humanness, only conscious awareness remains and Maharshi proclaims, "That I am." Nisargadatta Maharaj took a similar approach: "Do whatever you want, but never forget the reality, never forget what you really are. You are not the body, you are not the food, you are not this vital air. Whatever has appeared is a state, and as such it has to go … 'I am' is the witness; the entire manifest world is there because of this."[36]

This explanation of consciousness can make one uncomfortable. The mind combats this notion with, *No, I'm me. I'm separate. I'm an individual. I'm special. I'm my own self, different from all others.* The reply might be, *Who is this 'I' or 'me' of which you speak?* We'll address the source of our sense of separation later on.

Illustration 8

Consciousness can be likened to a telescope.[37] The observer looks through the telescope and sees the moon, the stars, and the planets, but the observer is not the telescope or what's being observed. Our mistaken identity with the body-mind organism, often called the ego, leads us to believe that we each possess a separate, individual self that views the world through its own telescope. The telescope, however, is simply the body-mind organism. What's looking through the telescope? The ego exclaims, *Me!* Sages report a different perspective: *Consciousness As Such* is the only Observer of the manifest world. The experience of a separate "me" is only an illusion, if but a persistent one.

Christian mystic Meister Eckhart noted, "The knower and the known are one. Simple people imagine that they should see God, as if He stood there and they here. This is not so. God and I, we are one in knowledge."[38] Zen master Huang Po said, "All the Buddhas and all sentient beings are nothing but the One Mind, beside which nothing exists."[39] And, "There is only the One Mind and not a particle of anything else on which to lay hold, for this Mind is the Buddha."[40] Even Einstein intuited an all-pervading, omnipotent field of Universal Consciousness:

A human being is a part of the whole, called by us "Universe;" a part limited in time and space. He experiences himself, his thoughts and feelings as something separated from the rest—a kind of optical delusion of his consciousness. This delusion is a kind of prison for us, restricting us to our personal desires and affections for a few persons nearest us. Our task must be to free ourselves from this prison by widening our circle of compassion to embrace all living creatures and the whole nature in its beauty. Nobody is able to achieve this completely, but the striving for such achievement is, in itself, a part of the liberation and a foundation for inner security.[41]

Once again, this information isn't to be simply assimilated by the mind. Einstein believed, "Nobody is able to achieve this completely," referring to this Oneness of Universal Consciousness. Indeed, the intellectual mind is restricted in its capacity to *know* this Universal Consciousness; it is limited to only *knowing about* it. The Sages, however, have transcended the mind through subjective realization and no longer identify with the body-mind organism but with Universal Consciousness As Such.

HAWKINS' MAP OF CONSCIOUSNESS

With our more intimate understanding of the nature of consciousness, we turn our attention to the exciting field of consciousness research. With a rare blend of science and mysticism, the Western world now has a framework, or "map," by which to understand the nonlinear domain and consciousness itself. This map, developed by David R. Hawkins through his pioneering work as the director of the Institute of Advanced Spiritual Research, highlights his discoveries in the area of human consciousness. For those grappling with existential questions about the nature of reality, this framework can lead to major leaps in one's understanding.[42]

Hawkins can be called an American Sage, although as Westerners, we generally don't value such a label. Trained as a psychiatrist and psychoanalyst with over fifty years of clinical experience, Hawkins possesses a unique combination of analytical, scientific explanation with subjective, spiritual Truth. Through his research, he developed a "map" categorizing the levels of human consciousness (also called the Scale of Consciousness). An elaborate discussion of the Map of Consciousness and its significance is outlined in his groundbreaking book *Power vs. Force* (Veritas Publishing 1995/Hay House 2002). Further explanation of Hawkins' study of the levels of consciousness is covered below and in appendix C, *A Theory of Everything.*

Hawkins' work has profound implications not just in the arena of science, but in virtually every aspect of sentient life. His work will be referenced extensively throughout this text as an authority on consciousness as his writings provide an unequaled level of clarity and truth concerning consciousness itself, which is critical to our understanding of creativity. (Additionally, we will refer to the work of brilliant thinkers like Jung, Bohm, Campbell, Maslow, Wilber, Freud, Gardner, Sheldrake, and Csikszentmihalyi for further context, clarification, and confirmation.)

The various levels of consciousness (LOC) are charted on a Map of Consciousness to illustrate the full range of human potential. Each LOC coincides with determinable human behaviors, points of view, predominant orienting emotions, central ways of processing information, and perspectives about life and God.

The numbers on the map range from 1 to 1000, representing calibrated levels of energy as measurable vibratory frequencies within the field of consciousness. The levels of human consciousness and its corresponding level of experiential reality are displayed on an exponential scale where the LOC of higher levels are profoundly more powerful than the LOC of lower levels.[43] The number range from 1 to 1000 is arbitrary; the significance lies in the relationship of one number (or level) to another within the relative framework of the Map as well as the meaning of each particular LOC. Hawkins observed that each calibrated level "implied a different way of not only seeing life but of experiencing it. An array of attitudes, beliefs, practices, philosophies, mental mechanisms, psychological sets, as well as healthy and unhealthy psychological defenses characterized each level of consciousness."[44]

Below is a brief description of the seventeen levels of consciousness from Hawkins' Map.[45]

Level 20: Shame. This highly-destructive level of consciousness houses the pain of "losing face," where we wish we were invisible. Those calibrated at Shame often commit suicide, or die in an avoidable accident, or become moral extremists. It is guided by an emotion of humiliation, takes a miserable view of life, and views God as despising.

Level 30: Guilt. The level of Guilt is often expressed as remorse, victimhood, and masochism, resulting in an unforgiving emotional attitude and a preoccupation with sin. Guilt is often used in society to manipulate and punish others. The dominant emotion at this level is blame, life is viewed as evil, and God is seen as vindictive.

Level 50: Apathy. The level of Apathy is denoted by poverty, despair, and helplessness where the future looks bleak. With the abandonment of hope, this is the level of derelicts in our society. The dominant emotional process is despair, where life is hopeless and God is condemning.

Level 75: Grief. The level of Grief is characterized by pervasive sadness, regret, and despondency. One sees sadness everywhere, and there's a feeling of constant loss, depression, and mourning. God is perceived as disdainful, life is tragic, and the overriding emotion is regret.

Level 100: Fear. From the level of Fear, a person can be easily manipulated and their world appears hazardous and threatening. Leading to inhibition, Fear is contagious and leads to mass hysteria and paranoia. Fear represents the favored tool for control by oppressive totalitarian governments. Governed by a frightening life-view and punitive God-view, the primary emotion is anxiety.

Level 125: Desire. As a major motivator in many human activities, Desire moves us to expend great effort to obtain rewards. Laced with accumulation and greed, Desire is the level of insatiable addiction. Led by the primitive emotion of craving, life is viewed as disappointing, and God is perceived as denying. This instinctual drive rules a great many in today's business world, where profits and the bottom line are prioritized above integrity and humanity's concerns.

Level 150: Anger. The level of Anger expresses itself as resentment and revenge. Stemming from frustrated wants, this level taps into a primal quality that can be dangerous and destructive. At this level, God is perceived as vengeful, life is antagonistic, and the dominant emotion is hatred. The lifestyle is exemplified by irritable, explosive outbursts. Anger can lead to destructive rage or hatred.

Level 175: Pride. The level of Pride is aspired to by the majority of mankind. Although socially encouraged, Pride is still a negative energy field—it feels good only in contrast to the lower levels of consciousness. The dominant emotion of Pride is scorn, and information is processed via inflation of the facts. The overriding life perspective is demanding and God is perceived as indifferent. Pride is the level of many extreme political activists, misguided theories like relativism, and CEOs of Fortune 500 companies.

Level 200: Courage. The level of Courage represents a major shift in the quality of consciousness. Whereas the energies below 200 are life-draining, above 200, true power emerges and the energy field is life-supporting. The negativity of the lower levels are balanced by the power of the levels above 200. This is the level of empowerment, determination, and fortitude.[46]

From Courage, life is seen as exciting, challenging, and stimulating, driven by the emotion of affirmation. Obstacles can now be overcome and true productivity can emerge. The collective level of consciousness of mankind currently calibrates at this level (approximately 204). From an economic perspective, this level is typified by unskilled labor and rudimentary trade.

Level 250: Neutrality. The level of Neutrality is relatively unattached to outcomes. A person doesn't feel driven to prove anything, as an inner confidence has emerged. Neutral people are nonjudgmental, with less positions about how things are supposed to go—they are easier to get along with and are not interested in conflict. Neutrality values freedom, with a governing emotion of trust and a satisfactory view about life, and divinity is perceived to be enabling and supportive. The semi-skilled laborers of the mid 200s transform into the skilled, blue-collar workers and tradesman of traditional industry in the high 200s.

Level 310: Willingness. At Willingness, human development and growth accelerate with increased self-esteem, genuine open-mindedness, and a commitment to participate at home, at the office, and in one's community. This level indicates friendliness and economic success, for they are helpful to others and willing to contribute to the good of society.

People at Willingness are excellent students, as they are self-correcting and ready to learn from positive feedback. The overriding emotion is optimism, life is seen as hopeful, and God is inspiring. Whereas at Neutrality, a customer support person just follows a script and does what is expected to fulfill the job requirement, at Willingness, the support person will make sure the customer is taken care of and that they feel good about the transaction. Technicians, advanced craftsmen, routine managers, and a more sophisticated business structure represent the emergence of the 300s.

Level 350: Acceptance. At Acceptance, a major shift in awareness occurs. People begin taking responsibility for their life conditions instead of playing the victim role that's prevalent in the lower levels. Happiness is now perceived as an internal realization and not something derived from the outside environment.

Living life on one's own terms with balance, emotional calm, flexibility, and stability, people are no longer polarized by conflict and opposition; instead, they are self-disciplined and motivated by long-term goals. This inclusive level is free from discrimination and intolerance, and honors the rights of others.

Led by the emotion of forgiveness, life is seen as harmonious and God as merciful. Educators, artisans and upper management emerge out of the mid- to high-300s. There's an informed awareness of public interest that goes beyond one's family or community to a more global concern.

Level 400: Reason. When the emotionalism of the lower levels is transcended, intelligence and rationality take center stage. The level of the intellect is capable of handling complex decision-making, understanding intricate details, and manipulating symbols as abstract concepts. Reason represents the level of science, medicine, law, academia, Nobel Prize winners, statesmen, and Supreme Court Justices.

Brilliant thinkers like Plato, Aristotle, Descartes, Newton, Freud, and Einstein resided in the high 400s. America currently calibrates at this level (421). This is the level of the professional classes, of higher education, and of true literacy. Homes are filled with books, educational materials, and even libraries. The primary emotion of Reason is understanding, life is viewed as meaningful, and God is believed to be wise.

The downside of the 400s is intellectualization, where there's an inability to differentiate between the symbols and what the symbols represent. It is easy to lose sight of the forest for the trees when there's an obsession with concepts, ideas, and theories as opposed to the meaning behind them. Although the intellect is powerful in our technical world, it tends to get lost in details and misses the essence or truth of complex issues. This level leads to great achievements in the physical world, but poses a major block to the higher levels of consciousness.

Level 500: Love. The level of Love is vastly different than the emotionalized love portrayed in the media—an addictive sentimentality with attractions, attachments, passions, pleasures, novelty, or dependency. In contrast, the level of Love is not dependent on external factors. It is characterized as unchanging, permanent, and unconditional. Love is a way of being with and relating to the world that is forgiving, nurturing, and supporting. Reason (400s) focuses on details, perceptions, and fragments, whereas Love discerns essence and evaluates situations holistically from a larger field perspective. The 500s represent the emergence of the nonlinear, subjective realm of consciousness, where thinkingness is replaced by an inner realization. There's a shift in the quality of experiencing where the details of a situation, which used to be of paramount importance, are replaced by "essence," the overall field of meaning.

Love is inclusive, expanding the sense of self, augmenting and uplifting those around it, and dissolving negativity. Exquisite music, art, architecture, and excellence in any field emerges from this level. This is the level of true happiness, guided by reverence, where God is loving and life is benign. A few notable figures who transcended the intellect and calibrate in the 500s include Nelson Mandela, David Bohm, Carl Jung, and Dante Alighieri. Only four percent of the world's population ever reach this level of consciousness.

Level 540: Joy. At 540, Love becomes unconditional and one begins to experience an inner joy that's not dependent on external events. Hallmark qualities of unconditional love are patience, compassion, and a persistent positive attitude even in the face of adversity. Everything in the world is experienced as an expression of beauty, love, and divinity as events unfold synchronistically. Life is complete and total, God is One with all things, and serenity prevails. This is the level of saints, spiritually-based twelve-step groups like Alcoholics Anonymous, and leaders of worldwide religious organizations like the current Pope and His Holiness, the Dalai Lama. A few other historical figures at this level (540-599) include Socrates, Father Pio, Brother Lawrence, Rumi, Confucius, and Saint Augustine. Only 0.4 percent of the world's population reach this level of consciousness.

Level 600: Peace. This extremely rare level of consciousness is attained by less than one in ten million people. This nondual level, where the distinction between subject and object no longer exists, represents the emergence of enlightenment, self-realization, or God consciousness. The state of bliss associated with this level usually precludes a person's engagement in normal worldly activities; however, some do become spiritual teachers.

All life is seen as radiant and vibrant, and the world is seen as exquisitely flowing and evolving. The mind goes completely silent (void of all conceptualization) and a stunning peace prevails. A few notable sages at this level include Sri Aurobindo, Saint John of the Cross, Karmapa, Muktananda, Ramakrishna, and Lao Tzu.

Level 700-1000: Enlightenment. These peak inspiration levels of the evolution of consciousness in the human realm are associated with Divinity and their sheer power influence all of mankind. At this level, there is no longer the experience of the individual or the personal self (the ego has been transcended), but rather, identification is with the Self (capital "S") as Divinity. The body is seen as a tool of consciousness, and the fate of the body is of no concern. The Self is eternal and complete.

This ineffable level of Divine Grace has been reached by only a few in human history. Sages at these levels included Mother Teresa, Mahatma Gandhi, Ramana Maharshi, Nisargadatta Maharaj, Dogen, Meister Eckhart, Patanjali, Rabbi Moses de Leon of Granada, and Saint Theresa of Avila. At the highest level of Enlightenment are the great "avatars" that transformed mankind, including Buddha, Krishna, and Jesus Christ.

The complete spectrum of human development is brought to light through the levels of consciousness. These calibrated levels determine experiences of "reality" with general social, emotional and intellectual attitudes, capacities for comprehension, occupational propensities, ambitions, interests, psychological and physical health, ethical and moral development, and overall behaviors. There are even high correlations between levels of consciousness and family orientation, socioeconomic status, buying habits, personality, capacity for happiness and love, selection of reading and entertainment material, as well as other forms of recreation. In essence, all aspects of human life—including creativity—can be contextualized within the various levels of human consciousness.[47]

*　　*　　*

At this point, a question may have arisen in your mind like, *Why is this information important?* or *What does this have to do with the creative impulse?* The answer is that the nature of the creative impulse cannot be revealed without an understanding of consciousness, and as we've observed thus far, this is no small endeavor.

The main blocks to this higher understanding are the Old World concepts that hold our beliefs in a linear, objective reality—independent of human consciousness—in place. The mind seems so enamored with this apparent objective reality that it doesn't realize the nonlinear, subjective function is allowing the experience of objectivity to unfold. We are mesmerized in disbelief at the snake ascending out of the basket until we understand that the snake, in actuality, is a rope. Until we see the rope as rope, we are not seeing things as they are. Once our eyes are opened, the creative impulse can be revealed.

Chapter 4
The Anatomy of Thought

All experience, to borrow an expression of the mystics, is bounded by the boundless. Every step on our journey adds to what we know but it also reveals there is no end to knowing.

—James P. Carse, *Breakfast at the Victory*

Now that we have a framework for understanding consciousness, we can apply a few advanced concepts to this new context to better understand the anatomy of thoughts.

Einstein's Elegant Formula

Although we may not be able to comfortably define thought, the New World does provide us with an interesting way of measuring its etheric presence. Thoughts, as it turns out, are energy. Each thought has its own vibrational frequency.[1] As human beings living in the physical world, we tend to ignore the formless. *If you can't see it and can't measure it, it's not real,* the material reductionist believes.

No one, however, denies the existence of thoughts, even though we can't point to them. This conundrum is what Descartes wrestled with: *res cognitas* (our internal, subjective experiences) versus *res extensa* (the outside world as it is). Are thoughts any less "real" than, say, a chair? A chair is a visible object, tangible, weighable, measurable, and easily identifiable with observation. Thoughts are none of these things, but does that make them any less "real"?

Our good friend, Albert Einstein, gave us the simple and elegant formula $E=MC^2$. Energy is equal to mass times the speed of light squared. In essence, energy equals matter (the speed of light squared is a mere detail). As Einstein said, "Mass and energy are both but different manifestations of the same thing—a somewhat unfamiliar conception for the average mind."[2]

Energy and matter are simply different *qualities* of the same thing. As strange as it may sound, thoughts and chairs are both *forms* of energy in the observable world. A chair, or any other physical manifestation for that matter, is no more "real" than a thought.[3]

Jung arrived at a similar conclusion, viewing mind (the "psyche") and matter as two qualities of the same thing: "Since psyche and matter are contained in one and the same world and moreover are in continuous contact with one another and ultimately rest on irrepresentable, transcendent factors, it is not only possible but fairly probable, even, that psyche and matter are two different aspects of one and the same thing."[4]

Advances in current consciousness research illuminate another important aspect of thought: *the level of energy of individual thoughts varies*. Hawkins' research reveals the various levels of human consciousness and the energy of thought arising from each level:

The energy of human thought, though minute, is nonetheless absolutely measurable. A thought which emanates from the 100 level of consciousness (Fear) will typically measure between $10^{-800 \text{ million}}$ to $10^{-700 \text{ million}}$ microwatts. On the other hand, a loving thought at the consciousness level of 500 (Love) measures approximately $10^{-35 \text{ million}}$ microwatts. The difference in power between a loving thought and a fearful thought is so enormous as to be beyond the capacity of human imagination to easily comprehend.[5]

Every thought is encoded with a particular level of energy, and thus holds varying levels of power. Negative thoughts like fear, anger, desire, guilt, shame, and pride have weaker energy, whereas thoughts aligned to love, joy, compassion, acceptance, gratitude, and peace are immensely more powerful.

PATTERNS OF ATTRACTION

Chaos theory demonstrates a vast world of connectedness in both the visible and invisible domains.[6] The term "chaos" refers to a mass of seemingly meaningless data in which an organizing pattern cannot be discerned. The study of chaos arose from the discovery of *Strange Attractors*, or attractor fields. Attractors exist in what physicists call *phase space*, an abstract reality beyond our three-dimensional experience. Attractor fields are highly organized energy fields that "magnetically" pull, or attract, everything in a given system toward it. In essence, behind the appearance of randomness is a world of organizing patterns, or order.

MIT meteorologist Edward Lorenz is credited as "accidentally" discovering the existence of attractors in 1960 while plotting a massive amount of weather data. Through a simple process called *iteration*, where feedback is produced by multiplying a factor by itself through a continual reabsorption of what has come before, "chaotic" patterns were discovered. Plotting three variables (temperature, air pressure, and wind direction) in a unique way over a period of time created what is now famously known as "Lorenz's Butterfly"—the first identified attractor pattern.

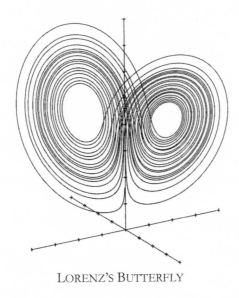

LORENZ'S BUTTERFLY

Attractor fields can have high or low energy, and their existence is not limited to nature. Hawkins' consciousness research uncovered that attractor fields of varying strengths exist behind every behavior, belief, and thought. Each level of consciousness is governed by a particular attractor field.[7]

When we're depressed, down, sad, angry, or spiteful, we are aligned with lower energy attractors, entraining us to these negative emotions. When we experience happiness, contentment, joy, gratitude, and peace, we are aligned with high-energy attractors.

Although our emotional states tend to wax and wane based on our environment, our level of consciousness tends to remain fairly steady throughout our lifetime.[8] One's level of consciousness, governed by a variety of attractors, dictates the stratum of thoughts a person is likely to align with.

THOUGHT ATTRACTORS

Consciousness research has revealed that all thoughts arise out of a particular level of consciousness, which is governed by an attractor.[9] *Thought Attractors* aligned with a higher calibrated level of consciousness (acceptance, gratitude, forgiveness, love, joy) are exponentially more powerful than Thought Attractors governed by lower levels of consciousness (anger, fear, guilt, desire, pride). Each person attunes to the thought field of his or her own level of consciousness like a radio receiver.[10]

For example, the concept of causality is aligned to an attractor field of Reason (mid 400s), representing an abstract concept and an innate limitation of mental perception. If a bowling ball is dropped on your foot, perception generally dictates that the bowling ball "causes" you to scream and get angry. Indeed, if a work colleague whom you didn't particularly like dropped the ball, screaming and getting angry is a likely scenario. Now, let's look at what happens in a different context: if a small child with tiny fingers accidentally drops a bowling ball on his mother's foot, she's still likely to scream, but she may not get angry. Why? The attractor field of Love (500) dominates, so the experience of the event is different. Attractors at higher levels of consciousness (500 and above) transcend all Old World concepts as they represent an ineffable, nonlinear domain of reality.

With this insight, let's see if we can formulate a conceptual illustration of how thinking really works. As previously stated, thoughts emanate from the collective field of consciousness, or Universal Consciousness, *impersonally*. Additionally, thoughts are a form of energy governed by attractor fields (Thought Attractors), arising out of a specific level of consciousness.

As Nobel Laureate Sir John Eccles pointed out, the brain acts as a conduit or a sending and receiving station for these energy patterns from the mind called thoughts.[11] The brain is like an air-traffic control unit which guides thoughts on and off the runway.

As "individuals," our particular levels of consciousness determine the predominant range of thoughts we're likely to engage. The mind acts as a communication gateway to an individual's corresponding energy field. Where the brain is rooted in the physical domain, the mind operates in an invisible, or etheric, realm.

Bohm provided a useful metaphor of the hologram to help us visualize the relationship between the physical and nonphysical domains. A hologram, like the three-dimensional metallic image on a credit card, represents both a visible and an invisible image created by the interference patterns of a split beam of laser light (light of a single wavelength). Bohm referred to the observable universe as the *explicate* order, or the visible "unfolded" reality. He denoted the *implicate* order as the invisible "enfolded" domain beyond measurement and conscious observation. As Bohm explains, "The essential feature of this idea was that the whole universe is in some way enfolded in everything and that each thing is enfolded in the whole."[12] Consistent with mystical teachings and more than just an abstract concept, the implicate order exists in an unobservable realm beyond the linear, space-time experience. This unobservable reality is what the Old World material reductionists are unable to accept.

Thought Attractors arise within the implicate/enfolded order and later manifest in the physical, explicate/unfolded domain. The idea of building Disney World emerges from a Thought Attractor in the implicate order and is received in the mind aligned to that particular attractor. As Walt Disney reflected, "It all started when my daughters were very young and I took them to amusement parks on Sunday ... I sat on a bench eating peanuts and looking all around me. I said to myself, dammit, why can't there be a better place to take your children, where you can have fun together?"[13] Then, with time, the thought manifests as the Magic Kingdom® in the observable explicate order.

THOUGHT'S BASIC ROADMAP

Let's attempt a crude visualization of how thought impulses are translated in the brain. The brain receives a thought pattern from the mind via the "right brain" or nondominant hemisphere—the nonlinear, intuitive, imaginative, and creative aspect of the brain. As we'll discuss in Book II, daydreaming and reverie, which are powerful tools to the unfolding of creative insight, are functions of this nondominant brain hemisphere.[14]

Thought patterns cannot be communicated by the highly abstract, intuitive, feeling right brain that receives them. If the information is to be structured linearly for communication in the form of language, it must be transferred to the linear left brain—the dominant, interpreting aspect of the brain responsible for temporal-sequential organization, recognition, and analysis of details. The relationship between the two hemispheres is symbiotic. Once the left brain obtains the information from the right brain, verbal and other forms of linear communication are transmitted. Creativity researcher J. C. Gowan suggests, "The left hemisphere seems to act as a problem solver, the right seems to act as a radio receiver."[15]

Perhaps it's more accurate to say the right hemisphere aligns to an idea and the left hemisphere must interpret, translate, verify, and then communicate it. Relegating ourselves to an "outside" observer of this process, we notice that thoughts are happening on their own as a sort of phenomenon inherent in nature. Thoughts and thinking are phenomena arising out of consciousness, and the body-mind organism can be viewed merely as a tool for the propagation and manifestation of thought.

IMPERSONAL THOUGHTS

When viewed "objectively," it becomes easier to see how thoughts are impersonal—without requiring a "you" to initiate the thinking. Thoughts do not arise from our brains. Thoughts arise out of an all-encompassing collective field, *happening* of their own accord.[16] The ego, however, takes credit and ownership of the thoughts in approximately $1/10,000^{th}$ of a second, immediately labeling them as "my" thoughts.[17]

In reality, although it may be difficult (if not impossible) for our minds to assimilate, there are no *personal* thoughts, a point emphasized by the Sages. All thoughts arise from a transcendent domain—a collective pool of consciousness. This domain—a single, all-encompassing, nonlocal field that Bohm called the implicate order—acts as a sort of communal gathering for our thoughts. This invisible domain constitutes an unmanifest realm devoid of form, but from which all form arises. This aspect of Universal Consciousness is the source of all existence, or as Bohm put it, "Deep down the consciousness of mankind is one."[18]

Despite what our Old World beliefs might tell us, thoughts are not personal, nor do they arise from within our heads, as we experienced through the illustrations in chapter 3.

*　　　*　　　*

Experiment: The Search for Oz

If your mind is experiencing some resistance—like wondering, *Don't I control my thoughts?* or believing, *My thoughts are personal!*—another experiment may be helpful. We already tried this experiment in chapter 3, but let's attempt it once more: try to have no thoughts for the next 60 seconds. Just clear your mind of all thoughts for 60 seconds. Close your eyes. Go.

Time's up.

Did you stop thinking for a single second? Are you still certain that you control your thoughts? If you control your mind and you tell your mind to "stop thinking," shouldn't it stop?

*　　　*　　　*

Thoughts arise of their own. The ego leads us to believe that we are our thoughts—that the locus of our thoughts resides somewhere in the brain. We believe we are the *thinker* behind the thoughts. The ego assumes it acts as a Great Oz hiding behind the curtain, pulling the levers and making all the decisions.

Left unchecked, the mind generally partakes in what Hawkins calls "thoughting," as opposed to thinking.[19] Thoughting is what you experience when you simply engage random thoughts arising in the mind. *Thinking* is a specialized way of focusing thoughts on a particular subject. When you're following driving directions to an unfamiliar destination, you're *thinking* when you read the directions and figuring out where to turn next. *Turn left at the next light and go straight for five miles.* After you turn, the mind engages in *thoughting*, where random thoughts come to mind until focused thinking is required for the next turn.

The mastery of thought—or more accurately, the taming of the mind—is not a popular discipline in the Western world (although this is beginning to change due to the efforts of His Holiness, the Dalai Lama, as well as various movements in self-growth and mindfulness-based practices). The East, however, has closely examined the inner terrain of the mind for millennia. The Eastern traditions put greater emphasis on "observing" the mind, or attempting to transcend one's thoughts through the practice of breath meditations, mantras, and contemplation to reach higher states of joy, peace, or what is traditionally termed "enlightenment."

Although enlightenment may not be a conscious directive to many of us in the West, "peace of mind" is desirable to those of us who attain a certain level of conscious awareness.[20] Furthermore, as we'll learn in Book II, this peaceful state is conducive for the manifestation of the creative impulse.

For our purposes here, understanding the impersonal nature of thought is imperative to our comprehension of the creative impulse. The *seeking* of creativity is counterintuitive when we realize it arises on its own without our volitional effort to "think creatively." The notion of thinking creatively arises from the Old-World view. As we shall see, a more fruitful question might be, "How might we allow the creative impulse to unfold, emerge, or reveal itself?"

BOOK II
Uncovering the Creative Impulse

If you've made it this far, congratulations! You now have the foundational context needed to explore the nature of creativity from a new and enlightened perspective.

Here in Book II we're going to explore the necessary conditions for creative manifestation, the blocks to the creative impulse, and a new way of approaching problems.

Chapter 5
The Creative Condition

Generally speaking, the germ of a future composition comes suddenly and unexpectedly ... It takes root with extraordinary force and rapidity, shoots up through the earth, puts forth branches and leaves, and finally blossoms. I cannot define the creative process in any way but [by] this simile.

—Tchaikovsky, *Life and Letters of Peter Ilyich Tchaikovsky*

IDENTIFYING CREATIVENESS

Many of us believe our level of intelligence, as measured by our IQ (Intelligence Quotient),[1] is the primary (or sole) indicator of that quality we often call *creative genius*. Indeed, brilliant scientists and mathematicians with high IQs reinforce this belief. But creative genius is not limited to having an advanced understanding of science and math, where a high IQ is a requirement for comprehension of the material. Interestingly, an unusually high IQ is not a prerequisite for genius in the arts like painting, music, or poetry.

In fact, in Lewis Terman's landmark "study of genius," which began with a group of children at Stanford University in 1921, found those with high intelligence (as measured by IQ) generally did *not* yield notable geniuses.[2] More recent psychological studies have confirmed Terman's findings.[3]

In business, there is a similar misconception. A high IQ or a keen intellect is believed to be the only hope we have for generating better ideas, more effective campaigns, or more innovative products. If intelligence *was* the most significant criteria, why aren't the "smartest" people always the most affluent?

Howard Gardner, Professor in Cognition and Education at the Harvard Graduate School of Education, has offered a more expansive approach to studying intelligence.[4] His "Multiple Intelligence" (MI) theory proposes that there are various forms of intelligence that have evolved in humankind. Whereas an IQ test mainly measures logical-mathematical intelligence, Gardner's research suggests that we also have musical, bodily-kinesthetic, linguistic, spatial, interpersonal, and intrapersonal levels of intelligence. Each of us has innate strengths and combinations of strengths in particular intelligences. While Gardner's model is vastly more sophisticated than traditional intelligence models, it still does not identify the core qualities of creativeness.

The root word of creativity is "create." Mihaly Csikszent-mihalyi, Professor of Psychology at the University of Chicago, notes that the term "creativity" originally meant *to bring into existence something genuinely new that is valued enough to be added to the culture.*[5] Quantum physicist Amit Goswami offers his definition of creativity as *the creation of something new in an entirely new context; newness of the context is the key.*[6] Humanistic psychologist Carl Rogers adds another layer to this view by defining the creative process as *the emergence in action of a novel relational product, growing out of the uniqueness of the individual on the one hand, and the materials, events, people, or circumstances of his life on the other.*[7]

This challenge of defining creativity has led academic researchers to distinguish "Big C" creativity from "little c" creativity. The criteria for Creativity generally includes a mix of originality, utility, a final "product," and recognition by the community. Creativity (with a capital "C") is reserved for those rare souls who society—especially colleagues—have labeled creative geniuses, such as Nobel prize winners, groundbreaking pioneers and inventors, master poets, artists, and composers. Creative geniuses also have an audience that admires their genius—think William Shakespeare, Robert Frost, Albert Einstein, Sir Isaac Newton, William Blake, and Vincent Van Gogh.

Creativity (with a little "c"), then, is used to denote everyday creative acts outside the world's limelight, like finding a new way to explain something, brainstorming a new business strategy, or creating a new recipe for lasagna.

While this somewhat arbitrary delineation might be helpful for studying creativity in an academic setting, it inhibits our ability to understand the essence of the creative impulse. The *essence* of "creativity" is present in ANY creative act—regardless of how big or small it may seem from society's viewpoint. Maslow challenged the limiting notion of "Big C" creativity, saying, "When a little boy discovers the decimal system for himself, this can be a high moment of inspiration, and a high creative moment, and should not be waived aside because of some *a priori* definition which says creativeness ought to be socially useful or it ought to be novel, or nobody should have thought of it before, etc."[8] Our current culture doesn't celebrate our individual discoveries sufficiently. As children, many of us rarely had our inner discoveries recognized and celebrated by adults, which can lead us to grow up with low self-esteem and self-worth.

In business, too, we seem to lack the ability to identify and evaluate new discoveries and ideas. Creativity consultant Edward de Bono calls it "value sensitivity," and he notes that during business meetings, people are often good at squashing new ideas, and poor at seeing their value.[9]

Maslow identified an internal environment from which to examine creative acts or inspirational, inner realizations and discoveries. The scientist in the laboratory, the mother caring for her family, and the child learning the decimal system all offer the same opportunity to demonstrate creativity.

THE CREATIVE PROCESS REVISITED

Theoretical biologist Rupert Sheldrake said, "Creativity is a profound mystery precisely because it involves the appearance of patterns that never existed before."[10] Creativity emerges when we set aside our linear, rational mind, and explore our inner, experiential terrain.

Given the inner, subjective nature of the creative impulse, we'll rely heavily on the testimonies of those revered as *creative geniuses* in this chapter. Their words will reveal a stunning tapestry of insights shared among composers, novelists, painters, scientists, poets, and philosophers as they describe their own creative processes.

We won't, however, invest much time discussing aspects of their personalities, their backgrounds, or social dynamics, which is a common practice in academic research in understanding creativity. Although it is interesting and even insightful to read biographical accounts of creative geniuses, examining creativity in this fashion aligns us with Old-World thinking and the Newtonian paradigm of *causality*. Looking for the common external factors of creative inspiration may provide clues, but they will not give us a complete understanding. In truth, creativity manifests in an infinite variety of shapes and sizes—all derived from the same eternal wellspring: consciousness itself.

In the 1933 publication *Modern Man in Search of the Soul*, Carl Jung expounded on this realization about the impersonal quality of creativity:

> The secret of artistic creation and of the effectiveness of art is to be found in a return to the state of *participation mystique*—to that level of experience at which it is man who lives, and not the individual, and at which the weal or woe of the single human being does not count, by only human existence. This is why every great work of art is objective and impersonal, but nonetheless profoundly moves us each and all. And this is also why the personal life of the poet cannot be held essential to his art—but at most a help or a hindrance to his creative task.[11]

With the framework we learned from Book I about the nature of consciousness as the source of existence itself, we can now state the conclusion of Book II: *creativity is an aspect of consciousness— governed by impersonal attractor fields of varying strengths within Universal Consciousness (or Consciousness As Such).* Creativity represents a leap from a particular level of consciousness to a higher level. ANY "individual" can align with this quality of consciousness under the proper "inner" conditions, discussed in detail throughout this chapter.

If you review the academic literature on creativity, you'll undoubtedly come across the English political scientist and psychologist Graham Wallas. In his 1926 classic, *The Art of Thought*, Wallas summarized the creative process in four basic stages:[12]

1. *Preparation*: The mind must prepare for the creative solution, which requires study and thinking intently on the subject—whether it be a musical composition, a new invention, a mathematical formula, or a business dilemma. One must research and evaluate the subject.
2. *Incubation*: A germination period follows where the person steps away from the problem and takes up some form of activity like daydreaming, walking, or meditating, where he no longer engages in thinking about the problem.
3. *Illumination*: Often as a flash, a brilliant idea shoots across the mind, frequently during a mundane task or while one is involved with something else. In the light of illumination, an idea manifests and is cognized by the mind.
4. *Verification*: The idea must be tested to determine its validity. The composition must be scored or the mathematical formula proven.

Although variations of this creative process were developed over the last century, Wallas' four-stage framework remains. Does this mean anyone can go through these stages and discover brilliant, life-altering ideas? Not necessarily. Naturally, there are other forces at work.

The challenge with this model and essentially any other "formula" for creative breakthroughs is that it perpetuates an Old-World, step-by-step process for what is actually a nonlinear occurrence. Therefore, it is helpful to view these four phases as *conditions*, rather than sequential stages. As you'll recall from *Beyond Causality* in chapter 2, when the conditions are appropriate, manifestation unfolds. The stages of creativity do not *cause* creativity; rather, they represent some of the conditions necessary for creativity to emerge. Put another way, when creative insights are discovered, these four conditions are generally present, setting the stage for creativity to occur.

CREATIVE ARCHETYPES

Behind each "condition" of creativity, a clear archetype emerges. Archetypes, as explained by Jung, represent patterns that exist in the collective unconscious, also known as "primordial types … with universal images that have existed since the remotest times."[13] These archetypes are, in many ways, synonymous with the attractor fields within consciousness, of which we are all part.[14]

Similarly, "creative genius" is also a quality of consciousness—it's not what someone *is*, but an aspect of Creation itself. As such, each of the four archetypes—as well as the inclusive archetype of the creative genius—are accessible to each of us.[15]

These four archetypes do not represent "people" or "personalities," but rather *styles*, qualities, characteristics, or ways of being in the world. The four archetypes aligned to Wallas's four conditions are:

CONDITION	ARCHETYPE
Preparation	The Student
Incubation	The Wanderer
Illumination	The Light
Verification	The Scientist

ARCHETYPES OF THE CREATIVE PROCESS

The preparation and verification conditions utilize the logical left hemisphere of the brain, while incubation and illumination are nonlinear, right-hemisphere occurrences. The creative process, then, can be viewed as a blending of two worlds: the linear, Newtonian paradigm (Old World) and the nonlinear realm of consciousness (New World).

THE STUDENT:
THE ARCHETYPE OF PREPARATION

The Student perceives the world at large from what the Buddhists call *Beginner's Mind*. With profound humility, the Student seeks wisdom and counsel from various sources of knowledge. The Student loves knowledge for knowledge's sake. A trademark quality of the Student is curiosity. Just like the tiger curiously sniffs, prods, and licks a newly-discovered object, the Student explores using all available intellectual and intuitive faculties.

The Student makes new connections, perceives new patterns, and sees old things in fresh ways as a consequence of his openness and humility, avoiding what psychologists call "functional fixedness" (looking at a problem from a familiar viewpoint).[16] The Student is dedicated to his craft, and ultimately, to some form of higher truth. This uncommon level of dedication and enthusiasm is also a hallmark quality of those we label as "genius."[17]

The capacity for intense focus is another attribute of the Student, who has the discipline to work tirelessly on a problem. These periods of intensity are often followed by periods of relaxation or reverie (discussed below) before cycling to the next period of intensity.

A common block to aligning to the Student archetype is the ego in the form of arrogance and the "I know" attitude. The true Student can be an expert in his field or a master at his craft; however, he still possesses the willingness to grow, a gratitude for his gifts, and a sense of profound humility for his own ignorance. From this position, the Student learns, evolves, and finds new creative insights. Jung remained a student of the psyche throughout his life. Maslow was a student of the human being. Campbell was a student of comparative mythology. Bohm was a student of quantum physics and the nature of reality. Mozart was a student of music. Even Albert Einstein noted the enchantment experienced by the Student: "The most beautiful and profound emotion we can experience is the sensation of the mystical. It is the source of all true science. He to whom this emotion is a stranger, who can no longer wonder and stand rapt in awe, is as good as dead."[18]

Wonder at Reality's nature drives the Student onward. The Student finds joy in the *search* for Truth. Perhaps the poet Rainer Maria Rilke best personified the Student archetype when he said, "Do not now seek the answers, which cannot be given you because you would not be able to live them. And the point is, to live everything. Live the questions now. Perhaps you will then gradually, without noticing it, live along some distant day into the answer."[19]

The true Student is resolute in asking questions and exploring the continually-increasing pool of knowledge. It is helpful when the Student is tenacious in his pursuit of "living the questions." Those who are prepared for them discover breakthrough ideas. In Gardner's research on creative geniuses, he found that at least ten years of steady work at a discipline or craft was required for mastery.[20] Howard Gruber's research concurs: "Perhaps the single most reliable finding in our studies is that creative work takes a long time. With all due apologies to thunderbolts, creative work is not a matter of milliseconds, minutes, or even hours—but of months, years, and decades."[21]

The better prepared we are—the more immersed we are in a particular topic—the greater probability of momentarily attuning to a higher attractor field in order to uncover a creative insight. Einstein's daydream into the nature of light likely would not have yielded the theory of relativity had he not been armed with the vast knowledge of a physicist.

Herein lies a notable challenge for today's Creative Professional: we lack the time and attention to thoroughly prepare ourselves for creative inspiration. Communication technologies like email, instant messaging, text messaging, and cell phones, along with rapidly-changing lifestyles and more information processing, greater choices, and new forms of entertainment and distractions like digital music players, video on demand, sophisticated gaming consoles, and the Internet all spell one thing: distraction! We are more distracted, with less time to study, to expand our knowledge in specific areas, and to focus intently on solving problems. Juggling one ball requires little skill, but few can juggle four balls successfully—it's simply too easy to drop a ball, losing one's focus needed to align with the Student archetype.

How much time do we invest in our continued education? How many new subjects do we explore each year? How deep do we dive into the areas that interest us? A little less than half of all Americans read more than five books each year and many of these books fall in the leisure-reading category.[22] Additionally, the average American spends two and a half hours watching television each day.[23] For the sake of our creativity, it seems prudent to find ways to carve out time for study and learning. Even with demanding work schedules, family, and extracurricular activities, the commitment of the Student is a necessary requirement for creative inspiration.

Ken Wilber, a leading academic writer and philosopher on psycho-spiritual development, reports that he often spends years in extensive reading and researching before sitting down to pen one of his voluminous works. Then, the writing pours out of him like a waterfall over a short, uncomfortably intense period of several weeks.[24] As busy professionals, most of us don't have a comparable luxury. Most of us can, however, commit to increasing the amount of time we invest in our personal studies.

Renowned mathematician Henri Poincare documented his own creative process. His recounting of the discovery of the Fuchsian functions (an important equation in mathematics) follows Wallas's four stages of the creative process and illustrates the Student's need to push the mind's limits:

> For fifteen days I strove to prove that there could not be any functions like those I have since called Fuchsian functions. I was then very ignorant; every day I seated myself at my worktable, stayed an hour or two, tried a great number of combinations and reached no results. One evening, contrary to my custom, I drank black coffee and could not sleep. Ideas rose in crowds; I felt them collide until pairs interlocked, so to speak, making stable combinations. By the next morning I had established the existence of a class of Fuchsian functions, those which come from the hypergeometric series; I had only to write out the results, which took but a few hours.[25]

Poincare engaged his work as a Student, working tirelessly at his worktable each day. After breaking his normal pattern and drinking coffee in the evening, he was unable to sleep, allowing the Wanderer to emerge. Next, the Light of illumination unfolds as "ideas rose in crowds" and he felt them "collide until pairs interlocked." The Scientist concludes by writing out and checking the results.

Preparation often includes an experience of utter frustration, where the Student has pushed his mind to the limit and exhausted every conceivable area of discovery. When the mind reaches an impasse, it prepares to leap to a new level, represented as a "quantum leap" to a higher attractor field.[26]

The Student is not afraid to delve into topics that are often labeled "taboo" by his field because his quest is for higher truth, and not validation from peers.[27] The true Student can be an expert in his field—a master of his craft—but still maintain the willingness to grow and learn, and have profound humility and gratitude for his discoveries. As Bohm observes, "One prerequisite for originality is clearly that a person shall not be inclined to impose his preconceptions on the fact as he sees them. Rather, he must be able to learn something new, even if this means that the ideas and notions that are comfortable or dear to him may be overturned."[28]

> The qualities of the Student include:
>
> - Humility and willingness
> - Commitment and devotion to discovery
> - Inner alignment with something greater
> - Capacity for intense focus
> - Drive and enthusiasm to learn and grow, no matter what

THE WANDERER:
THE ARCHETYPE OF INCUBATION

After the Student prepares through hard work and dedication, the knowledge must take root. The sought-after, illuminated idea must germinate via incubation.[29] The person's level of consciousness must align to a higher attractor, if only momentarily. This process cannot be forced by any "individual" volitional act. It happens of its own and it takes time for consciousness to resolve the problem.

The Wanderer archetype evokes images of the lone, aimless traveler—carefree and relaxed in the moment. The Wanderer moves with the wind, remains unattached to ideologies, concepts and theories, and stays present. As the proverb instructs, "Bend like the willow; don't break like the oak." The Wanderer is flexible and highly adaptable, not rigid and assuming. The overriding style of the Wanderer is that of *allowing*, as opposed to *doing*—a "Yin" feminine style as opposed to a "Yang" masculine approach. Taking volitional action (doing) is like swimming the breaststroke against the currents of a river, while letting go or surrendering (allowing) is akin to floating downstream with the current.

Although the Wanderer may appear detached from life or responsibility, he actually has an innate appreciation and love for the beauty around him and for life itself.[30] Because the quality of genius is complete in and of itself, a person aligned to the field of discovery tends to live simply, given that his basic needs have already been met.[31]

Wolfgang Amadeus Mozart reflects on his creative process, "When I am, as it were, completely myself, entirely alone, and of good cheer—say, traveling in a carriage, or walking after a good meal, or during the night when I cannot sleep; it is on such occasions that my ideas flow best and most abundantly. Whence and how they come, I know not; nor can I force them."[32]

Poet Rudyard Kipling also understood the need to lay the conscious mind aside and embrace the Wanderer: "When your Daemon is in charge, do not try to think consciously. Drift, wait, and obey."[33] Acceptance of the creative process is paramount, as novelist Henry Miller notes, "Every man has his own destiny: the only imperative is to follow it, to accept it, no matter where it lead him."[34]

The ego, however, often gets in the way. Our Western, male-driven society constantly challenges us to *do* something—to *always* take action. In our "doer" culture, we are not comfortable with the notion of *allowing* an idea to germinate.[35] In fact, the Wanderer is not a welcomed archetype in modern society, especially in business where we have deadlines that we must keep. We are expected to generate awe-inspiring ideas and creative results while sitting at our desks or in back-to-back meetings all day. Perhaps the only place where we still welcome the Wanderer is in the arts, where a poet or painter is allowed to wait for his muse while roaming the woods or sitting in cafés, staring into nothingness.

Philosopher Friedrich Nietzsche recalls how the idea of "Eternal Recurrence," a key component of his classic *Thus Spoke Zarathustra,* came to him: "That day, I was walking through the woods beside Lake Silvaplana; I halted not far from Surlei, beside a huge, towering, pyramidal rock. It was there that the idea came to me."[36]

The feminine energy of allowing respects the process of creativity and more easily surrenders control of the outcome. If the Student doesn't surrender to the Wanderer, creative insight is unable to manifest.[37] In the field of science, students who don't surrender are known as "technicians," working to confirm other people's ideas. Those who learn to surrender with humility are known as scientific geniuses or philosophers. Author Gary Zukav clarifies this distinction:

> In short, scientists discover and technicians apply. However, it is no longer evident whether scientists really discover new things or whether they *create* them. Many people believe that "discovery" is actually an act of creation. If this is so, then the distinction between scientists, poets, painters and writers is not clear. In fact, it is possible that scientists, poets, painters and writers are all members of the same family of people whose gift it is to take those things which we call commonplace and to *re-present* them to us in such ways that our self-imposed limitations are expanded. Those people whom this gift is especially pronounced, we call geniuses."[38]

Requiring a profound level of *letting go*, the Act of Creation is preceded by an effortless state of mind void of conflict and uncertainty. Csikszentmihalyi termed this state of allowing as *flow*.[39] Immersed in a particular activity, we may achieve a Zen-like one-pointedness of mind, where the mind becomes silent, or at least, the mind resides in the backdrop of conscious awareness. In this state of flow, events unfold effortlessly, whether one is in the process of writing a poem, washing dishes, peeling a potato, or pruning the garden. The "actor" behind actions and the "thinker" behind the thinking dissolve. We glimpse at what the Sages teach us: *everything is happening of its own.*

The "eureka moment" of creative inspiration often occurs after a period of reveries or trances. Walking peacefully after a meal, driving aimlessly on a country road, or taking a shower, we allow the creative impulse to shine upon the mind. In his later years, Jung would sit by the lake of his private Bollingen stone castle for weeks at a time, playing in the water, sand, and rocks until he felt the inspiration to write.[40]

The composer Johannes Brahms describes the Wanderer's way: "I have to be in a semi-trance condition to get such results—a condition when the conscious mind is in temporary abeyance, and the subconscious is in control."[41]

Brahms' observation is common to many musical composers. Creativity researcher John Curtis Gowan notes three ubiquitous phases of incubation:

(1) the prelude ritual;
(2) the altered state of consciousness or creative spell, during which the creative idea is born—starting with vibrations, then mental images, then the flow of ideas which are finally clothed

in form. This syndrome often unfolds with extreme and uncanny rapidity as a trance, dream, reverie, somnambulistic state, or similar altered condition; and

(3) the postlude in which positive emotions about the experience suffuse the participant.[42]

Playwright Neil Simon acknowledged this altered state of consciousness by saying, "I slip into a state that is apart from reality. My mind wanders—even when I talk."[43]

In the preparation phase, the question is identified. In the incubation phase, the mind remains open to receive the answer. Pablo Picasso divulges the secret to his art: "The painter passes through states of fullness and of emptying. That is the whole secret of art. I take a walk in the forest of Fontainebleau. There I get an indigestion of greenness. I must empty this sensation into a picture. Green dominates in it. The painter paints as if in urgent need to discharge himself of his sensations and his visions."[44]

"Emptiness" personifies the archetype of the Wanderer. In pushing the mind to its limits, the Student's mind becomes full. Now, the Wanderer must let go of everything he thinks he knows and come to a state of emptiness. As Neuroscientist Nancy Andreasen notes, the brain "disorganizes," which removes fragmentation momentarily to allow the creative impulse to arise.[45] If the mind does not eventually surrender the question, the "space" is not available for the answer to present itself.

Imagine the mind is the Midtown Tunnel in New York City. Average thoughts are like cars driving through the tunnel. A crisis erupts, and the more questions we ask, the more cars fill the tunnel, and a traffic jam ensues. How can an ambulance—the solution to the crisis—race through the tunnel if it's filled with bumper-to-bumper traffic?

A famous Zen parable echoes this notion: A student comes to a famous Zen master and asks to be instructed in the way of Zen Buddhism. The master begins to discuss several topics of Buddhism like emptiness and meditation, but the student interrupts the master in an attempt to impress him and says, "Oh, I already know that."

The master then invites the student to have some tea. When the tea is ready, the master pours the tea into a teacup, filling it to the brim, spilling tea over the sides of the cup and onto the table.

The student exclaimed, "Stop! You can't pour tea into a full cup."

The master replied, "Return to me when your cup is empty."

The goal of the Wanderer archetype is to remove all barriers—a momentary emptying of the mind—so the Light can shine through.

The qualities of the Wanderer include:

- Openness and patience
- Allowing / noncontrolling
- Flexibility and high adaptability
- Appreciation and gratitude
- Right-brain orientation
- Unattached to belief systems

THE LIGHT:
THE ARCHETYPE OF ILLUMINATION

In *The Varieties of Religious Experience,* James had this to say about mystical experiences:

> Although so similar to states of feeling, mystical states seem to those who experience them to be also states of knowledge. They are states of insight into depths of truth unplumbed by the discursive intellect. They are illuminations, revelations, full of significance and importance, all inarticulate though they remain; and as a rule they carry with them a curious sense of authority for aftertime.[46]

The Light has many names: God, Divinity, the Inner Teacher, Brahman, the Higher Self, the Kingdom Within, Intuition, Daemon, Inspiration, Revelation, Creation, Spiritual Vision, Universal Consciousness, the Muse—the list goes on.

The etymology of *intuition* is, "knowing from within." The root of *inspire* means "inner breath." What is this inner knower—this breath from within? The Sages, relying exclusively on the inner subjective realization, tell us that consciousness itself is the inner knower and the light within. As Maharaj explains, "Realize that your true nature is that of pure light only, and both the perceived and the perceiver come and go together."[47] And, "Because you are, there is light, the light of knowledge, and when you are gone the light of knowledge will be extinguished."[48]

What else but this all-pervading Consciousness—that which gives us sentience and is the source of all manifestation in the physical world—can be the creative impulse? The *Light of Consciousness* is the pure essence of creativity.

Jung called the Light the "primordial vision" and saw it as an impersonal quality, separate from the personality of the artist: "The poet's work is an interpretation and illumination of the contents of consciousness ... The primordial experience is the source of his creativeness; it cannot be fathomed, and therefore requires mythological imagery to give it form."[49]

Out of the infinite field of consciousness, Creation unfolds. We generally assume that Creation unfolds in a logical, sequential manner. Yet, new, never-before-seen crystal formations materialize from an unknown dimension. Out of 100 million black beetles, a new white beetle species emerges.[50] By what mechanism does this white beetle come into being? This is where even advanced theoretical science cannot help us. Sheldrake's Hypothesis of Formative Causation, for example, does an excellent job of explaining how memory is encoded in morphic fields, and how learning is transmitted through morphic resonance to those entrained to particular fields (see chapter 1). Even Sheldrake notes, however, the theory's limitation in explaining the creation of a new field, like the first white beetle or a new crystal compound that never existed before.[51]

How does a new morphic field come into existence? This question requires what Kuhn called a "paradigm shift"—a leap from the linear, provable Old World to the nonlinear, unmeasurable domain of subjectivity. As we've previously noted, no scientific theory, by definition, can contain the solution because a "theory" is a concept of the mind, not an experiential realization of what is. The nonlinear domain of consciousness is beyond the provable, measurable world. How do you measure the experience of love? What's the "meaning" of a sunset? Science dares not to address such questions. Only Sages and a select number of poets venture into such subjective arenas.

As we learned in Book I, thoughts arise from the nonlinear field of consciousness—an invisible realm beyond perception, measurability, or provability. Creativity comes about when there's a jump from a particular level of consciousness governed by an attractor field to a higher level of consciousness. As all of these "levels" of consciousness represent a stratum within a "single" unified field of Consciousness, they are impersonal in nature. Throughout time, great creative geniuses intuited this phenomenon, and responded to their genius with humility, knowing the ego/self/individual cannot take credit for what unfolds during the illumination phase.

William Blake called God the "Poetic Genius."[52] Puccini said his greatest opera *Madame Butterfly* was "dictated to me by God."[53] Both Brahms and Beethoven appealed directly to the "Creator Himself."[54] Like Aristotle before him, Rudyard Kipling looked to his "Personal Daemon" for inspiration.[55] And, in recounting his experience with the creative process, Wolfgang Amadeus Mozart said, "What has been thus produced I do not easily forget, and this is perhaps the best gift I have my Divine Maker to thank for."[56]

Composer Richard Strauss had this to say about the source of his inspiration:

Composing is a procedure that is not so readily explained. When the inspiration comes, it is something of so subtle, tenuous, will-o'-the-wisp-like nature that it almost defies definition. When in my most inspired moods, I have definite compelling visions, involving a higher selfhood. I feel at such moments that I am tapping the source of Infinite and Eternal energy from which you and I and all things proceed. Religion calls it God.[57]

The words these creative individuals used to describe the Divine vary greatly; however, they all clearly point to a power beyond themselves—a subjective experience of a Higher Source— for their creative inspiration.

Campbell, who spent a great deal of his lifetime studying aspects of Divinity as a professor of comparative mythology, gave us a wonderful summary of Light's manifestation:

> The effect of the successful adventure of the hero is the unlocking and release again of the flow of life into the body of the world. The miracle of this flow may be represented in physical terms as a circulation of food substance, dynamically as a streaming of energy, or spiritually as a manifestation of grace ... An abundant harvest is the sign of God's grace; God's grace is the food of the soul; the lightning bolt is the harbinger of fertilizing rain, and at the same time the manifestation of the released energy of God. Grace, food substance, energy: these pour into the living world, and wherever they fail, life decomposes into death.[58]

To understand the Light requires a paradigm jump beyond the notions of causality and duality to the nonlinear, spiritual domain. The Light has no opposite; as such, it is "One." The Light cannot be accurately described with words. It is said to be ineffable, only realizable through an inner subjective realization—the realization of the nature of Divinity within.[59]

Words can only point the way to an internal reality that transcends the limitations of the linear, dualistic mind. Science faces this same challenge in its attempt to understand the nature of consciousness. The source of creative inspiration is not found in a concept, a formula, a theory, or a process. Instead, the Light can only be *realized* through the source of our own existence—consciousness itself.

Indian sage Nisargadatta Maharaj explains:

> Understand only one thing: That godly principle is there, that 'I-am-ness' or consciousness—that is the godliest of principles. It is there only so long as the vital breath or life force is there … This beingness at present is your nature—you are that only. So worship that principle. That quality, the touch of "I-am-ness" or consciousness, is something like the sweetness of the sugar cane.[60]

The source of creative inspiration is the same source as the field of consciousness. When unimpeded, manifestation can come upon a person very suddenly. The genius often envisions the entire answer in a flash. Mozart, for example, would experience an entire piece of music in his head, all at one time, not through a linear progression:

> All this fires my soul, and provided I am not disturbed, my subject enlarges itself, becomes methodized and defined, and the whole, though it be long, stands almost complete and finished in my mind, so that I can survey it, like a fine picture or a beautiful statue, at a glance. Nor do I hear in my imagination the parts *successively*, but I hear them, as it were, all at once. What a delight this is I cannot tell![61]

English poet Samuel Taylor Coleridge was reading the words of another poet when he fell asleep. Coleridge recounts in the third-person how his famous poem, Kubla Khan, was created:

> The Author [Coleridge] continued for about three hours in a profound sleep, at least of the external senses, during which time he has the most vivid confidence, that he could not have composed less than from two or three hundred lines; if that indeed can be called composition in which all the images rose up before him as things, with a parallel production of the correspondent expressions, without any sensation or consciousness of effort. On awaking he appeared to himself to have a distinct recollection of the whole, and taking his pen, ink, and paper, instantly and eagerly wrote down the lines that are here preserved.[62]

French poet and novelist Jean Cocteau describes a similar experience of illumination that occurred for the creation of *The Knights of the Round Table*: "I was sick and tired of writing when one morning, after having slept poorly, I woke with a start and witnessed, as from a seat in a theatre, three acts which brought to life an epoch and characters about which I had no documentary information and which I regarded moreover as forbidding. Long afterward, I succeeded in writing the play and I divined the circumstances that must have served to incite me."[63]

Friedrich Nietzsche explains the condition of illumination quite elegantly:

> The notion of revelation describes the condition quite simply; by which I mean that something profoundly convulsive and disturbing suddenly becomes visible and audible with inde-

scribable definiteness and exactness. One hears—one does not seek; one takes—one does not ask who gives: a thought flashes out like lightning, inevitably without hesitation—I have never had any choice about it ... Everything occurs quite without volition, as if in an eruption of freedom, independence, power, and divinity.[64]

For the Light to unfold, the individual must surrender to it. The person must, at least momentarily, rise above the ego, which creates a sense of detachment from everything "out there." True creative inspiration is void of personal, egoistic attributes (which is the discussion topic of the following chapter).

The creative genius simply becomes the channel for the Light. As Pablo Picasso explains,

How would you have a spectator live my picture as I have lived it? A picture comes to me from far off, who knows how far, I divined it, I saw it, I made it, and yet the next day I myself don't see what I have done. How can one penetrate my dreams, my instincts, my desires, my thoughts, which have taken a long time to elaborate themselves and bring themselves to the light, above all seize in them what I brought about, perhaps, against my will?[65]

Neil Simon accentuates the humility of the genius: "I don't write consciously—it is as if the muse sits on my shoulder."[66]

Although reading the accounts of those who we might consider genius is helpful, it is only through our own inner realization of embracing the Student and then surrendering to the Wanderer that we're able to invite the Light of illumination and experience creative inspiration.[67]

> The qualities of the Light include:
>
> - Nonlinearity
> - Humility
> - Faith in a higher power
> - Inner knowing of something greater than oneself

THE SCIENTIST: THE ARCHETYPE OF VERIFICATION

Following the unfolding of illumination, the Scientist takes over. The role of the Scientist is to verify the discovery and to translate the revelation into something comprehensible to others. Once again calling upon the resources of the left brain utilized previously by the Student in the preparation phase, the Scientist now employs intellectual prowess to communicate the discovery to the world.

In the verification stage, the mathematical formula is proofed, the composition is performed, the image first presented to the mind is drawn onto the canvas, and the prose of a literary masterpiece is captured on paper.

The term Scientist is used rather loosely as the act of translating the intangible to the physical domain. The moment of "creation" unfolds through illumination, preceded by preparation and incubation, and now the Scientist must confirm and communicate the revelation. In the verification phase, the illumined ideas become crystallized.

Translating the revelation into a cohesive, comprehensible form can be painstaking. Many notable creatives like Friedrich Nietzsche, Jackson Pollock, and Vincent van Gogh went mad while trying to verify their internal inspirations.

Artist Vincent van Gogh attempted to describe the process of translating the nonlinear into the linear: "How it happens that I can express something of that kind? Because the thing has already taken form in my mind before I start on it. The first attempts are absolutely unbearable. I say this because I want you to know that if you see something worthwhile in what I am doing, it is not by accident but because of real intention and purpose."[68]

Van Gogh found the verification stage "absolutely unbearable," as many other creative geniuses can attest. Other times, the Scientist's verification is effortless. Poincare, quoted previously, received his mathematical discovery and "had only to write out the results, which took but a few hours."

Chemist Dmitri Mendeleev, the creator of the Periodic Table of Elements, reported falling asleep while he struggled through exhaustion to categorize the elements by atomic weight: "I saw in a dream a table where all the elements fell into place as required. Awakening, I immediately wrote it down on a piece of paper. Only in one place did a correction later seem necessary."[69]

One of the challenges to an expansion of creativity in Western culture is that the scientist (with a lower case "s"), or what Zukav labeled as the technician, reigns supreme. The technician generally foregoes subjective, inward experience for intellectual, objective knowledge. The technician is generally an Old-World material reductionist who gives no weight to an inner reality that isn't objectively measurable. As such, the creative impulse, residing in the nonlinear, subjective domain, remains elusive and hidden.

Modern science and academia appear to be on the hunt to verify everything with quantitative data. This creates a problem in understanding the subjective realm, which lacks quantifiable data. In fact, the technician is skeptical of the subjective, nonlinear domain of consciousness because it can't be measured or proven—a prerequisite for Old-World, Newtonian science. Living in a land of symbols, abstraction and theory, the technician is the champion of the intellect. Wilber's Integral Map offers scientists, politicians, academics, and business people a more expanded operational viewpoint by pointing out that any truly Integral Model must incorporate both the subjective and the objective domains.[70] Hawkins' Map of Consciousness also demonstrates how the linear, objective domain is limited to levels of consciousness at 499 and below (Reason), whereas the nonlinear, subjective domain begins to emerge at consciousness level 500 (Love) and up (see chapter 3 and appendix C).

Interestingly, even though much of the scientific community denies the existence of a nonlinear, universal field of consciousness (Radical Subjectivity), all breakthroughs in science have come about through this divine Light of Consciousness. When a group of people is entrained to a particular belief, it is unable to see the reality beyond its own belief systems. A leap from one paradigm to a "higher" paradigm represents a jump to a higher attractor field—a higher level of consciousness. This jump requires humility, surrender, and the aforementioned conditions of preparation, incubation, and illumination.

With observation, we come to view creativity as a quality of the human condition. The experiential realization of our innate creativeness diminished the drive to have evidence-based proof (a restriction of the linear domain) of its existence. Anyone who has ever had a breakthrough idea enter his or her mind can give testament to this fact.

The qualities of the Scientist include:

- Dedication
- Linear / left-brain orientation
- Skilled / knowledgeable

QUALITY OF GENIUS

While discussing the archetypes that tend to unfold as creativity becomes available at the highest levels, we explored many of the inner conditions generally present when creativity manifests. Let's explore those inner qualities more closely.

If thoughts reside in this collective pool of consciousness as suggested in Book I, the belief in the privacy of thought is an illusion. The dualistic nature of the mind sees a "this" perceiving a "that," and the ego's identification with the mind as a "me," creates this illusion of privacy. (These ego mechanisms will be discussed in the following chapter.) This ego identification and the impersonal nature of thought are even more profound when we consider a trait commonly shared by those we call genius: humility.[71]

As we observed in the subjective recounting of geniuses in *The Light*, it is common for them to demonstrate tremendous humility by attributing their insights to a higher power.

Letting go of one's volitional choice or free will is a challenging task for most. Perhaps this is one of the reasons why genius is so rare. But this humility is indeed a prerequisite, as Jung observed: "Art is a kind of innate drive that seizes a human being and makes him its instrument. The artist is not a person endowed with free will who seeks his own ends, but one who allows art to realize its purposes through him."[72]

If all thoughts are rooted in a collective field of consciousness, then how can we claim authorship of our thoughts? True geniuses intuit this Higher Ground concept. Humility, it seems, aligns us with attractor fields of the higher levels of consciousness, which, in turn, facilitates the manifestation of *genius*.

Becoming a genius is, in essence, the process of *getting out of one's own way*—slipping past the ego's proclivities that block creative inspiration. Perhaps this is what Blake meant when he said, "The true Man is the source, he being the Poetic Genius."[73]

A true genius, then, does not wrestle between the polarities of false modesty and overt narcissism. If your thoughts aren't personal, who or what is going to take credit for them as "mine"?

Genius is a Latin word derived from the Greek *Ginesthai*, which means, "to be born or come into being."[74] As stated, both genius and creativity are innate qualities of consciousness, accessible to all mankind. The role of the genius—and anyone looking to manifest greater levels of creativity—is to become a channel for inspiration by removing the barriers (discussed in the following chapter) we subconsciously create.

INNER TERRAIN OF CREATIVENESS

Other than humility, what additional traits or qualities are common to the expression of creativity? In *The Farther Reaches of Human Nature*, Maslow identifies eighteen "determinants" of creativity, but he acknowledged that there can be thousands of influences. Anything that helps "the person move in the direction of greater psychological health or fuller humanness would amount to changing the whole person."[75] Put another way, "fuller humanness" is actualized through fully accessing consciousness by removing the barriers to creativity.

It is helpful to view the inner qualities of creativity as impersonal attributes as opposed to personal characteristics. Instead of representing an aspect of a creative person's personality, these impersonal qualities signify the removal of the barriers to creative potential.

Let's discuss a few noteworthy, interrelated, impersonal characteristics of the inner terrain.

The Present Moment

The creative person gives up the past—the way things have always been done. In so doing, he is not subject to the paradigm blindness that plagues the "uncreative" in our society. The mind tends to toggle between past and future, lamenting and retelling the past, and anxiously awaiting the future. Locked in a seemingly-endless loop of "what was" and "what might be," the mind misses out on the present moment. Additionally, the creative person surrenders the future, which otherwise distracts from the problem at hand.

The Light can only be *realized* in the Now, beyond the notions of past and future. While staying completely and totally present, the creative person is able to focus with a Zen-like one-pointedness-of-mind,[76] blocking out all distractions, and narrowing his awareness to align to the creative impulse.

The Beginner's Mind

The Zen Buddhist concept of the Beginner's Mind implies a high level of openness, free of preconceived notions. Maslow called this quality "Taoist Receptivity" to encapsulate this non-interfering way of being.

So how can one "be open"? Openness requires the removal of the ego's limitations and barriers, the opposite of psychological defensiveness. Openness helps one avoid the "lack of rigidity and permeability of boundaries in concepts, beliefs, perceptions, and hypotheses."[77]

Openness is aligned with the feminine quality of *allowing* versus the masculine energy of *doing,* as discussed in the Wanderer archetype section. Allowing creativity to unfold is very different from attempting to force creativity through some kind of "technique." Although our modern world operates on a demanding timeline, creativity is not personal and it cannot be "controlled" by an individual—a difficult concept for many to grasp. The openness of the Beginner's Mind allows a high degree of receptivity to the creative impulse when backed by the tenacity and dedication of the Student.

Internal Evaluation

Although society or the members of a particular field of study must verify the results of one's Inspiration before one is labeled "genius," the creative person seeks his or her validation internally. The creative person's evaluation comes from within first, before being subjected to outside judgment. This awareness allows the creative person to see things more lucidly, to tap into a reservoir of inner strength, to make connections that others miss, and to transcend the collective beliefs of the masses. Additionally, a person is less likely to fear judgment and criticism if he or she is evaluating the work produced internally.

Devoid of Judgment

The creative person creates without judgment. This isn't to say that he doesn't evaluate his own work or have personal preferences, but he simply doesn't judge it with the arbitrary indicators of "good" and "bad." Judgment, or the pathway of the critic, is a surefire way to shut down creativity.[78] Judgment is a double-edged sword that cuts you as you swing at others. Few critics, professional or otherwise, produce anything of creative value. Author Henry Miller explains, "It didn't matter to me if what I wrote should be considered bad. Good and bad dropped out of my vocabulary. I jumped with two feet into the realm of the aesthetics, the non-moral, non-ethical, non-utilitarian realm of art."[79]

With judgment arises the fear of not being good enough. This fear blocks the Light of illumination, hindering all hopes of creativity. (More on this in chapter 6.)

Spontaneity and Play

The ability to be spontaneous—to play with ideas in a variety of ways—is a common condition found in creative geniuses. Perhaps best expressed in the imagination of a child, the genius is willing to go beyond the bounds of "reasonability" to dance with the absurd, the bizarre, and the downright weird.

With play comes a certain zest for living that can be channeled into creative work. Bohm notes that the creative state of mind requires wholehearted interest in the topic of study, like that of a spirited young child.[80]

Tenacious Devotion

A lack of tenacity may be one of the most prevalent reasons notable creativity appears so infrequently in society. In today's world of endless entertainment, single-minded focus and tenacity are infrequently exhibited qualities. Few souls seem to display the necessary level of focus, commitment and devotion for unique discovery.

Although many of the creative geniuses highlighted above had faith or an inner knowing of Divinity, this is not a prerequisite. Devotion need not be to a "higher power," per se. For example, Freud was an atheist. No one, however, will deny Freud's tenacity to explore, discover, and understand the human psyche. This unyielding drive to advance one's understanding, as well as the collective knowledge of mankind, elucidates the creative genius. Ultimately, regardless of the field of endeavor, it's one's devotion to the truth that drives the wheels of Creation.

Transcending the Ego

In moments of creativeness, the individual may achieve a sage-like subjective state that transcends the everyday identification with the body-mind apparatus. In this state where the ego is held in abeyance, fear disappears (because all fear arises through ego-identifications), leading to reduction of defenses and inhibitions. Concurrent with the loss of fear is an inner sense of strength and courage that comes from a Higher Source. Devoid of the ego's need to control every moment, a person trusts this inner Source and is accepting of his Divine gifts.

Creativity is observed as a natural occurrence, where the creative act is the Act of Creation. When the individual removes enough barriers to the creative impulse through the momentary transcendence of ego identification, the Light is able to shine through the individual as an expression of Divinty. Of course, depending upon the level of consciousness of the individual, moments after the Act of Creation unfolds, the ego may claim authorship of the Creation.

From the Linear to the Nonlinear

In the creative state, internal processing shifts from the intellectual abstraction of the conscious mind to an "aesthetic perceiving" or a discernment of the essence of Reality. This subjective state allows for unbridled spontaneity and spiritual expression as the imposed boundaries of the ego dissolve into the oneness of all that exists.

Maslow noted the limitations of the linear mind: "Our conscious intellect is too exclusively analytic, rational, numerical, atomistic, conceptual and so it misses a great deal of reality, especially within ourselves."[81]

What lies beyond the sophisticated, complex processing of the intellect is the nonlinear, spiritual domain—the realm of direct, subjective realization of Divinity (not of a personal subjective state as implied by phenomenology, but rather, a direct experience of the progressive levels of realization of the field of consciousness). We might state it like this: for the Light to enter, the mind must Wander.

The Impersonal, But Natural State

We can reiterate that the inner qualities of creativity are *not* personal traits of the individual. In fact, personal traits or characteristics often hinder the unfolding of one's innate creativeness. Creativity is an impersonal quality of consciousness that presents itself when the inner conditions are appropriate. Jung noted, "Every creative person is a duality or a synthesis of contradictory aptitudes. On the one side, he is a human being with a personal life, while on the other side he is an impersonal, creative process ... [W]e can only understand him in his capacity of artist by looking at his creative achievement."[82]

One's inner terrain—mental health combined with a degree of alignment with a high-energy attractor field (higher level of consciousness) set by intention—establishes the potential range of one's creative genius. When preconceived notions, limiting beliefs, and negative emotions like fear are held in abeyance—when we are of sound mental health—creativity unfolds as a natural occurrence.

Consider how radical this concept is: creativity is our *natural state*, not an anomaly that arises from time to time.[83] The conditions for creativity are the innate qualities of a fully "self-actualized" human being.[84] Granted, the demands from society and ourselves are not supportive of our natural state, and this disrupts the creative process. Our business culture, for example, reinforces the opposite of creativity by celebrating and rewarding time spent on the job rather than the creative results achieved.

The mind rides a wave that either worries through projections into the future (the front of the wave) or laments about old stories of the past (the back of the wave). Only by staying in the present moment (on the crest of the wave) can we manifest our natural state. To paraphrase Hawkins, the sun is always shining; we need only remove the clouds.[85]

THE CREATIVE ENVIRONMENT

Creative inspiration arises in some of the most unexpected places, defying the patterns creativity researchers often identify. In contemplating creative manifestation, there is much we can say about our current "Creativity Crisis" and the external conditions helpful for fostering creativity within a community—or even within humanity.

It is important to reiterate that these external conditions do not *cause* creativity, nor are they even requirements. Creativity is an internal, subjective state that transcends the Newtonian paradigm of the measurable world. All of the external conditions for creativity can be present without an inkling of creative inspiration manifesting; without the inner conditions, one cannot align to a higher attractor field within consciousness.

Carl Rogers addressed two important external conditions that nurture creative potential: psychological safety and psychological freedom.[86] Psychological safety requires an environment where people are empathic and accepting of the individual's worth unconditionally, without judgment. Psychological freedom encourages free symbolic expression, allowing individuals to think, feel, and transcend prior conditioning or beliefs. Essentially, repressed, censored, and controlled societies are likely to inhibit creative output more than free, democratic environments. If you're afraid of getting your head chopped off or going to prison for manifesting creative ideas, you may be less likely to pursue them.

These external conditions support the internal conditions discussed above: when all our basic human needs are met and we're in a state devoid of fear or judgment, the creative impulse is more likely to manifest.[87]

Exclusively examining "Big C" creativity through a "systems approach," Mihaly Csikszentmihalyi identifies three critical elements for the unfolding of creative genius:

1) A culture that contains symbolic rules,
2) A person who brings novelty into the symbolic domain, and
3) A field of experts who recognize and validate the innovation.[88]

Creative ideas, products, or discoveries manifest from a system composed of the above three components. "Big C" creativity requires approval and confirmation from a field of experts. For example, Einstein's Theory of Relativity needed to be confirmed—or at least validated—by his peer physicists before his theory could be heralded as a stroke of genius.

Within these criteria, however, Emily Dickinson cannot be considered an artistic genius since during her lifetime, she was unknown and unaccepted by literary experts. Her genius was acknowledged years after her death, when she became a celebrated American poet of the modern era.

The creative genius doesn't need external validation from others to enhance her self-worth. The inspiration and fulfillment of the genius's work is internally derived. Perhaps more importantly, the work of the genius must be separated from that of the individual, as Jung noted. The creative expression of the artist, in the form of a painting, poem, theory, story, photograph, recipe, or piece of music, stands on its own. From this perspective, Dickinson's acts of creation were creative even without the validation of a community—or even herself.

In an attempt to figure out what leads to the "creative brain," neuroscientist Nancy Andreasen points out that there were specific periods of time when creativity flourished. For example, in fifth- and fourth-century (B.C.) Athens featured Western philosophers like Pythagoras, Socrates, Plato, and Aristotle. The Italian Renaissance of the fifteenth century showcased the artistic genius of Leonardo da Vinci and Michelangelo Buonarroti. The late nineteenth and early twentieth centuries in the United States offered brilliant inventions like Eli Whitney's cotton gin, Samuel Morse's telegraph and Morse code, Alexander Graham Bell's telephone and Thomas Edison's light bulb and phonograph.[89]

Andreasen observed distinct environmental conditions present during these periods of monumental creativity, such as freedom, novelty, a critical mass of creative people, a competitive atmosphere that is free and fair, mentors and patrons, and economic prosperity.[90]

Notice how the external conditions necessary for creativity to thrive supports internal creative development. For example, a free and fair outer environment may encourage an inner freedom that doesn't fear criticism or judgment. A competitive environment may energize the archetype of the Student, similar to how it's easier for college students to study when their peers are studying.

The common themes of freedom, support, and growth are consistently mentioned in Andreasen's study. The creative environment is devoid of fear, harsh judgment, prejudice, and other destructive energies. It is here, in the sea of infinite potentiality, that our creative expression shines like a child joyfully playing in his imaginary world.

Chapter 6
The Guard to Creative Genius

The mind, in its identity with the ego, cannot, by definition, comprehend reality; if it could, it would instantly dissolve itself upon recognition of its own illusory nature. It is only beyond the paradox of mind transcending ego that that which Is stands forth self-evident and dazzling in its infinite Absoluteness. And then all these words are useless.

—David R. Hawkins, *Power vs. Force*

THE EVOLVING HUMAN BRAIN

Millennia ago, reptilian creatures represented the highest form of evolution on earth. The simple *lizard brain* supported basic life functions—digestion, circulation, respiration and reproduction.[1] There was no advanced information processing at this early stage of the brain's development. Eat. Breathe. Mate. Fight. Survive.

Through evolution, mammalian creatures developed a more advanced brain. Extending from the lizard brain's stem, the *leopard brain*, or limbic system, developed. These more advanced species possessed the capacity for emotion and sophisticated coordination of movement. Primal instinctiveness like Walter Canon's famed *fight-or-flight response*[2] and Hans Selye's *stress alarm reactions*[3] ran the show at this level.

The next stage of brain evolution was the development of the impressive prefrontal cortex, or the *learning brain*, which included the ability to remember, solve problems, use language and numbers, and create. The learning brain brings us to present-day Homo sapiens.[4] Still superior to a high-tech computer, the human brain is capable of extraordinary information processing. Think about all the filters the brain is using from instant to instant. While driving a car, the brain is processing an impressively large amount of data, determining which bits of information are important and which are not. We're simultaneously talking on our hands-free cell phones, contemplating where to go to dinner with news radio playing in the background, all while navigating to our destination (hopefully) without smashing into another car.

It's significant that each human embryo undergoes these three basic stages of development during its nine months in the womb. The fully-developed human brain contains the more primitive lizard and leopard brains, which reveals the primary challenge to our creativity: our ancestral, animalistic heritage is still an integral component of our brain physiology.

What happens when someone drops a bowling ball on your foot? You scream—an inherent reaction of the animal brain. How does a lion respond when a tiger approaches his den? How does a man respond when an intruder enters his home? Any difference?

Keep in mind that the same drivers for survival in the animal kingdom exist in humans. As the animal is always on the move—hunting, running, eating, drinking, communicating, protecting, and mating—the human, too, has a similar instinctive drive. While our brain functioning is more sophisticated, we still have the same biological inheritance, a primal drive running in the background.

The human brain can be likened to the personal computer (PC) operating system, Microsoft Windows®. Bill Gates built Microsoft Windows on a primitive operating program called DOS in the early 80s. DOS is a programming language that requires technical knowledge of codes and commands. Microsoft Windows enables the PC user to interact with a variety of software programs with reasonable ease, using a mouse or keyboard to navigate, clicking on icons and words, without any programming knowledge. While the Windows operating system allows us common folk to use the computer, primitive DOS, was (and still is) running in the background often leading to instability, inconsistent performance, and system crashes.[5] Like the PC, the human brain is built on an old operating system that includes the lizard and leopard brain.

Contained within the brain's stem, there's a loosely knit system of neurons called the *reticular activating system* (RAS) which essentially acts as a toggle switch between the limbic system (the leopard brain) and the prefrontal cortex (the learning or thinking brain).[6] When we are emotionally charged, the learning brain shuts down and our instincts take over. With the leopard brain in control, we are subject to the flight-or-fight response as if we're on automatic pilot. When we are in a relaxed state, the learning brain is activated and the animal brain is switched off, allowing for the activation of creative intuition and logical reasoning—the tools needed for higher creativity.

Consciousness can be compared to the hardware of a computer. The software is all the programming society inputs into the hard drive via beliefs, opinions, and social patterns. As the hardware of the computer (consciousness) is innately innocent, it is merely at the effect of its programming.[7] The animal brain lives on in mankind. Instincts as learned patterns of behavior developed over millennia are continually reinforced and reconditioned by society.

THE SPIRITUAL BRAIN

Hawkins' consciousness research has uncovered a new evolution in brain physiology. What he calls the "Etheric Brain" is now available to approximately 15% of the world's population.[8] Not anatomical in structure, the Etheric Brain is purely energetic in construction and it picks up high-energy frequencies aligned with higher levels of consciousness.[9]

For the majority of mankind, information moves quickly from the thalamus or nerve relay station to the amygdala or the emotional center of the brain. Within this structure, information moves very slowly to the cerebral cortex (the learning brain) and moves quickly to the emotional center, resulting in a highly reactive individual who often fires off knee-jerk reactions without logic or reason. A driver with "road rage" exhibits this type of brain physiology. Concordant with this emotional instability, Hawkins' research discovered an increase in stress in the form of adrenaline and a decrease in the neurotransmitter serotonin, a condition found in most cases of depression and anxiety.[10]

In contrast, for those who are more evolved, the cerebral cortex, the thalamus, and the Etheric Brain process information very quickly before reaching the emotional center. Within this information blueprint, individuals are able to access both logic and intuitive processing before getting emotional, which leads one to be less reactive and more rational. Along with higher-brain processing comes increased levels of endorphins, which are associated with feelings of inner peace and pleasure, and higher levels of serotonin, making people less susceptible to depression and anxiety.

The Etheric Brain is accessible to anyone committed to integrity and truth. Its presence is not a consequence of one's level of intelligence as measured by IQ, but rather a function of one's prevailing level of consciousness.

The discovery of brain plasticity, or neuroplasticity, gives us an optimistic perspective on a person's ability to make positive changes. As Andreasen explains:

> Sigmund Freud and the psychoanalytic movement gave us an awareness that early life experiences affect emotional development and attitudes in later life. Neuroscience adds a new dimension: it makes us aware that experiences *throughout* life change the brain throughout life. We are literally remaking our brains—who we are and how we think, with all our actions, reactions, perceptions, postures, and positions—every minute of the day and every day of the week and every month and year of our entire lives.[11]

It seems apparent that mindful practices like meditation and contemplation will affect the brain's physiology as well. Richard Davidson, director of the Keck Laboratory for Functional Brain Imaging and Behavior and University of Wisconsin professor of psychology, discovered that meditative practices alter brain activity involving various mental processes. Teaming up with the Dalai Lama, the study compared the brain activity of Tibetan Buddhist meditation practitioners with nonmeditators of the same age. Davidson and his colleagues found that the Buddhist monks had a higher level of brain impulses associated with higher mental activity such as learning and conscious perception than nonmeditators, suggesting long-term meditation practices can change the brain's physiology.[12]

In another study, Sara Lazar of Harvard Medical School used Magnetic Resonance Imaging (MRI) to compare the brain's physical structure of daily meditators who practice the Buddhist "Insight" meditation with a group of nonmeditators. Lazar and her colleagues found that the brain structures in the group of meditators featured a thicker cortex (a bigger "learning brain") compared to the sample of nonmeditators.[13]

A meditation study on Raja yoga by B. K. Anand and associates from the All India Institute of Medical Sciences in New Delhi offers further evidence of altered brain function in the spiritually adept. In this study, the brainwaves resulting from the electroencephalogram (EEG) readings demonstrate a deeper state almost devoid of any reaction to sensory input in meditators compared to the various brainwave frequencies activated by sensory stimuli of normal adults.[14]

Finally, A. Kasamatsu at the Tokyo University Branch Hospital conducted EEG testing on Zen practitioners. Kasamatsu found that brain waves of meditators rapidly shifted from beta waves of waking consciousness to alpha waves and, in some cases, theta waves associated with sleep appeared, a phenomenon uncommon in normal subjects.[15]

The basic animal brain was designed to preserve survival of the animal body. Although meditative and even artistic practices can aid the animal body's survival, these practices appear to serve a "higher" need that transcends one's physical drive. Current neuroscience shows that music, art, nature, spirituality, and altruism all demonstrate positive effects on the physiology to the nondominant brain hemisphere.[16]

The Etheric Brain developed as a consequence of the evolution of consciousness. With the capacity for spiritual exploration and self-realization, this Etheric Brain represents an entirely new domain for creative insight. The guard of the Etheric Brain, ironically, is what served mankind's survival: the ego in the form of the animal brain. In better understanding the mechanisms of this primitive self, we can transcend its urges, freeing our minds to align with creativity.

THE EGO: A FOREVER WANTING ANIMAL

An understanding of the brain's evolution helps us decipher the mechanisms of the ego as our biological inheritance. From a psychoanalytic perspective, the ego performs a complex juggling act, aligning one's personality with the external social reality and simultaneously balancing and resolving conflict between the conscience (Freud's "superego"), the inner idealized standards ("ego-ideal"), and the animal instincts ("id").[17] The psychologically healthy individual has a well-rounded, realistic, and balanced personality, implying a survival value to the ego. Unhealthy individuals may have a "weak ego" and low self-esteem, or the converse, an over-inflated ego characterized by "egotism."

In spiritual parlance, the ego is equated with what Deikman calls the "survival self,"[18] compared to the Self (with a capital "S"), which represents a universal aspect of Divinity within.[19] From this perspective, the "ego" implies a negative quality more closely aligned with the primal drive of Freud's id, representing something to be transcended through one's spiritual evolution. The Sages tell us that identification with the body-mind organism is the main block to experiencing nonlinear Reality. This ego identification leads us to experience a sense of separateness from everything else, creating a duality of the world "out there" against the world "in here" (Descartes dualistic dilemma of *res cognitas* and *res extensa*.)

To avoid confusion with various definitions of "ego" from psychological and spiritual phraseology, let's define the ego as a *mechanism responsible for our sense of self.* The ego represents a collection of thoughts presumed to be representative of one's personal identity. This composite of thoughts and beliefs and their associated meanings create the illusion of a personal self as the "cause" of one's thoughts, emotions, actions, and ultimately, one's existence.[20]

In transcending the ego's limitations, we pave the way for the emergence of the creative impulse, symbolized by a jump to higher attractors as we progress to ever-higher levels of consciousness. To understand creativity, we need to consider the programs the ego is constantly running in order to transcend them. Our wants, cravings, and desires, for example, are a function of the ego's survival drive to *acquire.* As noted above, our animal tendencies are wired into our brains. The animal is always on the move—searching for food or water, hunting, mating, protecting, hiding, sniffing, tasting, testing—longing to survive and prosper. The squirrel doesn't find and store only enough acorns to survive a harsh winter. Given the opportunity, the squirrel continues to accumulate more acorns than it can consume, guided by a ceaseless drive to acquire. This drive to perpetuate one's existence through survival and acquisition is intrinsic to the human being as well.

WANTS VERSUS NEEDS

Let's distinguish between wants and needs. A *need* represents what one is required to have in order to survive; once the need is satisfied, the drive to satisfy that need dissipates. For example, once you have a roof over your head, you no longer *need* shelter. You may *want* a fancier house in a nicer neighborhood, but your need for shelter is satisfied. You may *need* a watch to help you get to work on time, but you may *want* a Rolex to impress your friends.[21]

Self-help teachers generally prescribe emotional intensity for realizing our goals. In the perennial self-help text *Think and Grow Rich*, Napoleon Hill highlights "intense desire" as a common trait of successful people.[22] Personal development coach Tony Robbins advocates passion as the building block for achievement.[23] Although this instruction is well intended, it may be misguided.

Strong desire and emotional intensity can actually block the manifestation of your goals. Consciousness research reveals that strongly desiring something can block your realization of it. Desire (125), as a level of consciousness, with its concordant emotion of craving, is governed by a weak attractor field calibrating below the critical level of integrity.[24] Desire is the driver behind the animal brain, not the Etheric Brain or the Higher Self.

Another important distinction here is between intention and emotion. Intending to grow your business, for example, so that you can provide for your family and the community doesn't require emotionality. A high intention, driven by a purpose beyond your personal wants or needs, like serving your family, your community, or your country, is all that is required. Various attractor fields govern levels of intention in consciousness. Higher intentions are represented by something bigger than personal wants, aligning a person to a more powerful attractor field. In contrast, intense desire switches your brain into "survival mode," inhibiting creativity and higher functioning, and aligning a person to a weaker attractor field. The ego is always seeking control of a situation; in fact, the narcissistic core of the ego believes it is sovereign over everything and is the source of existence itself. When aligned with Spirit, a person is able to surrender the ego's need for control and even the desired outcome for a situation. The act of surrender, which the ego views as a weakness, actually calls upon the powerful energy of the Light.

As Maslow noted, the creative person is able to set the personal ego aside, at least momentarily, to allow creativeness to manifest. When desire, the fuel of the ego, is in charge, the inner conditions necessary for manifesting creativity are crippled. Maslow aptly acknowledged that "man is a perpetually wanting animal."[25] Similarly, the spiritual text *A Course in Miracles* asserts that the ego's basic doctrine is "Seek, but do not find."[26] When we are motivated by Love, in contrast, we align with an energy that is self-sustaining and ever-present. Love has no needs or wants—it is complete within itself—whereas wantingness, by definition, arises from a feeling of incompleteness.

Left unchecked, the ego locks us into an endless cycle of cravings, wants, and desires. It is the primary block to accessing creativity or channeling the creative impulse.

Although this insight may appear paradoxical (be aware of what you want, but don't actually *want* it), references from your own subjective experience will probably help your understanding. When someone desperately wants to be in a relationship—be it romantic, professional, or cordial—isn't that relationship often elusive? And what happens when this person surrenders the desire for the relationship? Often, the relationship presents itself. (For further discussion on this topic, see *Weapon 4: Attachments* below.)

FOUR WEAPONS OF THE UNCREATIVE

If the ego is the guard who keeps creative inspiration at bay, what are its tools or mechanisms? The ego employs four primary weapons in defense of its identity: judgments, positions, opinions, and attachments. By understanding these weapons, we can learn to transcend them and in so doing, access higher creativity.

Weapon 1: Positions

Positions or *positionalities* are the bedrock of the ego's defenses against creativity. Positionalities represent errors in the mind's programming, the consequence of the "duality of opposites" discussed in chapter 2. Once the mind takes a position ("this is good"), it instantly creates its opposite ("that is bad"). The lens of perception becomes more and more distorted every time an additional position is taken.[27] The ego/mind holds an incalculable number of positions about every aspect of life. These positions become the core filter with which the ego/mind evaluates the external world.

The mind believes *this is how it is*, negating other potentialities, assuming its position is accurate and fortifying its positions to the point of absurdity even in the face of striking evidence to the contrary. For example, author Robert Henderson wrote three books trying to disprove Einstein's theories and expose him as a fraud.[28] (It appears no one has told this octogenarian about the atomic bombings on Hiroshima or Nagasaki.) Furthermore, turn on any news broadcast or open any newspaper and you will be inundated with an endless stream of positionalities.

Hawkins notes that the ego is a compilation of positions bound together by fear and vanity.[29] He identifies four primordial positionalities that hold the structure of the ego in place and drive the thinking mechanism and its related content. These four core ego positions are:[30]

[1] *Ideas have significance and importance.*

Ideas are important because the ego claims them as "mine." Thoughts are imbued with "specialness" and provide the framework for our "personal" worlds. Seeing ideas through the lens of the nonlinear, spiritual domain, however, we begin to see the impersonal nature of thoughts, which weakens this primordial position of the ego. Thoughts are not personal assets, but rather components of Universal Consciousness, accessible by all.

[2] *There is a dividing line between opposites.*

Since the mind takes "positions," it perceives reality through the duality of opposites. In so doing, it is incapable of seeing the infinite gradations of potentiality in a single variable. In contrast, as we discussed in *Transcending the Opposites* in chapter 2, instead of there being "light" and its opposite, "dark," we see a gradient scale of light and various degrees of the absence of light. The mind sees a dividing line between opposites and it thinks it is capable of discerning the difference between the two.

[3] *There is a value of authorship—thoughts are valuable because they are "mine."*

Similar to number one above, thoughts are special because they are "mine." Yet, the humility and the lack of authorship shown repeatedly by creative geniuses testify to the universal aspect of the creative impulse. In fact, we are not the *authors* of our thoughts; we're a mere channel for Divine inspiration in one form or another.

[4] *Thinking is necessary for control, and survival depends upon control.*

The mind believes that it must think in order to survive—if it doesn't have "control" of the situation, it will be at the mercy of the environment. *If I don't plan dinner, I won't eat.* This is an understandable sentiment. As the Sages remind us, however, everything is happening of its own—nothing is "causing" anything to occur. *Everything is the expression of its own essence and is self-existent.*[31]

When the mind is silent, the world doesn't stop. Instead, everything in the physical world unfolds on its own—only now, the busyness of constant thoughting is replaced by profound peace and the creative impulse flows freely.

These deep-rooted positionalities form the basis of the opinions (discussed below) and beliefs that are created and energized each day by the mind. Through introspection, contemplation, and self-inquiry, we are able to identify, examine, and surrender these limiting positionalities. Positionalities lock us into paradigm blindness, hindering our development to higher levels of consciousness.

With humility, we can acknowledge that we *know* very little (although we may *know about* a great deal). The mind can know about a diverse range of topics; however, to know something requires one to *be* it. As previously mentioned, we can intellectually know a lot about dogs, but we can't know what it is to be a dog. As Maharaj proclaims, "All knowledge is ignorance, that 'I do not know' is the only true statement the mind can make."[32] Once this is fully comprehended, a person is less likely to turn ideas into positions, leading to a more flexible, relaxed, and creative individual.

Weapon 2: Judgments

Deeply-rooted positions power a more obvious ego tool: judgment. Due to the nature of perception through the dualistic mind (me versus the world), the ego is incapable of seeing anything as it is. Experiencing the world through our perceptual filters leads us to judge everything in our environment: good versus bad, friend versus foe, light versus darkness, right versus wrong. Although judgments can be rationalized by the mind ("He deserves it because ..."), they never serve the individual since the end does NOT justify the means, as ethics dictate. Such rationalized sentiments can justify any barbaric behavior.[33]

The Bible tells us, "Judge not, lest ye be judged," and, "'Judgment is mine,' sayeth the Lord." Hawkins points out that judgment is simply an inappropriate tool to evaluate internal and external events, like using a ruler to measure water. In order to accurately judge something, one would need to know an infinite number of details and understand the entire, dynamic context of a situation, which is virtually impossible. Since human beings are not omniscient, we lack the ability to accurately *judge* anything.

Discernment, by contrast, is a quality of evaluation from Higher Ground, devoid of condemnation or judgment. Discernment is a quality of consciousness available to those who have tamed the animal brain.

How can we attempt to move beyond judgmentalism, then? By seeing things unfold through the lens of compassion. With compassion, one can seek to understand instead of condemn, realizing that "everybody is doing the best they can with the resources they have."[34] From here, we understand the innate limitations of the human condition and feel compassion for others.

In judging another human being, we may say, "They shouldn't have done that." With compassion, we understand that each of us perceives and evaluates events differently based on our beliefs, memories of past experiences, and our prevailing level of consciousness. Compassion breeds understanding, and we then realize that the options or choices available vary from person to person. For example, when you give someone a gift that you spent a great deal of time picking out, you might expect the recipient to respond with gratitude for your efforts. In truth, the recipient may not have the capacity to express gratitude in the way you want it due to his current psychological state or current state of awareness. In seeking to understand rather than condemn, compassion for the ungrateful arises—instead of judgment.

Transcending judgment has another benefit. As we said above, judgment acts as a double-edged sword: the judgments we project onto others are subconsciously projected back onto ourselves via our inner critic. This inner critic squashes creative ideas and blocks their manifestation. The inner critic cleverly sabotages our development and, left unchecked, will continually drain the joy from one's life experiences. The inner critic is silenced once we surrender judgment of others. When we stop critiquing others, we're less likely to project the criticism inward onto ourselves.

Once we begin to see that everything *is how it is* (without any additional commentary), an "okayness" evolves, leading to a kinder, gentler, more easy-going way of being—the qualities crucial for manifesting a creative life.

Weapon 3: Opinions

Opinions are an even more refined type of judgment, tightly held in place by an underlying position. Opinions are the mind's projections of how things "should be" based on its own ideals. The mind loves having opinions about almost everything. In fact, for many of us, the idea of *not* having an opinion on a topic of discussion seems foreign. If you ask someone, *What's your opinion on the price of tea in China?*, you'll usually get an answer, regardless of one's knowledge about the subject in question. Pay close attention during elections and other political discussions and you'll witness the endless opinions voters have on topics they often know little about. Additionally, most of the information the voters do have is learned via propaganda from various media sources that each have their own opinions (fueled by positions) about world events and their meanings.

That our opinions are nothing but the ego's vanities is difficult for the mind to accept. Consider how many "opinions" you may have about politics, religion, or another controversial topic like abortion, stem cell research, or capital punishment. Possibly, you believe these opinions as fact, and the ego energizes those opinions with emotional intensity. Just as judgment can be a counterproductive way to engage life and channel creativity, opinions can impede the creative process as well. Opinions inhibit our ability to understand the context of a situation; in apperceiving the context from Higher Ground, we note that our opinions simply contribute to the ego's nonsensical rhetoric.[35] When people are given more information on a particular subject, their perspective tends to shift because they now have a better understanding of the context (see *Transcending Conflict* in the following chapter).

Note the difference between opinions and perspectives. An *opinion* is "how it is" from the ego's position, without the possibility of fallacy. A *perspective* is how things "appear to be" from the individual's vantage point. Someone with an opinion might say, "What they are doing is wrong!" Someone with a perspective might say, "It appears, from my perspective, that what they are doing is not serving the greater good." An opinion is derived from an egoistic, self-centered reality whereas a perspective acknowledges with humility that the mind is incapable of discerning truth from falsehood.

If you picture a chair projected in front of you, the three-dimensional image is going to change depending on your position. From one standpoint, you see the back of the chair; from another, the front; and there are numerous angles in between. The image of the chair isn't changing—only one's perspective changes based on his or her position in the room.

How do we transcend the mind's proclivity to generate opinions? The answer is the potent by-product of the creative genius: humility. With humility, the mind is able to penetrate its own self-infatuation and self-indulgences, uncovering the vanities that all opinions represent. The mind can only speculate about something through the use of concept manipulation; it can't *know* anything directly because to know something would require one to *be* it.[36] (The Sage, in contrast, speaks with authority not based on citation of ecclesiastic doctrine, but rather, on a subjective realization of the Presence of Divinity within.)

One needs profound humility to undo the vast fortress of opinions, judgments, and positions that the mind creates. True creative geniuses, possessing the trademark quality of humility, are less likely to have judgments, positions, and opinions within their particular area of mastery during periods of creative inspiration.[37]

Weapon 4: Attachments

Ah, the joy of *things*. Look all around you. We have stuff everywhere. Our culture has a near obsession with things of all types, shapes, and colors. HSN. QVC. Wal-Mart. Target. Amazon.com.

Things abound.

Things aren't the problem; the challenge is we latch onto things and they become part of our identity—who we think we are. Imbued with a sense of importance or "specialness" from being labeled as "mine," we now think we can't live without them. In fact, the use of the possessive adjectives "my" or "mine" generally reveals an attachment. Cars, jobs, houses, books, jewelry, clothing, pets, and even our spouse or friends become objects of attachment. Furthermore, similar to how the mind gets attached to things, it also gets attached to intangibles—the content of the mind—like beliefs, opinions, and ideologies. The attachment to the Old-World paradigm, for example, keeps the collective culture from embracing the exciting New-World understanding. The attachment to an old paradigm creates a barrier to the creative impulse by inhibiting the leap to a higher attractor field.

Why do we get attached? We believe our attachments will bring us happiness. *If I get that new car, then I'll be happy. If I find the love of my life, then I'll be happy.*

As previously stated, "Man is a perpetually wanting animal." Ultimately, the core drive behind all wantingness and cravings is the search for happiness. As Aristotle noted, "Happiness, therefore, being found to be something final and self-sufficient, is the end at which all actions aim."[38] The ego searches for happiness in the external world, to no avail.

Happiness is a worthy aspiration. The most important distinction in pursuing happiness is, as the Sages assert, to search for happiness *within* rather than in the outside world. As Krishna explains in the *Bhagavad-Gita,* "For the man who doeth that which he hath to do, without attachment to the result, obtaineth the Supreme."[39] If the source of happiness was "out there," how elusive would happiness be, always subject to the whims of the environment. Those addicted to drugs, sex, gambling, or food are on a perpetual quest for happiness, but since the "highs" that feed these addictions don't last, they constantly need more.

Taoist Chuang Tzu expressed the dynamics of desire and attachment very logically:

When an archer is shooting for nothing
He has all his skill.
If he shoots for a brass buckle
He is already nervous.
If he shoots for a prize of gold
He goes blind
Or sees two targets—
He is out of his mind!

His skill has not changed. But the prize
Divides him. He cares.
He thinks more of winning
Than of shooting—
And the need to win
Drains him of power.[40]

The mind often creates a series of rules for what it thinks it needs to experience happiness. If it has so much money in the bank, a certain kind of relationship or family, and certain material things, THEN it can be happy. Many people believe if they win the lottery, all of their problems will be solved and they'll be happy. The reality, of course, is quite different. Studies have shown how depressed lottery winners often become,[41] and we have numerous examples of high-profile celebrities like Elvis Presley, Marilyn Monroe, Chris Farley, Anna Nicole Smith, or John Belushi who appeared to "have it all" and ended up over-dosing on drugs or alcohol.

After reading this, a person might say, "But I really *will* be happy when I get _____." Or, "But I really *do* experience happiness when _____ happens."

Now, stop and think: *does that event or thing actually bring you happiness, or do you allow yourself to experience happiness when it occurs?* Through honest introspection, one will note that happiness is always internally derived. With observation, it becomes apparent that happiness arises within consciousness as a consequence of the removal of lower attractor thoughts and emotions; an event, in and of itself, has no magical power to do this.

If you've ever spent time with someone who is genuinely happy, they maintain that outlook regardless of the experience of the moment. Understand this is not simply "positive thinking" or a "mood"—these genuinely happy people require no act of volition to be joyful or at least experience life as "okay."[42]

As we see through the ego's desires and cravings, we naturally discover the eternal wellspring of joy within—the joy of existence itself. Once this primal energy is diffused, there's no drive to attach one's happiness to anything outside of oneself.

THE WAY OF NONATTACHMENT

To serve the transcendence of craving and wanting, the spiritual practice of *nonattachment* is useful. The notion of non-attachment often brings up the fear of complacency or passivity. It can be helpful to make a distinction between the Buddhist practice of detachment versus the way of nonattachment.[43] *Detachment* leads to formal renunciation, where one leaves the world and enters a monastery, for example. This Eastern pathway is not socially appealing or acceptable in Western culture.

Nonattachment, in contrast, allows full participation in life and is more aligned with Western living. You engage the world full on, but without the limiting attachments that bind us or stunt our growth. Having a home and car you enjoy are aspects of modern living; they do not represent a problem. Our *dependence* upon our things and our belief that we can't live or be happy without them poses the problem because it energizes the primitive survival self arising out of fear and projects our quest for happiness "out there."

By practicing nonattachment, we understand that fear of compla-cency is groundless, an illusion of the ego. In a state of non-attachment, you're better-equipped to navigate daily decision-making because you're not emotionally attached to certain outcomes.

Another drive behind our attachments is a fear of loss. The fear of loss is generally a consequence of the mind's projection into the future. *What if I lose my job? What if someone steals my idea? What if it doesn't work?*

This type of fearful projection into the future tends to bind us to the current conditions. If you're afraid of losing your job, by default, you're attached (or bound) to the job—whether you like the job or not.

As we've noted, the mind continually jumps from replaying past experiences to projecting out toward future potentials. In so doing, it blocks the reality of the present moment—the NOW where happiness is discovered.[44]

The idea of nonattachment is very challenging for most Westerners to practice. The ego clings to its attachments as if they represent its source of life. One of our deepest attachments is to our thoughts and the thinking process itself. In claiming our thoughts as "mine," like we do with material things, the mind imbues significance to the thoughts, leading us to cherish our thoughts with "specialness."[45] With honest observation, however, we note that the vast majority of our thoughts are mostly the same, only rehashed in different ways.

As we discovered in chapter 4: The Anatomy of Thought, thoughts arise out of the infinite field of consciousness and they are, in fact, *impersonal*. If we are attached to our thoughts and our belief systems, we're more susceptible to paradigm blindness. In releasing our attachments to our thoughts, we free our minds to function creatively in a more intuitive, nonlinear manner. (This practice takes time to master.)

Operating in the world, we are constantly choosing a specified direction or path. As soon as our course is set, the ego wants to attach itself to the outcome. As soon as your chips hit the green felt on the casino table, you have an attachment to winning. But in this ever-changing, transitory world, the target is always moving. As the context of a situation changes, the objective holds different meaning. Today, your company may be at the top of your industry; tomorrow, a pioneering technology can deem you irrelevant to your customer. If you are attached to the way things are right now, you'll be unable to adapt to the shifting landscape. In surrendering your attachments to how things "have to be," you are free to maneuver to Higher Ground and navigate your course more effortlessly.

To participate in the Act of Creation, we leap from our current field of information to a new context of understanding. To facilitate this leap, we release all attachments to the way things are or to the way we believe things *should be*. By moralizing about how things *should be*, we cloud the landscape with illusions that hinder our apperception of reality. In letting go of our attachments, we eliminate our paradigm blindness and open ourselves to creative breakthroughs.

Blake's poem *Eternity* beautifully explains how to avoid the trap of emotional attachment. We learn to "kiss joy," not "bind" ourselves to it:

> He who binds to himself a joy
> Does the winged life destroy;
> But he who kisses the joy as it flies
> Lives in eternity's sunrise.[46]

Saint Francis of Assisi echoes Blake's poetry with his suggestion of "wearing the world like a loose garment."[47] Once one realizes that happiness is indeed derived from within, the mind's silence grows, paving the way for our creativity to manifest. From nonattachment, we exponentially increase our creative potential.

OUR LOVE FOR BUSYNESS

One additional mechanism of the ego requires attention, especially for the Creative Professional, because it is attached to an attractor so powerful and widespread that it impacts ongoing creative output in our culture. Particularly in business, we can easily observe this powerful drive in areas like project management, inter-office communication, leadership, corporate meetings, and routine daily affairs. This attractor is governed by the ego's need for movement, or "busy-ness." In fact, *busyness* is so pervasive in Western culture that it is often mistaken for *business*.

In classic Hindu philosophy, this drive for activity is called *rajas*, one of the three in-born qualities of consciousness.[48] Activity or movement is a quality of consciousness; it's present whether we ask for it or not. Try sitting quietly under a tree. See how long you can sit there before your stomach reminds you that you're hungry, your parched mouth tells you that you're thirsty, your bladder reminds you of the need to urinate, your thoughts remind you of something you forgot to do, or someone comes over and tells you to leave because the tree you're sitting under is on private property.

Although activity is an innate quality of life, the ego is unnecessarily aligned to activity in a counterproductive manner. The survival self thrives on being busy. Our brief tour of the brain's evolution helps explain our animal heritage and our drive for busyness and continual activity. The reptilian brain keeps us on constant patrol—hunting, running, eating, interacting—to survive.

According to the ego, to stop and incubate—to be void of thoughts or "meaningful" activity—is equal to death. As a consequence, the ego does whatever it can to stay busy and resist succumbing to the archetype of the Wanderer. The ego thrives on a sense of control, whether it be of thoughts or actions, while the Wanderer freely relinquishes control and *allows* answers to present themselves.

To reinforce this primitive drive, our social programming has linked our sense of significance to how busy we are. The ego gets its sense of worth not from the results it manifests or the contributions it makes, but by how busy it continues to be. Executives, for example, may brag about the number of hours they log each week or how little sleep they're getting.

Phone calls, emails, instant messages, meetings, passing thoughts—these are all easy hooks for the ego. The question, *What do I need to do?* is one of the ego's primary programs for staying occupied, reinforcing its sense of importance and significance with an endless series of details.

Please understand: it doesn't serve us to feel bad or shameful about the ego's tendencies; rather, we simply need to see the ego for what it is. The ego's drive to be busy and to always be *doing* is conditioned into the collective field. *You* didn't create this drive—it is simply an attribute in the field of consciousness, reinforced over millennia via our animal inheritance.

With awareness of the ego's mechanisms like the need for continual activity, we are able to shift gears and align with the observer. Now, we become the audience in the theatre instead of the actor performing on stage, which limits the ego's ability to direct the show. (See the exercise called "Be the Watcher" in the next chapter.) Through inner honesty, we can identify this innate drive for busyness and move beyond it. With compassion, we can witness the busy "doer" begin to emerge in consciousness, and rather than fall victim to it, simply note its presence.

The social conditioning of a busy culture is powerful. In high school and beyond, we're conditioned to think in terms of to-do lists, tasks, and checklists. While a checklist for groceries can be useful when food shopping, using action lists in your business activities is not only inefficient, but it often plants the "seed of your own destruction" because it guarantees a lot of busyness without necessarily moving you toward greater achievement.

There's nothing "wrong" with being busy. In fact, as a quality of consciousness, it's innate to our humanity. If we are unable to transcend this primal drive of the ego, however, we greatly limit our creativity. The general lack of creativity in the majority of mankind is a testament to this animalistic drive.

Locked in this endless pattern of activity, it's difficult, if not impossible, to find the Higher Ground (the focus of the next chapter). High-level evaluation and doorways to the creative impulse are closed to the person overwhelmed by continual busyness.

The wise transcend the survival instinct that often hinders our ability to manifest creatively. In a relaxed, centered state with a higher intention, we increase the potentiality of attuning to a more powerful attractor field within consciousness. The minds of those often denoted as "genius" are able to, at least momentarily, transcend the instinctual drive for busyness, allowing the Light of illumination to manifest.

Chapter 7
Finding Higher Ground

All avenues of questioning lead to the same ultimate answer. The discovery that nothing is hidden and truth stands everywhere revealed is the key to enlightenment about the simplest practical affairs and the destiny of mankind.

—David R. Hawkins, *Power vs. Force*

NO TECHNIQUES

There are numerous books written about creativity, most offering a variety of techniques for increasing creative output. Although certain techniques may be helpful within a specific context, like learning strategies to discover new ways of solving problems, becoming more creative is not a consequence of following a technique or formula. Bohm beautifully illuminates this truth:

[F]or thousands of years people have been led to believe that anything and everything can be obtained if only one has the right techniques and methods. What is needed is to be aware of the ease with which the mind slips comfortably back into this age-old pattern. *Certain kinds of things can be achieved by techniques and formulae, but originality and creativity are not among these.* The act of seeing this deeply (and not merely verbally or intellectually) is also the act in which originality and creativity can be born.[1]

As we've stated, creativity is a nonlinear occurrence—an innate quality of consciousness that arises when the proper conditions are present. We learned how the ego blocks this quality of consciousness through mechanisms like fragmented, dualistic thinking, energized lower emotions, or the drive for constant movement. The consciously evolved, "whole" human being transcends enough of these ego proclivities to allow his innate creativeness to manifest.[2]

Breakthrough discoveries are not the result of a linear progression of ideas. In shifting from the Student to the Wanderer, all techniques and formulas must be relinquished. In fact, a technique or formula can actually inhibit creative insight by locking the mind into circular patterns and habits. For example, asking a specific question repetitively can stall the free association of ideas especially when asking becomes mechanical and without intention. The Wanderer, in contrast, resides in a nonattached, unstructured state, allowing illumination to unfold.

While a technique for active learning, reading, or even overcoming procrastination can be valuable for one's personal development and can improve one's role as a Student, creativity itself cannot be produced via a "technique." A formulaic, linear technique cannot lead to *nonlinear* discovery.

"Letting go" or "surrendering to the moment" are abilities few possess in our Western, get-it-done culture; and yet, as we've noted, surrendering is the precursor to the creative impulse. We must rise above the drive of the ego to control every moment and lock us into an automaton-like state. Transcending this conditioning can help us produce works of ingenuity and originality.

While understanding our intrinsic ego drives, it becomes apparent that our "work" is in eliminating the barriers set up by the ego rather than in moving toward creativity via a technique. This notion was the theme of the film *The Legend of Bagger Vance*, directed by Robert Redford and starring Will Smith and Matt Damon.[3] A young golfer with a tumultuous past, Randolph Junah, lost his way both on and off the golf course. A mystical golf caddy named Bagger Vance instructs Junah on how to find his "authentic swing." "To find your authentic swing," Bagger Vance instructs, "you've gotta' get out of your own way and let your swing find you."

This act of getting out of our own way illustrates what's needed for the creative impulse to manifest. To get out of your own way, embrace an *allowing* state of mind in the present moment, as opposed to a *doing* state. The mind bounces from the past to the future. In the present moment of NOW, what the Eastern teachings often call "No Mind,"[4] we remove the influence of the ego, leaving behind commentary, judgments, and opinions. In the No-Mind state, silence and peace prevail. In reading the introspective accounts of creative geniuses like Mozart, Picasso, Poincare, Coleridge, Cocteau, and Miller, a pattern that includes a period of reverie occurs prior to their revelations. This state of *allowing* helps attune the person to a higher attractor field (higher level of consciousness), which precedes the Light of illumination.

Instead of searching for a technique to increase our creativity, it is more useful to adopt a *style*—a way of being in the world—that loosens the ego's drive for control and allows our innate creativeness to manifest. Through a deeper understanding of the nature of thought and creativity, combined with a contemplative way of being in the world, a creative lifestyle develops that permeates more than just one's vocation—it affects who one becomes at a deep, spiritual level.

Two Minds

The "busyness syndrome," which we're all too familiar with, is a consequence of what some traditions call "Monkey Mind." Imagine thoughts jumping from place to place, like a monkey swinging through the trees. Many of us live in Monkey Mind.

Monkey Mind is too busy to enjoy the beautiful landscape and tranquility of the forest; instead, it's preoccupied with chopping down the tree. With this limited viewpoint, we don't see on-coming storms and other potential calamities. In Monkey Mind, the fly keeps smacking itself against the window while trying to escape to fresh air, leading to an early demise.

Monkey Mind is reactive to the circumstances of the moment. With the animal brain in charge, the "learning brain" is not engaged. Living in Monkey Mind, most of society shuts off its creative potential, slipping into a coma-like state suited for mind-lessly watching television. Living in this state, a human being blocks the Light and therefore lacks ingenuity and inventiveness.

Contrast Monkey Mind with what we might call *Aware Mind.* Aware Mind aligns to the bigger picture. When Aware Mind is activated, the problem is approached from a "higher" per-spective—perceiving a more "holistic system" from which the problem is arising. From Aware Mind, the fly would back up and see the entire window, noticing that the window is cracked open, allowing for an easy escape.

Aligned with a more powerful attractor field, Aware Mind taps into the creative potential of human consciousness. Whereas in Monkey Mind you tend to entrain to a single position, in Aware Mind you are able to evaluate issues and situations from a global or holistic viewpoint. Aware Mind seeks to understand the context of the situation without getting stuck on a particular detail (see *Transcending Conflict* below). The Great Law of the Iroquois Confederacy personifies Aware Mind: *In our every deliberation, we must consider the impact of our decisions on the next seven generations.*[5]

Small-business expert and author of *The E-Myth Revisited* Michael Gerber reveals that most entrepreneurs work *in* their business as opposed to *on* their business. When people work *in* their business, they operate from Monkey Mind and become a slave to the everyday details and demands of the business such as customer support, manufacturing, or technical problems as well as an endless stream of phone calls, emails, and faxes. This person is in survival mode, operating in a continuous state of crisis, barely getting through the day. This business owner is likely to be exhausted, stressed out, and nominally engaged in creative thinking or higher thought. In contrast, entrepreneurs who work *on* their business have a healthy detachment from the work; they set up necessary boundaries, establish efficient systems, and operate the business from a higher field. When operating *on* a business, Aware Mind is active, enabling you to think through the business from a more global perspective (Higher Ground) without becoming imprisoned by the day-to-day minutia of your work.

If you think about the corporate environment, it's somewhat incredulous how we evaluate employee performance. Corporate structure primarily centers around how much a person works as opposed to the quality and results generated by that work. The overall emphasis of the work environment implies that productivity is generated by busyness. Monkey Mind rules the office, leading us from email to email, phone call to phone call, and meeting to meeting in an endless series of directionless discussions and debates. By contrast, Aware Mind generally prefers a quiet atmosphere with less worldly distractions. Aligned with the Wanderer archetype, Aware Mind benefits from weekend retreats, drives in the country, walks through the woods, and even coffee shop interludes.

Most of us read from Monkey Mind—the goal is simply to finish the book rather than to evaluate the work from a higher perspective. From Aware Mind, we learn to clarify our objectives and purpose for reading the book, and embrace an "active learning" approach. We may review the front and back cover, table of contents, and skim the chapter and subtitle headings through the text. We might determine our key questions and skim the book in search for answers. Do you see how reading in this fashion can become a tremendously valuable, efficient, and fulfilling process? (See Mortimer Adler's classic *How to Read a Book* for further instruction.)

In Monkey Mind, we sit in front of our computers or with our BlackBerry® or iPhone® in hand, waiting for the "ding" or "buzz" of a new email. Always online, we watch our inboxes like hawks. When the cell phone rings, we immediately pick up. Management-by-Crisis, guided by the demands of the moment, is how most of us operate. By living in reaction to the conditions present in our environment, we live at the mercy of our environment. In today's high-speed, highly-connected world, the demands of the environment are great indeed.

In Aware Mind, we pause and strategically evaluate our objectives before diving into the task. With a higher understanding, we see beyond the problems at hand and move forward with greater clarity, patience, and compassion. This holistic alignment helps us discern a more reliable path to success, eliminating the temptation to start checking things off our list of "to-dos," which may or may not manifest the results we want. Aware Mind brings clarity and direction, the key guides to Higher Ground.

Aware Mind is characterized by nonlinear leaps in understanding—quantum jumps, so to speak—where one stares into the great white unknown and takes a leap of faith, believing the answers will appear. In essence, one aligns to a power beyond the linear, fragmented capacity of the thinking brain and allows creation to unfold. As Maslow observed, "Creating tends to be the act of a whole man (ordinarily); he is then *most* integrated, unified, all of a piece, one-pointed, totally organized in the service of the fascinating matter-in-hand. Creativeness is therefore systemic; i.e., a whole—or Gestalt—quality of the whole person ..."[6]

Monkey Mindedness is strictly linear and intrinsically perceives things as "black-and-white." Dualistic thinking—driven by the concepts of opposites and causality discussed in chapter 2— inhibits breakthrough discoveries, moments of inspiration, and advancements in human understanding.

Scan the table on the following page to see the contrast between Monkey Mind and Aware Mind.

Are you aware of which side of this chart you spend most of your time? It's not that we're either one or the other. Qualities of both Monkey Mind and Aware Mind are aspects within consciousness. In fact, there are infinite combinations and degrees of both minds; they aren't polar opposites (see *Transcending the Opposites* in chapter 2). One's ability to manifest creative results is directly correlated to the degree of attunement with the higher attractor of Aware Mind. Dominated by Monkey Mind, a person's achievements are limited; aligned with Aware Mind, great creative potential can manifest.

MONKEY MIND	AWARE MIND
Doing	Allowing
Reacting	Flowing
Busy	Free
Stressed-out	Calm / Peaceful / Relaxed
Emotional	Centered ("Jedi"-like)
Mindless	Mindful / Aware
Environmentally conditioned	Catalyst for change
Fragmented	Whole picture
Everything is black and white	Gradients of all things
Mechanistic	Systems thinking
"Misses the forest for the tree"	True vision
Focuses on details (content)	Looks for larger context
Linear	Nonlinear
Rigid	Flexible
Limited perception	Holistic perspective

MONKEY MIND VERSUS AWARE MIND

The style of Aware Mind is akin with the archetype of the philosopher whose mind is allowed to free associate with ideas, make unique connections, and identify patterns that are elusive to common observation.[7] The way of the philosopher, however, isn't exactly encouraged in modern society. Unless you're a college student waxing intellectual in a coffee shop, musings of this nature are replaced by the drive to "make a living." A select few modern philosophers find careers as writers/lecturers, but the rest of us are expected to "go to work."

In spite of these obstacles, Aware Mind can be utilized in any profession. In any meeting where a team is trying to tackle a problem, you can always take a step back, clear your mind, and observe the problem from a more expansive viewpoint. What are the underlying assumptions already brought to the table? In truth, what exactly is the problem? (The actual problem is often different than the perceived problem.) Why is it always done *this* way? Is there a better or more effective way of doing this? The physicist David Bohm spoke and wrote passionately about the need to have group "dialogues," where all assumptions are examined and a shared meaning is eventually reached.[8]

If you're a fan of J.R.R. Tolkien and/or the Lord of the Rings trilogy, you will recognize Aware Mind as the mythological race of Elves: steady, centered, peaceful, fully-integrated beings with foresight and vision. The Race of Men, in contrast, is aligned with Monkey Mind: fragmented, fearful, often war-like creatures unable to see the whole picture. The Elves represent the transcendent aspect of the Self, while the Humans are indicative of our more primitive, animal heritage.

In Aware Mind, we are peaceful and centered. In Monkey Mind, we are at the mercy of the ego's chaotic emotions: desires, wants, cravings, fears, worries, angers, and anxieties. Naturally, both of these terms are somewhat arbitrary concepts being used to illustrate a point. The qualities of Aware Mind are closer to our higher state of being, a more evolved form of what we call *humanness* that transcends our animalistic heritage and allows our innate creativity to manifest. Or as Bohm states it, "Thus, originality and creativity begin to emerge, not as something that is the result of an effort to achieve a planned and formulated goal, but rather as a by-product of a mind that is coming to a more nearly normal order of operation."[9]

*   *   *

Experiment: A Practice of Mindfulness

To temper the erratic and capricious nature of Monkey Mind, the practice of *mindfulness* can be very useful. Mindfulness helps you become more aware of your sensory experience by focusing on a particular information-processing modality. The practice of mindfulness can reveal a completely new world hidden within your everyday experiences.

Here are four activities you can try:

1. *Mindful eating*: Focus all of your attention on what you're eating (perhaps try a raisin). Experience the various textures of the raisin as you place it on your tongue. Move it around your mouth and notice how the experience of the food changes. Now, slowly bite down into the raisin. Perhaps you'll become aware of different flavors and textures you've never noticed before. Chew slowly and continue to focus 100 percent of your attention on eating

the raisin. Be sure not to judge or evaluate the taste of the raisin or the overall experience. Just stay completely present with the experience of eating.

2. *Mindful listening.* Sit outside, close your eyes, and listen. Don't try to label or judge the various sounds by calling them pleasant or disruptive. With all of your attention on your hearing faculty, simply listen to the variety of sounds in your environment.

3. *Mindful seeing.* Now, open your eyes and look around. Again, without judgment or evaluation, calmly survey your environment solely with your eyes. You can focus in on particular things and notice specific details like colors, shapes, dimensions, and textures (without labeling them). Let only your eyes guide your experience.

4. *Mindful breathing.* Close your eyes again. This time focus all of your attention on your breath. Don't try to take a deep breath or breathe in any particular way. Simply observe your breathing for a few minutes without descriptions or commentary. With all of your attention on your breathing, you shouldn't be able to pay much attention to your thoughts, but if you find your mind wandering, simply bring your attention back to mindfully breathing.

You can conduct this type of mindful activity with any of your senses. The idea is to focus intently on a single sensory experience, thereby blocking the endless phantasmagoria and avalanche of information processing that we've become accustomed to in today's world.

Experiment: Be the Watcher

Next, you can take a step beyond mindfulness and learn to watch the reactionary nature of Monkey Mind with a simple technique called *watching*. Whereas mindfulness requires an intense focus on the *experiencer*, you can shift your awareness to that which is *watching* the experiencer. You can watch the mind do what it does without playing an active role. Instead of playing the movie's lead actor, you can sit in the theatre and watch the movie. From the perspective of the watcher of the film (instead of the actor), your experience of the moment radically changes.

As the actor, we get locked into the demands of the moment, reacting to the conditions of the environment (like the animal). As the watcher, your perspective changes and you can actually catch the ego of Monkey Mind trying to create a continuous sense of busyness.

Watching Monkey Mind at work tends to diffuse its dominance. In the relaxed state of the watcher, you'll naturally move into Aware Mind and beyond.

*　　　*　　　*

ACTIVATING ATTRACTORS WITH QUESTIONS

Physicist Werner Heisenberg asserts, "What we observe is not nature itself, but nature exposed to our method of questioning."[10] When we ask a question, we activate an attractor field.[11] As we've learned in chapter 4, attractors have varying levels of power. Higher quality questions aligned to higher intention activate higher attractors (and levels of consciousness) and vice versa.

The Student is the perpetual questioner, coming from Aware Mind. The mind uses questions for evaluation, understanding, and problem solving. Genius is often simply knowing what questions to ask and being relentless about discovering the answers. In fact, questions are as important as answers. As creativity researcher Howard Gruber noted, "Rather than thinking in order to solve problems, the person striving to develop a new point of view solves problems in order to explore different aspects of it and of those problems and of those domains to which those problems apply."[12]

The "brilliant" question may identify a problem which others didn't perceive as a problem. A quality of genius is the ability to locate unsolved problems hidden in plain sight. As author David Lindley observed, "A judicious questioning of the obvious may well be a mark of genius."[13]

Asking quality questions is an art, not a science. Like any craft, we get better with practice and with a commitment to improvement. You wouldn't pick up a paintbrush for the first time and expect to be Rembrandt; similarly, learning to ask superior questions takes time to master and only the true Student commits with necessary resolve.

Asking *What do I need to do?* is a lower-quality question (coming from Monkey Mind) that generally leads to a lot of busyness with very little accomplishment. Lower quality questions provoke a linear thought process (or "tunnel vision") that limits our ability to see a more important global perspective with many options.

Remember the fly and window illustration above? The fly doesn't know to ask a better question, like, "What am I smacking into, and how big is it?" As the old proverb goes, "If you know all the answers, you haven't asked the right questions."

Few understand the value of questioning more than Albert Einstein, who asserts, "The important thing is not to stop questioning. Curiosity has its own reason for existing. One cannot help but be in awe when he contemplates the mysteries of eternity, of life, of the marvelous structure of reality. It is enough if one tries merely to comprehend a little of this mystery every day. Never lose a holy curiosity."[14]

In addition to knowing *what* questions to ask, it's important to know *when* to ask them. The best questions asked at the wrong time will yield poor results. A well-conceived combination of questions asked at the right time can reveal profound solutions to even the toughest problems. For example, if you're brainstorming the solution to a problem within a work group, asking, "What's potentially wrong with this idea?" can have a deleterious effect *if* you don't ask for positive feedback regarding the idea first. Inviting the devil's advocate into the discussion too early is likely to squash any new ideas your team might bring forth. Cautionary thinking, however, can save your business millions of dollars if it's used at the appropriate time.

TRANSCENDING CONFLICT

To reach Higher Ground, one of the fastest ways to disarm the ego's positions, judgments, and opinions is to understand the critical difference between *content* and *context,* and the relationship they play in personal, professional, and international conflicts.

Arguments, debates, and other forms of conflict pervade business and politics, and every area of life. Do you ever wonder why? Is conflict an inherent aspect of the human condition? It seems that way when we retrace our course throughout history. Was there ever a time in human history where, on a global level, there was no war? If there was, this period was certainly short-lived. As humans, conflict appears to be part of our nature.

What is the mechanism behind conflict—between two people, a group of people or nations? How can two intelligent people have completely contrasting opinions on a particular topic?

We can bypass the very root of all inherent friction by understanding the difference between content and context.[15] *Content* includes the details of a particular situation. *Context* is the overall field of meaning from which the details arise. Without context, content is meaningless. This statement bears repeating because understanding it opens the floodgates to the resolution of any conflict: *without context, content is meaningless.*

Illustration 1

What is the value of an acre of land? You can't accurately answer this question without additional information. The acre of land is the content. The context is the quality of land, its zoning, and its surrounding environment. What is the current market condition? Is the property in a high-value area with a good school system? Can you build on the land? Is the property situated on wetlands, next to a toxic waste dump, or by a stream with a mountain view? The value of an acre varies greatly depending on the context of the surrounding environment.

Illustration 2

A bacon double cheeseburger (the content) from your favorite fast food chain might sound delectable to you. The thought of this tasty meal with a side of fries and a soft drink makes your mouth water. After years of delighting in your favorite meal, your arteries clog and you have a heart attack. This life-altering event changes your perspective on bacon double cheeseburgers—although you may still crave it, you don't indulge in it. What's different? The *context* of the burger has changed. Before, eating the burger represented pleasure in the moment. Now, the burger represents possible death.

Illustration 3

A continent (the content) can be viewed in terms of the earth (the context). The earth can be viewed within the context of the solar system. Where the earth was the context in the first observation, when looking at the entire solar system, the earth becomes the content. The solar system can be examined within the galaxy. Again, the context shifts—the solar system is part of the galaxy. The galaxy can be examined from the position of the universe. Once again, the context shifts—this time, our galaxy is contextualized within the universe at large.

Illustration 4

As author John Gray noted in the national bestseller, *Men are from Mars, Women are from Venus,* men and women are not the same. Each sex experiences a completely different view of the world (context) and as a consequence, men and women respond to situations, information, and problems (content) differently.

The *context* denotes the larger field within which the *content* exists. Data is meaningless unless the context of the information is defined. Herein lies the source of all conflict and arguments. When you "take something out of context," you remove the foundation that made the content relevant. Newspaper editors often intentionally play this game. They offer opinions on a particular issue without providing the reader with sufficient information (context) to fully understand the issue. Without your awareness, you may be swayed by an argument that is unfounded because of a lack of background information (context).

To visualize the relationship between context and content, look at the arrow in the following illustration. The shaded rings of the target represent various levels of context, or the various ways in which a piece of information can be evaluated and understood. The entire target itself represents the overall field of knowledge and potential ways of understanding the information. The place where the arrow lands represents content, a specific piece of information, like an acre of land from Illustration 1 above. Content is a specific and often arbitrary point of focus within a particular field of context.

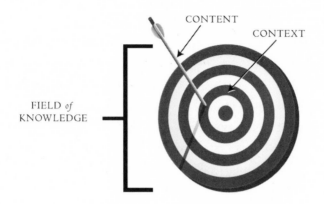

CONTENT VERSUS CONTEXT

Arguments arise when two or more people discuss qualities of an arrow from the perspective of two different rings on the target, and sometimes two completely different targets. If the potential land purchaser is evaluating the price of the acre based solely on the surrounding landscape and the seller is only concerned with the last sale price of an acre in that area, it's unlikely that an understanding will be reached. When people discuss a matter from different contexts, resolution is often impossible. Often, context remains hidden, while content takes the center stage.

LEVELS OF CONTEXT

As we discussed in chapters 3 and 4, all thoughts and beliefs are aligned to various attractor fields. Hawkins' Map of Consciousness, denoted by highly specified fields or levels of consciousness, helps us better understand the nature of context.

Each level is governed by highly-organized patterns of perception, meaning, emotion, and behavior. Each person, place, and country has a calibratable level of consciousness.

For example, the level of consciousness of the United States currently calibrates at Reason (400s), denoting a highly logical, academically-driven culture. As rational beings, we expect and assume every other nation will behave and process information in the same logical, understanding manner. The challenge is that countries vary in their calibrated levels of consciousness—the context through which they view the world is different.

When dealing with a country that calibrates at the level of Pride (175), which is a level of consciousness void of integrity, the United States expects a logical response to their diplomacy and interests.[16] The level of Pride, however, includes a life view full of demanding, scornful emotions, irrationality, and a desire for control.[17] Negotiating from the level of Reason versus the level of Pride is like comparing apples and elephants.

As a consequence of different levels of context, the United States is often surprised by the actions of other nations—think Pearl Harbor, the Cuban Missile Crisis, and 9/11. We assume people will act and behave similarly to how we act and behave. Resolution's only hope is for diplomats to leverage an understanding of context and content in relation to the levels of consciousness in matters of world diplomacy.

On an individual level, you can incorporate this awareness into your daily activities. If you find yourself getting angry with someone, perhaps you can consider the context of the disagreement from their perspective (which, incidentally, may be unknown to us). Maybe that guy driving like a lunatic down the freeway is trying to get home to his wife who is in labor. Perhaps your boss is grumpy because his child got suspended from school for doing drugs. Maybe your best friend forgot your birthday because she was worried about something her doctor just told her.

It is helpful to remember Socrates' observation: all people are only able to do what they think is good, even though they are unable to discern good from bad. Or, as Tony Robbins states, "Everyone is doing the best they can with the resources they have."[18] Both of these contextualizations help us find compassion rather than defensiveness or anger.

Albert Einstein is often quoted as saying that no problem can be solved from the same consciousness that created it. Think about it: A problem is only a problem from a particular point of view. From a higher perspective, our problems are recontextualized and later disappear.

Let's say, for example, you're having a real challenge working with someone on your corporate team. They seem disconnected, unhappy, and their productivity is unimpressive. As a team leader, you want to address the problem. You hire a consultant to conduct personality profile testing for the whole team. You discover that your "troubled" team member is highly introverted. To some introverts, meetings are worse than funerals. You may also discover other problematic conditions that were negatively impacting the productivity and emotional fortitude for him and other team members.

What happens next? With your willingness, change occurs as a consequence of awareness at Higher Ground. Because of your expanded understanding, in a short time frame, the problem will no longer exist as it currently stands. You'll become conscious of your colleague's need for space and only include him at critical meetings. You will probably also learn about other personality dynamics that will benefit your team's productivity in both observable and intangible ways.

"Seek to understand, not condemn."

Any time conflict of any size arises, you can trust a shift in context exists—certain information isn't currently known by you. This realization alone can provide tremendous relief from suffering, opening the gateway to resolution and greater peace.

Conflict and its resulting negative emotions fuel the ego, which blocks the creative impulse. Problems tend to disappear from a higher context. The skill of recontextualizing a problem is of infinite value to anyone seeking greater creativity.

MULTIPLE PERSPECTIVES

Finding Higher Ground is not possible when we're only able to perceive our own point of view. Even if that viewpoint is aligned to a higher truth, perceiving other viewpoints facilitates understanding and better communication. Obviously, if everyone was "on the same page," corporate meetings would be faster, more productive, and generally conflict-free.

Wilber's Integral Model offers a holistic approach to understanding multiple perspectives.[19] He points out that all major languages have first-person, second-person, and third-person pronouns. The first-person perspective refers to the person who is speaking, the "I" or "me." The second-person perspective refers to whom you're speaking to, the "you" or "yours." And the third-person perspective refers to the person or thing being spoken about, such as "he," "she," "they," or "it."

These three dimensions also manifest as the Beautiful, Good, and True (referred to by many philosophers), the dimensions of art, morals, and science, or that of self, culture, and nature. These three dimensions also coincide with the three basic levels of moral development: 1) egocentric, where a person can only perceive the world from his or her own point of view, 2) ethnocentric, where a person is aligned to the perspective of a group or culture, and 3) worldcentric, where a person realizes a global perspective.

The awareness of these various dimensions can help one find a more expansive viewpoint by ascertaining their subjective experience (first-person), multiple perspectives from others through dialogue and empathy (second-person), and objective, verifiable facts or conditions about the situation which help set the overall context (third-person).

Creativity consultant de Bono offers a fun and effective way of viewing multiple perspectives. In his Six Thinking Hats method for creative team collaboration, he identifies six hats, or perspectives, that can be "worn" during a meeting. The white hat is for offering facts and figures; the red hat is for emotional and gut reactions; the black hat is for cautionary thinking; the yellow hat is for positive perspectives; the green hat is for creative ideation; and the blue hat is for process and organization.[20] While in a meeting, a group using the Six Thinking Hats will each wear the same hat at the same time. A team of six people will each wear the red hat, for example, and provide their individual emotional reactions to an idea or problem. No one is permitted to shoot down a person's reaction while the team is wearing the red hat. Only when the black hat is worn can team members play devil's advocate. The power of this model lies in its simplicity as it forces everyone on the team to adopt numerous perspectives instead of aligning to only one or two.

Bohm observed that one of the greatest blocks to collective understanding is the assumptions we knowingly make about particular issues.[21] Remember, opinions are a primary tool of the mind, which thinks it needs to have an opinion about everything. Our assumptions and opinions often cloud the third-person realities of the situation. Perception is not reality—our interpretations are filtered through our beliefs, thoughts, experiences, definitions, and levels of consciousness, and we must be willing to honestly examine these subjective filters and discard those beliefs that no longer serve us.

To achieve Higher Ground, all assumptions, opinions, and beliefs must come under examination, even those that we hold dear, if shared meaning within a group of individuals is to be achieved.

NAVIGATING THE MAP

As we realize the importance of understanding multiple perspectives, we must contemplate how to truly understand someone else's perspective without walking in their shoes.

Hawkins' Map of Consciousness provides us with the various levels of evolutionary development and offers profound insight into the multitude of human experience. Comprehending the entire stratum of human consciousness, one can pinpoint which level a particular individual, group of people, company, or even product is coming from and then act accordingly.[22]

For example, in advertising, if the calibrated level of consciousness of the target audience is in the 400s (Reason), it would be advisable to create an ad that calibrates at a similar level to this target audience to build rapport and create a more powerful connection.

By closely examining the levels of consciousness, we observe that each level offers a different experience of reality.[23] Below the critical level of Integrity (the level 200 or Courage), the levels are guided by the more primal, animal instincts, or the survival self. Perspectives that negate the existence of an absolute truth like pluralism, sophism, secularism, relativism, or the entire post-modern movement represent calibrated energy fields below 200. These perspectives calibrate between 165 to 190, representing a prideful, infantile energy field.[24] Companies that fall below the critical level of integrity are eventually exposed in today's society—the truth is eventually revealed (consider Worldcom, Enron and Martha Stewart, which all calibrated below 200). Two hundred, the level of Courage or Integrity, represents a profound shift from destructive and harmful behaviors to life-promoting and integrity-driven lifestyles.[25]

Hawkins' consciousness research also reveals that integrity translates to the bottom line in business. Wal-Mart, the world's largest enterprise, is often vilified in the media and by special interest groups. The company's massive size and the concomitant disappearance of the "mom and pop shops" of old America make it an easy target. Yet Wal-Mart, at 365 (Acceptance), calibrates higher than most other companies.[26] Companies that are driven by the profound dedication to serve their customers instead of simply turning a profit actually have an edge.

In *The Power of Cult Branding*, brand expert Bolivar J. Bueno identified numerous companies that developed a cult-like following (in a benign and positive sense) by understanding and serving the customer's needs better than anyone else. Interestingly, we can observe a direct correlation between these cult brands and higher-than-average levels of consciousness. For example, Southwest

Airlines, a customer-centered, personable airline that managed to stay profitable while the rest of the industry struggled post-9/11, calibrates at 345, guided by Willingness and an optimistic viewpoint. Other notable companies and their calibrations include L.L. Bean (330), Harley-Davidson (300), FedEx (340), Ben & Jerry's (340), Dillard's Department Stores (350), Home Depot (305), Lowe's (300), and The Oprah Winfrey Show (505).[27]

Further discussion on the levels of consciousness is found in appendix C; however, please see Hawkins' *Power vs. Force, Truth vs. Falsehood,* and *Transcending the Levels of Consciousness* for a thorough discussion. With familiarity and practice, you become adept at discerning the level of a particular person, group, or issue, which provides the necessary context for transcending the situation.

THE ESSENCE OF PROBLEMS

Highly creative people are willing to grow and evolve, making them adaptable to change. Remember that curiosity combined with humility is a trademark attribute of the Student archetype—a prerequisite for creative inspiration. Willingness allows for alignment to more powerful attractor fields, leading to greater understanding and the elimination of conflict.

The solid circle in the center represents you. The outer circle represents your entire "field of influence." Any "problem" or "challenge" that falls within your field of influence will not be perceived as a problem. Like a fallen branch in your path, you'll toss it aside or simply step over it.

EXPANDING YOUR FIELD OF INFLUENCE

As individuals, we characterize situations or circumstances as "problems" when they fall beyond our current field of influence. As Einstein observed, a different level of consciousness is needed to effectively solve the problem. Here, you have a large oak tree lying in your path—too big to climb over or walk around. Until you figure out a way to either slice through the tree, dig beneath it or scale it, the problem will persist. By determining a solution, you've effectively expanded your field. You've grown—you're no longer the same as you were before. Now, when a similar issue arises, it will no longer require growth, nor will it be perceived as a problem.

With willingness to grow, we can flow with the events of life, always seeking Higher Ground. We can avoid rigidity and fragmented thinking because we know that when we are inflexible, our problems become insurmountable and our personal and professional growth is limited.

A PRACTICAL APPROACH TO PROBLEM SOLVING

Although we may not be able to guarantee creativity through a linear process, we can utilize the principles we've learned to better assess problems and derive solutions.

It is helpful to view the following approach to problem solving as a basic framework for thinking through ideas—one that can be tailored to the needs of the individual based on the context of the situation.

What follows is a very basic but highly effective system of thinking for solving the most troubling problems. This process can be applied to most areas of your life, including building a business, growing your career, managing your daily affairs, working with teams, developing projects, and even planning vacations.

If applied diligently with a high level of commitment and flexibility, you'll begin to break out of the *busyness attractor* to which most of us are entrained. You'll know this new thought system is working when you begin to experience a greater degree of freedom, significant results, and a reduced drive toward busyness.

Step 1: Clearly Define the Result You Want

As Yogi Berra foretold, "If you don't know where you're going, you'll end up someplace else." First, you must clearly define the results you're seeking within a given situation. A "result" is the quantifiable, measurable target you want to move toward, stated in the positive. You may know you want to decrease customer attrition, however, you may not realize your objective is to build customer loyalty. The more clearly you define your objectives, the better. Often, it is necessary to invest time in clearly identifying and articulating the problem at hand before the objective can be clarified. "Lose weight" is ambiguous and hard to measure; achieving a desired weight of 145 lbs is clear, actionable, and stated in the positive. *More money* is a *want*, not a result; $20,000 in revenue generated per month is a clearly stated and actionable objective. Considering to develop a new website for your business is nice; creating a seamless online customer experience with a ten percent sales conversion rate and annual sales exceeding $250,000 by January of next year is a clearly stated, measurable result.

Don't be too quick to define the result. This result represents your "end picture"—how things will look when you're done or when the problem is solved. This ultimate vision captures the larger field and provides the context to evaluate your strategic next move. All decisions will be made from the result you define.

Notice we're not focusing on tasks or action steps here. Monkey Mind always wants to jump into a posture of *doing* and it requires tasks and actions to maintain constant activity. Defining your end result is an Aware Mind function and evaluating the problem from multiple perspectives gives you an enlightened perspective of the problem.

Find a relaxed, centered state, from which you'll be better prepared to see the larger field and to envision the entire "system" from which you're making your decisions. It is okay if you don't feel that you completely nailed your result right away—you'll have the opportunity to tweak this end picture later on in the process.

Step 2: Determine the Necessary Conditions

In order to better quantify the result you want, do your best to identify the conditions needed for your result to manifest. At this stage, you often have to accumulate more information to help you better understand the necessary conditions.

For example, if you want to have a net worth of over $1 million and your job currently pays $35,000/year (with current yearly expenses at $40,000), you may need to clarify the conditions needed to attain a net worth of $1 million. For example, you may need to learn about starting your own business, compound interest, tax strategies, budgeting, financial planning, real estate investments or other vehicles for generating wealth (or find a different job).

Gathering data often requires researching on the Internet, interviewing a few knowledgeable experts, or devouring a few books on the subject. During this stage, accumulate as much relevant data as your brain can handle (and it can absorb more than you think).

To review: in order to discern the necessary conditions needed to manifest your objective, hold your result in mind and ask the question, "What conditions are necessary for [state the result or solution] to manifest?" Let's say your result is to achieve a weight of 145 pounds and you're currently resting at 180. Your intention is to be healthier so you have more energy to play with your kids. Now, what has to happen in order to achieve the weight of 145 pounds? You brainstorm possible conditions and jot them on a sheet of paper: learn some keys to good health; eliminate all the toxic and overly fattening foods you keep in the house; drink half your body weight in ounces of water; minimize social drinking; take up an aerobic activity; join a gym and get a trainer.

Continue to capture all the thoughts that come to mind. After you jot down an idea, restate the question. This is not the time to be critical of the ideas that arise; simply free associate ideas and get them all down on paper. If you're doing this process by yourself, you can state the question in your mind or aloud. If you're conducting a group session, it's important that you continually pose the question to the group: *what other conditions must be in place in order for this result to manifest?*

Remember, the mind is conditioned to think in terms of "to-dos"; by restating the results-driven question you're actively pre-framing the mind to think in terms of results. Over time, this new system of questioning becomes wired into your brain.

Before moving to the next step, it is often helpful to push the mind to the point of exhaustion or utter frustration. Brainstorm all your ideas until steam starts rising from your head.

Step 3: Step Back & Incubate

This step is next to impossible when Monkey Mind is running the show. The drive for never-ending busyness compels most to level off at "go-go-go!" Monkey Mind sees your list of ideas and wants to immediately dive in. But Aware Mind understands the value of letting an idea simmer for a while—to give way to the Wanderer so the Light of illumination can manifest. We need to give the answer time to present itself. Remember, the purpose is not to execute ALL of our ideas—if we do, we'll trap ourselves into a never-ending cycle of busyness. No, we are trying to determine the most fruitful actions for moving us closer to our objectives. And, generally speaking, we need to let the mind incubate and align to the appropriate Thought Attractor first.

If you recall from chapter 4: *The Anatomy of Thought*, thoughts and ideas flow from a collective field, through the mind field,[28] to the "right brain." This nondominant hemisphere is the receiving center for our intuition and abstract thinking. We must let it do its job and avoid letting the linear, left brain interfere. You've probably noticed that great ideas often come to you at the most unlikely times and in the most unlikely places: as soon as you awake in the morning, while rinsing in the shower, or driving a car. When the mind is relaxed, creativity flows (through alignment to more powerful attractors).

In this stage, taking a walk, playing with your kids or your dog, meditating, or reading poetry or a good novel all serve a useful function. Ralph Waldo Emerson understood this principle all too well: "The whole course of things goes to teach us faith. We need only obey. There is guidance for each of us, and by lowly listening, we shall hear the right word."[29] We must learn to have patience to wait and *listen* for the answers.

Have a Moment of Genius

In the advertising classic *A Technique for Producing Ideas*, James Webb Young aptly called this experience "Eureka! I have it!" This isn't really a "step," but rather an unfolding or allowing. It happens of its own when the aforementioned process has run its course. In essence, the Eureka moment is that point in time when you're attuned to a powerful attractor and the brain successfully interprets it. In a flash, a critical idea pops into your mind as the Wanderer gives way to the Light. It's often this single idea that secures the likelihood of the manifestation of your results. Here, your patience and relaxed mind pay enormous dividends.

Step 4: Craft your Results Plan

Armed with your new idea(s), clarifications, and distinctions, it's fruitful to revisit your specified result/solution and the conditions you've identified. Often, the clarity afforded by incubation helps you state your result more succinctly, and perhaps more convincingly. After you've made any desired changes to your result, check in with your answers from Step 2—the necessary conditions needed for the manifestation of your result. Have you identified any targeted action steps you can take that will be infinitely more productive than the ones you've already listed? Can you eliminate certain action steps as being unnecessary?

Staying with our healthy, weight-related result, maybe you determine that you need to stop getting a McDonald's Big Mac® every day on the way home from work; or you need to kick your late-night ice cream addiction; perhaps you remembered how you love bike riding and how it can be an enjoyable way of getting into shape.

To craft your Results Plan, write out the specified result you identified in Step 1. Then, ask the same questions from Step 2, capturing only the absolute necessary actions (the critical conditions) needed for the achievement of your result. Eliminate all other tasks that don't serve your intention.

Step 5: Take Strategic Action

Now, armed with your brilliant ideas and an understanding of the necessary conditions for manifesting your results, it's time to move on to the final step. Staying in Aware Mind, begin taking thoughtful or *strategic action* toward your result. Aimless action (defined as action taken without a mindful objective) results from being entrained to Monkey Mind, which leads to busyness. Strategic action (deliberate action focused on your result) is a function of Aware Mind.

Start by reviewing your Results Plan. Avoid getting entrained to Monkey Mind and being affected by your environment. When taking strategic action, here are a few suggestions to minimize distractions and the likelihood of entraining to Monkey Mind:

- Close your email program (like Microsoft Outlook®). We've become conditioned to leave our email inbox open whenever we're sitting at our desk. This puts us at the whim of the moment and creates an ongoing distraction in our environment. The value of email is that it enables communication's demands to be managed more efficiently than a phone call. Block off time for email or check email during your "down time"—don't use email as an excuse to be "busy" for the sake of busyness.

- Shut off your cell phone and send your incoming calls to voicemail. Again, we've become conditioned by an environment that is pulling our attention in infinite directions. Answer and return calls during down time, when you're Higher Mind isn't running the show.

- Close your door. If you're an executive with your own office and you have an "open door" policy, that's terrific. There are times, however, when you need to stay completely focused on creating your results. Any interruption breaks your "flow" and often toggles you into Monkey Mind. (When you don't need to be mindfully focused, of course, keep your door open.) As Thomas A. Edison noticed, "The best thinking has been done in solitude. The worst has been done in turmoil."[30]

- Manage meetings from Aware Mind. Meetings dominate the business world. Look at the schedule of any high-level executive and, in most cases, you'll see a sea of appointments. The challenge is that most meetings are to "discuss" things. With such poor clarity, these discussions are often unfruitful and quite frankly, a waste of time. By applying results thinking to your meetings, they will become infinitely more productive and take less time; and you'll need fewer meetings.

  Always start off your meetings by clearly stating the objective(s) of the meeting. If your objective is to come to a definitive decision on a particular issue, state it. If your objective is to brainstorm at least ten ideas for a new service offering or marketing promotion, state it. The more clearly you can set the context of the meeting, the more fruitful your meeting will be. Next, as the meeting's moderator, your role is to constantly guide the team back to your objective. Every time a member gets off track (which will invariably happen), simply guide the discussion back to the objective at hand.

Summary

To recap:

1. Clearly define the results you want.
2. Determine the necessary conditions.
3. Step back & incubate.
4. Craft your results plan.
5. Take strategic action.

That's it. Sound easy enough? The magic comes when we integrate and condition this new thought system into our daily activities. The minor course corrections that you take from the many subtleties and nuances you'll learn will enhance your mastery of this results-oriented methodology.

Although it appears that we've created a linear process to solving problems, we can note the nonlinear aspects of many of the steps involved. The above functional "process" is merely an overall framework useful in its application to knowledge work. Ultimately, the solutions that present themselves are a result of the attunement to the creative impulse, not the consequence of our linear progression of thought. As such, it is of great value to keep the inner qualities of creativeness (discussed in chapter 5) in mind when approaching problem-solving endeavors.

Epilogue

A few closing remarks and a summary of what we've learned.

Final Thoughts

I AM, THEREFORE I THINK

Who might have thought that an exploration into the nature of creativity would lead us to the core of what we are? The answer is too obvious, really—even exceedingly brilliant minds generally miss it. What else but consciousness could be the source of our creativity? If our consciousness is the only true capital we have, as sages like Nisargadatta Maharaj reveal, then what else but consciousness could be the source of divine inspiration?

Understanding the nature of our creative consciousness is no easy task. In fact, while the issue appears complex or irrelevant to many people, there are a growing few who are experiencing an inner awakening, and for whom understanding consciousness is of paramount importance. We're all acquainted with Descartes' well-known conclusion: *I think, therefore I am.* The implication is that because I can think—because I can actively access, interpret, and use thoughts—I exist, I know that I am. This type of sentiment leads us to believe that we are our minds, equating the mind with one's consciousness. This is the error of Cartesian Dualism.

In a peaceful, aware state, the mind goes completely silent (called "satori" in the Zen tradition); thoughts cease or are simply no longer cognizable. In this tranquil state, you still *are* even though you do not *think*. Your sense of existence—the knowledge that you are—does not require thinking. Look into the eyes of a dog like a Labrador Retriever. There is little question about his existence: the dog knows he *is*, without words or thinkingness.

It would be more accurate to inverse Descartes' statement to, *I am, therefore I think.*[1] A step in the right direction. Still more accurate might be: *I am, and thinkingness occurs of its own.*

And perhaps the most accurate statement posed by all the great traditions—both East and West—is, *I am That.*[2] It is the "That" which we must come to understand first and then to *know* by inner experience. "That" refers to undifferentiated Universal Consciousness, unconfined by any form like a physical body, unrestricted by any field like a mind, and not limited to concepts like space and time. Through contemplation and introspection, we acquaint ourselves with that precious capital called *consciousness*, which we generally take for granted.

And what happens next? The texture of life changes. Everything becomes more peaceful, more benign. We become less affected by our environment as the survival self takes a back seat to Aware Mind, which just witnesses events without commentary. There's an overwhelming sense of gratitude and joy for our existence. The mind might even give you a break from time to time, allowing a stunning silence to be experienced, like the tame ox in the famous Zen ox herding pictures.

The Zen ox herding allegory illustrates how the mind is transcended. The ox represents the mind. First, the ox is running wild, representing the uncontrollable, chaotic nature of the mind's thoughts. The farmer must first catch the ox, where the person becomes fully aware of the mind's activities. Next, the ox is disciplined and then tamed to the point where the ox remains motionless. Now, the farmer and the ox can sit peacefully by a pond. Once the ox/mind is tamed, it no longer runs the show and a degree of peace prevails. Finally, the ox is transcended and disappears. In the state of the realized Sage, the ox/mind is no longer present.

With the mind tamed, love begins to radiate—not as a transitory emotion, but as a way of *being* in the world. Love, just like Creativity, is an innate quality of consciousness. Love and Creativity are, in essence, qualities of Divinity, of Universal Consciousness. As such, when the survival self is tamed, these qualities of Divinity are able to shine forth with greater brilliance.

As we've stated repeatedly, a trademark quality of true creative genius is humility. Humility and its accompanying surrender to our own ignorance opens the doorway to the reality of subjective experience. In the West, this doorway is vaulted shut and camouflaged in plain sight. The "what-you-see-is-what-you-get" material reductionist is blinded by the Newtonian paradigm of the physical domain. They are only comfortable with their current model of the world. Don't blame them; instead, have compassion. In their defense, science and academia's belief in the Newtonian paradigm as the ONLY reality is not only understandable, it's expected. For many, because of the fear of sounding "new agey" or being professionally discredited, negating the spiritual domain appears a safer bet.[3]

The mind loves theorizing, hypothesizing, and mentalizing; embracing a reality beyond these mechanisms is not only unappealing, it is often uncomfortable. With time, through the evolution of consciousness, limited perception gives way to the reality of subjective experience.

HIGHLIGHTS OF WHAT WE'VE LEARNED

A lot of this information is counter-cultural; as a consequence, the mind may resist it. Through familiarity and self-inquiry, the information begins to be assimilated at deeper and deeper levels. The more aware you become of your internal reality, the more this information will resonate. Self-honesty and a commitment to uncovering the truth is all that is required.

Here are a few key points to keep in mind from each section:

Introduction

- We are evolving into the "Creative Age," where our ability to solve problems and innovate is becoming more important than ever before.
- The Creative Professional represents a growing breed of knowledge workers who "think" for a living.

Chapter 1: Collective Mind

- Our perception of reality is NOT Reality itself.
- We very rarely see things as they are; through the mind's perceptual lens, we see only our interpretation of "events," which generally leads to false assumptions and limiting beliefs.
- Morphic fields help explain the collective memory and habits encoded in nature.
- Different species as well as various collective fields like cultures, religions, and ethnicities, entrain to a single field and thereby demonstrate similar characteristics.

- A paradigm is a prevailing set of beliefs about a particular area of understanding.
- "Paradigm blindness" hinders our ability to grow beyond limiting concepts and belief systems.

Chapter 2: Concepts from the Old World

- Our predominant Western, mechanistic worldview of cause and effect was solidified by Isaac Newton and René Descartes (among others).
- The Newtonian/Cartesian paradigm views the world as a machine where we understand the whole by merely examining the parts.
- The material reductionist believes that if you can't see it or measure it, it isn't real. This paradigm negates the reality of subjective experience and the overall spiritual domain.
- The concepts of cause and effect and duality (or opposites) are two major obstacles to understanding the New-World perspective and the subjective domain.
- Instead of one thing *causing* another, we note that when the conditions are appropriate, manifestation unfolds. We can observe *emergence*, not causes.
- Instead of seeing opposites like light and dark, we note that there is only one variable—light—and the infinite gradations of that variable, including its absence ("darkness").

Chapter 3: The New World and Beyond

- In quantum mechanics, we learn that observation in the form of human consciousness affects what is being observed, so you can't take consciousness out of the equation (as classical physics assumed).

- Consciousness cannot be intellectually understood; instead, it can only be subjectively experienced through internal realization.
- The quality of consciousness, which gives you the sense that *you are*, is so subtle that its presence generally goes unnoticed.
- Exploring the nature of consciousness brings us to the core of our existence—the Self-Realization of Divinity within.
- Hawkins' consciousness research revealed a Map of Consciousness that illuminates the full stratum of human development and paves the way for a true science of consciousness.

Chapter 4: The Anatomy of Thought

- Every thought has a calibratable energy frequency; thoughts are a form of energy similar to matter.
- Thoughts flow of their own accord. This thought flow is impersonal; *you are not your thoughts.*
- Our minds entrain to certain thought patterns in the form of attractor fields.
- Thought Attractors have varying degrees of power— thoughts aligned with uplifting qualities like love, peace, gratitude, and joy have infinitely more power than the lower emotions of hate, revenge, resentment, greed, desire, and anger.

Chapter 5: The Creative Condition

- Creative genius does not necessarily translate to a high IQ; you can have a very high IQ and access very little creativity.
- A trademark of creative genius is humility. Creative geniuses acknowledge the higher source of their ideas and inspiration.
- Creativity is an internal phenomenon that has outward consequences. To effectively examine creativity, we must set the conditions both internally and externally for the creative impulse to manifest.
- The creative process takes one through the preparation of the Student, to the allowing of the Wanderer, to the emergence of the Light of illumination, and finally to the verification of the Scientist.
- The Student demonstrates an internal drive to learn, grow, and discover through persistence, dedication, and unending curiosity.
- The Wanderer illuminates the value of allowing and surrender, creating a space for the creative impulse to emerge.
- The Light is the archetype of Divine inspiration, where the survival self is momentarily transcended and the creative "flash of illumination" manifests in the mind.
- The Scientist verifies the nonlinear creative impulse of the right brain, translating it into a linear, creative medium as an expressible idea, a poem, a painting, a recipe, or a formula.
- In order for creativity to be expressed, the inner conditions for creativity must be present.

Chapter 6: The Guard to Creative Genius

- In becoming aware of the evolution of basic brain physiology, we acknowledge that the reactive "animal brain" is still a component of the more advanced human brain.

- The spiritual or "etheric" brain is a new development in brain physiology that leads to a more benign, rational human being.

- The ego—the identification with the body-mind organism—is a "perpetually wanting animal." Although this survival self is not what we really *are*, this aspect of our animal heritage keeps us entrained to society's endless programs.

- The ego, with its constant wanting, craving, and desires, is constantly anticipating the next moment. It thrives on busyness, mistaking it for "business."

- The ego is the main block to the creative impulse.

- The four primary tools of the ego are positions, judgments, opinions, and attachments. In understanding these mechanisms, we are able to transcend them.

- The practice of nonattachment allows us to operate in the world without the ego's wants and desires.

Chapter 7: Finding Higher Ground

- There is no "technique" for realizing our creativeness; we need only eliminate our (the ego's) self-imposed obstacles.

- When aligned to Monkey Mind, we are unable to stay centered and focused. When Aware Mind is activated, creativity can flow effortlessly.

- The willingness to grow, another quality of the Student archetype, is a key component of problem-solving and manifesting creativity.
- Questions activate attractor fields. High-quality questions activate more powerful attractors.
- Conflict can be transcended by understanding the *context* of a situation instead of merely focusing on the *content*.
- An awareness of multiple perspectives and levels of consciousness help breed compassion and higher understanding.

A CREATIVE ADVENTURE

The landscape continues to change as we're once again reminded of Emerson's observation: "Everything looks permanent until its secrets are known." In a world of increasing complexity with its expanding technologies, vast interconnectivity, "always on" mentality, and every kind of "on demand" entertainment one can imagine, we have an uphill climb ahead to nurture our creative souls. This isn't to say that any or all of these modern advancements are "bad," only that they present a never-ending series of distraction that greatly limits our creative time. It's too easy to fill our days with responding to emails, phone calls, and instant/text messages, going from meeting to meeting, conducting business during our commute home, then flipping on the TV and surfing through 300+ channels to decompress from an intense day. Breaking this never-ending flow of busyness seems like a daunting task, but our creative lives depend on it.

We can continue to find ways to carve out time from our hectic lives for reflection, contemplation, introspection, and simply staying quiet. We can learn to listen more deeply to our environments. Whether at the office, in a car, in a restaurant, at home, or walking through the woods, we can learn to tune into the silent backdrop behind the various sounds and noises. Silence is not a quality we often pay much attention to, however, the Sages generally do. As Maharshi noted, "That state which transcends speech and thought is silence; it is meditation without mental activity. Subjugation of the mind is meditation: deep meditation is eternal speech. Silence is ever-speaking; it is the perennial flow of 'language.' It is interrupted by speaking; for words obstruct this mute language."[4]

Silence is ever-present; sounds are heard and distinguishable only because of the silence resting behind the sounds. The silent field is always available to us. What wonderful news! Sure, it may be a bit more challenging to be in that field while sitting in a business meeting where people debate irrelevant points, but the silence is available nonetheless.

Of course, the silent field is easier to detect while walking alone in the woods. Immersed in nature, it is often easier to connect with that deeper part of ourselves—that part which transcends identification with our personalities, our behaviors, our bodies, and our minds—and reminds us of something greater. It is in connecting with that powerful Source that our souls become renewed, recharged, and reborn. From here, creativity is able to flow of its own—undisturbed, unedited, and pure. This is the precious gift bestowed upon all those who honor the Presence of Spirit by providing the space for Its emergence.

Surrendering to the creative impulse can seem impossible at times. The ego's innate proclivity to feel like it is in control is in direct opposition to the stance of letting go and surrendering to a higher power. The ego always chooses to fight the current and swim forcefully upstream while surrender requires relaxing and floating downstream with the current.

With practice and training, however, we can tame the ego-mind and then enjoy a nice, peaceful ride downstream. When the ego's constant drive of desire and wantingness is kept at bay, one can introduce the notion of simplicity as a way of life. Simplicity is unattainable when the drive for wantingness and continual gain is present. For example, the ego may want a new house or a new car, but once attained, it will want a nicer, more luxurious car or a bigger house with more amenities. Each new thing adds an additional layer of complexity. Managing one house takes a good deal of time and often aggravation; managing an additional summer home, for example, increases the amount of time, aggravation, and complexity. Now, there are more decisions to be made and more time is required to manage and maintain the home.

Think back to the original promise of such applications as email, instant and text messaging, and even cellular technologies: they were supposed to make our lives easier. How has it worked out for you? The majority of executives report being overwhelmed by emails alone, many receiving over 60 messages each day.[5] Although these innovations have provided certain conveniences, the demands upon us have spiraled to a far greater degree. These additional demands have increased the level of complexity in our lives, not decreased them. Put simply, most of us don't have the time to be creative.

All of this isn't to say that simplicity is unattainable—only that, ironically enough, we must work at creating simplicity. By becoming aware of where we spend our time and making conscious effort to eliminate unnecessary complexity (focus and sacrifice where needed) and keeping the ego's desires in check, a more simple, creative life filled with greater levels of peace and joy can be achieved.

A profound and wondrous creative adventure lies before all those who choose to take the unmarked path. Within the context of your profession, the more you learn to "get out of your own way" and *allow* the archetypes of the creative process to unfold, the more creativity you can manifest. Choose this uncommon and unfamiliar route and allow the miracles that await you to unfold on their own. Such has been the trademark of the masters of ancient and recent times; such will be your destiny as well.

Appendix A
A Brief History of Quantum Theory

Over the last century, scientific thought in the form of advanced theoretical sciences has begun discovering what sages have experienced and taught for millennia: the existence of an invisible reality, oneness or interconnectivity beyond our three-dimensional, sensory experience.

In the 70s, modern classics like Fritjof Capra's *The Tao of Physics* and Gary Zukav's *The Dancing Wu Li Masters* highlighted the extraordinary discoveries of quantum mechanics and their parallels with timeless mystical teachings. Over the last several decades, major leaps in understanding have occurred as the nature of consciousness itself has been recontextualized.[1]

A brief overview of these discoveries will help you become better-acquainted with this paradigm-shifting science. Additionally, the abovementioned books are highly recommended for deepening your understanding.

*   *   *

The whole "problem" really started with light. In the late nineteenth century, Scottish physicist James Clerk Maxwell discovered that light was nothing more than a chain of electric fields intertwined with magnetic fields, or electromagnetic waves. Around 1900, German physicist Max Planck discovered that light was made up of energy packets (particles). Albert Einstein furthered Planck's work with his analysis of the photoelectric effect in 1905, demonstrating that light was indeed made up of tiny particles. Light is a particle; light is a wave. The duality of light emerged.

Viennese physicist Erwin Schrödinger hypothesized that electrons were nothing more than standing waves or vibrations. Another German physicist Max Born took this wave interpretation to the next level by saying that these waves are not "things;" they're *probabilities*. So how could light be reduced to a "probability" that is both a particle and a wave?

As Zukav clearly explains, "[T]he Schrödinger wave equation governs the development in isolation of the observed system which is represented mathematically by a wave function. A wave function is a mathematical fiction that represents all the possibilities that can happen to an observed system when it interacts with an observing system (a measuring device)."[2]

The logical absurdity of a wave function is often explained by Schrödinger's famous thought experiment: A cat is placed in a closed box with a radioactive substance, giving the cat a 50/50 chance of survival after one hour. Until an observer opens the box to determine whether the cat is alive or dead, according to Schrödinger's equation, the cat is said to be both dead and alive (and everything in between). Once the cat is observed, the wave function collapses into either a dead or living cat. So according to many theorists, the *collapse of the wave function* creates our experiential reality—each collapse creates a change in reality. (We'll come back to the wave function shortly.)

Let's further consider the significance of observation as it relates to scientific thought with German physicist Werner

Heisenberg's famed *uncertainty principle* (discussed in chapter 3). Basically, you can either know a particle's momentum or its position, but you can't accurately measure both. The uncertainty principle says that any attempt to observe an electron alters the electron. Now we're getting to the good stuff. Zukav illuminates, "This is the primary significance of the uncertainty principle. At the subatomic level, we cannot observe something without changing it. There is no such thing as the independent observer who can stand on the sidelines watching nature run its course without influencing it."[3]

As we've stated, the Old World thinking of classical physics is based on the idea that the physical world is comprised of tiny bits of matter and energy that interact in definable, measurable ways. With this mechanistic paradigm, everything in the physical world has a causal relationship with everything else. In a Cartesian, machine-like universe, each motion *should* have a calculatable outcome and a clearly-observable causal force. We should be able to *determine exactly* (hence the term *determinism*) how electrons interact just like we can predict how billiard balls interact. For centuries, this concept of causality has applied to cosmic interactions within our solar system, natural phenomena on our planet, and the functioning of the human body. Within this paradigm, scientists perform experiments as an outside observer assuming that an objective "outside" world exists.

As physicist Henry Stapp points out, however, this Newtonian worldview is inaccurate because the observer is an integral part of the system in which the research is being conducted:

> Classical physics is merely *an approximation* to a more accurate theory—called quantum mechanics—and quantum mechanics says just the opposite. Quantum mechanics incorporates the

causal effects of mental intentions upon physical systems, and explains how your mental effort causes your arm to rise. Quantum theory converts science's picture of you from that of a mechanical automation to that of a mindful human person.[4]

According to quantum mechanics, when you witness something, like an electron, it changes. In classical physics, everything is assumed to be knowable. In quantum mechanics, nature is uncertain, as expressed through probability. At the quantum level, the choices you make—your intention—shifts the probability of a potentiality. In fact, at the Copenhagen Solvay Conference in 1927, the founders of quantum mechanics made the following conclusion: *the observer and that which is observed are inextricably linked and must not be viewed as separate*. Stapp explains:

> Copenhagen quantum theory is about the relationships between human agents and systems that they act upon and observe. Thus that formulation separates the physical universe into two parts, which are described in two different languages. One part is the observing human agent and his measuring devices. That part is described in mental terms—in terms of instructions to colleagues about how to set up the devices, and what we then "see," or otherwise consciously experience. The other part is *the system that the agent is acting upon*. That part is described in physical terms—in terms of numbers assigned to tiny space-time regions.[5]

So with quantum mechanics, theorists are able to incorporate human thought and conscious observation into the equation, whereas in classical physics, the reality of the mind is not and cannot be taken into account.

Now, there are two "choices" related to quantum theory. There is the *Heisenberg Choice*, where an observer chooses which question will be asked of Nature. The observer's question determines which aspects of Nature are to be observed, confining Nature to a finite vacuum, and places the observation within specific parameters. The observer also constructs the measuring instruments and reads their recording. The Heisenberg Choice is the decision of consciousness via a human being.

Additionally, there is the *Dirac Choice* (or Process), named after physicist Paul Dirac, which is the random choice on the part of Nature represented by a collapse of the wave function. The observer determines what question to ask and then must recognize the answer provided by nature. As Stapp explains, "According to quantum theory, the Dirac Choice is a choice between alternatives that are specified by the Heisenberg Choice: the observer must first specify what aspect of the system he intends to measure or probe, and then put in place an instrument that will probe that aspect."[6]

This brings us to Hungarian mathematician John von Neumann who published *Mathematical Foundation of Quantum Mechanics* in 1932. Aware of the determinations from the Copenhagen Conference, von Neumann applied his wizardry as a logician and mathematician to these new "quantum distinctions."[7] The result was a reformulation of the theory which effectively incorporates both mind and body, observer and observed.

He split the formulation into two simultaneously occurring processes: Process I and Process II. Process II represents the physical world governed by laws that are both local and deterministic, similar to what is observed in classical physics, but in a more general way. Process I ties in the role of the observer—the human experiencer—which classical physics precluded, accounting for the effects on a physical world by the intentions of a human observer with "free choice" not determined by any known law of nature.

Once again from Stapp: "In actual empirical practice, it is the prerogative of the observing agent, not the system being observed, to determine, from a continuum of possibilities, what kind of information or knowledge will be gathered by the agent during his act of observation. The system being observed does not make this choice."[8] Nature responds to conscious choice—to the intention of an observer; nature does not select what the observer chooses to observe.

Our conscious *choice* about what question to ask affects the system of which we are inquiring. According to this interpretation of quantum theory, each response to our inquiry in nature represents a collapse of the wave function.[9] But what's causing the collapse of the wave function and the creation of reality? This is where the field of science generally hits a brick wall because it requires a radical leap from the linear to the nonlinear. The understanding provided by the Sage is Consciousness itself collapses the wave function. The body, brain, and the surrounding system or environment are at the effect of the infinite field of Consciousness.[10]

In *The Tao of Physics*, Capra beautifully illustrates the parallels between quantum theory and Eastern philosophy. Physicist Amit Goswami picks up where Capra left off, exploring the reasons why these parallels exist in *The Self-Aware Universe: How Consciousness Creates the Material World*. In his theory, which he calls *monistic idealism*, Goswami sides with the Sages, saying that nothing exists outside of consciousness. Further, "Consciousness is the agency that collapses the wave of a quantum object, which exists in potentia, making it an immanent particle in the world of manifestation."[11]

The understanding one can derive from the foregoing is that although we appear to be separate, autonomous beings, we are all aspects of a single unity of consciousness. We are like waves within the ocean: although we may appear to have separate, identifiable waves or forms, we are all momentary crests in a unified, infinite ocean. Interestingly, this is the subjective, experiential reality proclaimed by mystics, sages and spiritual teachers throughout time, and now, advanced science is pointing to a similar understanding.

Appendix B
The Perennial Philosophy Revisited

The mind's fragmented and dualistic mechanisms hinder our ability to see beyond the either-or, black-or-white, this-or-that nature of human perception. From a more expansive viewpoint, one moves beyond perceiving "opposites" and even observing the "relationships" among various things. Instead, only the Whole is apperceived—a single, unified field beyond conceptualizations. The mind immediately tries to conjure up a visual image of this Whole, but the dimension is beyond perception, visualization, cognition, or linear understanding. The Whole is an infinite, nonlinear, nonlocal field comprising Absolute Truth.

Within the Whole exist gradients, degrees, levels, and hierarchies. An understanding of these levels doesn't necessarily help us apperceive the Whole (although it does point the way); rather, it helps us contextualize the entire strata of human experience.

The concept of the Perennial Philosophy, a term popularized by Aldous Huxley's 1945 book by the same title, offers a powerful framework for understanding the relationship between the physical (local/linear) and spiritual (nonlocal/nonlinear) via an ordered hierarchy of understanding relative to Absolute Truth. An examination of the Perennial Philosophy helps us contextualize the meaning behind the levels of human consciousness, and provides a way of interpreting the complete strata of human experience, both worldly and internal.

The notion of an Absolute Truth is in concordance with the world's great traditions, the teachings of all Sages, and the foundation for all sophisticated branches of philosophy. Absolute Truth implies the existence of a Godhead, Divinity, Universal Spirit, or Source (or whatever name feels appropriate). This Presence is ever-present, eternal, and non-transitory; it is not subject to personal beliefs, opinions, and positions of an individual. In contrast, the philosophic position of relativism negates the existence of an absolute (law, morals, ethics, or truth). This sophomoric ideology is the pinnacle of the ego's narcissism, where the ego assumes it is God and the creator and source of the universe. From an Absolutist's perspective, however, Divinity is viewed and experienced as the source of all Creation. From the Absolute or Unmanifest, the manifest world emerges. The emergence of Creation unfolds within various domains or realms of potentiality and actuality where the "lesser" is contained in the "greater," but not vice versa (which the relativist does not understand).

Ken Wilber, one of today's most well-known American philosophers, offers a concise explanation of the Perennial Philosophy from a detailed study of the world's great traditions, demonstrating that a universal philosophy must contain all of the following levels in this particular order:[1]

1. *Physical*: The physical level includes all nonliving matter/ energy, like inanimate rocks, the earth, water, and the entire solar system.

2. *Biological*: The biological level includes all living, sentient matter/energy, from the animal kingdom all the way up to modern humans.

3. *Mental*: The mental level is the etheric level of thinking, logic, emotions, and ego identification. This is the domain of psychology, psychiatry, and philosophy.

4. *Subtle*: The subtle level is the nonlinear realm of archetypal energy (Jung's archetypes and the unconscious), intuition, creativity, and what Wilber calls "trans-individual."

5. *Causal*: The causal level is the domain of ineffable formless Consciousness in the nonlinear realm. There is no "otherness" in the causal domain; there is only the radiance of Divinity as Self.

6. *Ultimate*: The Ultimate level is the Supreme Absolute, beyond consciousness—the state of pure awareness—the source and nature of all other levels. Huxley noted that throughout all of the great Eastern and Western traditions, there exists an Absolute, a Godhead, a Supreme from which everything else arises.[2] It is from this unmanifest Absolute, similar to the philosophy of Hegel, that all else springs forth.

Any topic that can be discussed will fall into one of the above levels. The levels within the Perennial Philosophy represent the fields of context discussed in chapter 7. These levels do not represent "better thans," but rather, degrees of spiritual evolution in which the lesser is contained within the greater. For example, the physical domain can be discussed within the biological framework, but not vice versa. The first level is contained within the second and the first two levels are contained within the third.

All of the levels are contained within the Ultimate (the sixth level), but none of the lower levels can offer any distinctions or "clues" about the Ultimate.

The Perennial Philosophy in Hinduism and Buddhism

This notion of multi-dimensional levels or hierarchical degrees is found throughout all spiritual teachings, including Hinduism and Buddhism.[3]

LEVEL	BUDDHISM	HINDUISM
Physical body and the five senses	The five *Vijnanas*	*Annamayakosa*
Biological function	Included in *Vijnanas*	*Pranamayakosa*
Mind-ego	*Manovijnana*	*Manomayakosa*
Subtle or Higher Mind	*Manas*	*Vijnanamayakosa*
Causal	*Alayavijnana*	*Anandamayakosa*

In the Hindu philosophy we also have the three *gunas*—the three "constituents of the Cosmic Substance"—or qualities of consciousness: *tamas*, *rajas*, and *sattva*.

1. *Tamas*: In Sanskrit, *tamas* (meaning darkness, inertia, passivity, and restraint) represents the base level of consciousness, and is responsible for the ego's claim of "doing." In essence, the *tamas* quality identifies the body-mind organism as being a "me."

2. *Rajas*: In Yoga, *rajas* (meaning activity, energy, to be colored, affected, moved) refers to the "activating aspect of Nature, without which the other constituents could not

manifest their inherent qualities."[4] While *tamas* creates the sense of personal doership, *rajas* activates the constant drive for movements. (*Rajas* is the source of the "busyness attractor" discussed in chapter 6.)

3. *Sattva*: The third constituent of the Cosmic Substance is *sattva* (meaning being, existence, reality itself). *Sattva* is the quality of goodness and purity, standing for balance and harmony which allows us to be aware of the higher Self. It also represents the quality of creativity, intelligence and illumination existing as an aspect of Creation itself.

Notice how the levels of the three gunas demonstrate a progression from "lesser" to "greater," from inertia to activity, and finally, to harmony.

The Levels of the Cakra Energy System

Another example of the hierarchal structure in nature is found in the *cakra* (pronounced "chakra") energy system of the ancient traditions. The system is comprised of seven energy centers, concomitant with various organs in the body, from which the life force or spiritual energy called *kundalini* (or "chi") flows. These seven *cakra* centers represent various stages of spiritual development:

❶ The base or root *cakra* is called the *Muladhara*, located in the region between the genitals and the anus. This is the primal, animalistic level where there's no active psyche—only reaction and survival instincts ("flight or fight response").

❷ The sacral *cakra* or *Svadhisthana* is located in the groin. This is the center of the sex drive, as well as emotions like excitement, hatred, jealousy, revenge, lust, and sexual frustrations.

❸ *Manipura* is located in the naval or solar plexus. This is the level of selfishness and greed, and the drive for possession, winning, control, and power. Along with the drive for power comes the fear of losing it.

The first three *cakras* are represented by our animal heritage—Freud's id and Jung's shadow. Here, you find the ego's proclivities at work: the drive to compete, to acquire, to conquer, to control, and even to kill are all rooted in these first three *cakras*. As a consequence of these energy fields, which are associated with lower levels of consciousness (below 200), civilizations develop social law (or *dharma*) and what can be called "popular religion," providing moral standards of "right" and "wrong."

Once the spiritual energy rises beyond *Manipura*, it enters an entirely new strata of human development aligned to the fourth *cakra*.

❹ *Anahata* represents the level of the heart, the center of love, forgiveness and transformation. The basic drive of the animal are now tamed as a Divinely loving energy now prevails.

❺ *Visuddha* is located in the throat area and is related to communication, creativity and expression through growth. By this level, the life force energy projected out toward conquering others (from the third *cakra*) is now turned back against oneself, called "turning about of the *Shakti*" energy.[5]

❻ *Ajna*, the third eye *cakra*, located in between and slightly above the eyes (linked to the pineal gland), means true authority and power (impersonal, not of the individual). Spiritual discernment and vision originate from this spiritual level.

Levels one through six represent duality or opposites—this or that, subject and object. In the Indian philosophy, these levels of reality are denoted as *maya*, or illusion. Once the spiritual energy transcends these six *cakras*, it returns back to its Source.

❼ *Sahasrara*, located at the crown of the head, is the *cakra* of Universal or God Consciousness—the Radiance of God. This is the master cakra that controls and encompasses all the other levels. The crown *cakra* represents the Ultimate level of the Absolute where "I and the Father are one."[6]

Once again, the ancient *cakra* system highlights a hierarchical structure where the lesser is contained in the greater, but not vice versa. The Perennial Philosophy demonstrates the progressive levels of human evolution and development.

THE CAKRA SYSTEM

The Four States of Consciousness

Composed some 3,000 years ago, the ancient Hindu text *The Upanishads* offers perennial spiritual teachings in a collection of engaging parables and enlightening poetry. In the shortest *Upanishad*, titled "Mandukya," there are four states of consciousness of the Self (with a capital "S"). The Self is the Universal Spirit or Brahman: "Brahman is all, and the Self is Brahman."[7] The four states of consciousness are:

State 1: Vaishvanara. This is the dualistic, external experience where one is only aware of the physical world.

State 2: Taijasa. This is the subjective, internal dream state where the subject and object are part of the same thing.

State 3: Prajna. Without internal dreams or external desires, the state of deep sleep prevails. In this state, there is no dualistic mind, no sense of separation, and as such, no ego identification. There is only Consciousness As Such—joyful and at peace.

State 4: Turiya. This fourth, superconscious state is ineffable, beyond the senses, thoughts, or anything that can be pointed to. It is Allness, the Ultimate, the Absolute—All That Is. "He is the supreme goal of life. He is infinite peace and love. Realize him!"[8]

The Upanishads represents the earliest known text where the Perennial Philosophy is first recorded.

Maslow's Hierarchy of Human Needs

The hierarchical levels of being found in the Perennial Philosophy are not restricted to ancient Eastern philosophies and spiritual teachings. We can observe degrees of *beingness* in contemporary psychological theory as well. Maslow's famous Hierarchy of Human Needs, which is generally pictured in a triangle, offers the various stages of human needs. The basic, primal needs must be met before an individual can experience the higher level needs.

The human needs are as follows:

1. *Physiological needs*: These biologically-rooted needs come first in the form of food, water, and basic homeostatic requirements like sleep and sex.
2. *Safety needs*: Safety needs include shelter, protection, and stability.
3. *Love and belonging needs*: The need for affection, relationships, and a sense of belonging emerges once our physiological and safety needs are met.
4. *Esteem needs*: Next we see the need for status (esteem from others) as well as an internally-derived sense of personal worth (self-esteem).
5. *Self-actualization*: Finally, as one continues to grow, so does the drive for self-fulfillment—to actualize one's potential nature.

As Maslow explains, "Human needs arrange themselves in hierarchies of pre-potency. That is to say, the appearance of one need usually rests on the prior satisfaction of another, more pre-potent need. Man is a perpetually wanting animal. Also no need or drive can be treated as if it were isolated or discrete; every drive is related to the state of satisfaction or dissatisfaction of other drives."[9]

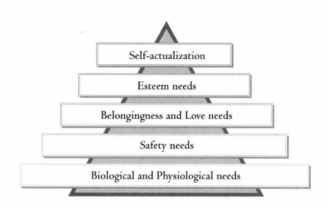

MASLOW'S HIERARCHY OF HUMAN NEEDS

Once again, we see various levels or degrees of development, where the lesser is contained in the greater, but not vice versa. The need for belonging to a group is not present when someone is starving to death—the drive for nourishment overwhelms the potentiality to experience higher needs. In cultures where few are hungry or homeless, the focus is on the higher level needs of belonging (to a church, a community, or a specialized group), esteem (often in the form of "keeping up with the Joneses"), and self-actualization (in the form of self improvement and personal growth).

In Maslow's later writing, he eluded to a sixth level called the "transcendent" level.[10] This subjective experience, beyond self-actualization, transcends the personal ego and taps into a "trans-personal" reality. Again, the lesser is contained in the greater, but not vice versa.

*   *   *

The mind has difficulty discerning how to categorize different things, generally lacking the context to make such decisions. With an awareness of the reality of levels and hierarchies within nature and the spiritual domain, we can turn our attention to what is arguably the clearest description of the Perennial Philosophy, Hawkins' Map of Consciousness.

Appendix C
A Theory of Everything

David R. Hawkins, to whom we've referenced extensively throughout this text, developed a "map" of the levels of consciousness that uses a muscle-testing technique called the physiologic response to document the nonlinear realm of consciousness. An elaborate discussion of the Map of Consciousness and its significance is outlined in his groundbreaking book, *Power vs. Force: The Hidden Determinants of Human Behavior.*

Aligned with the Perennial Philosophy discussed in appendix B, the Map of Consciousness represents the various levels of human development through the evolution of consciousness. Each level of consciousness coincides with human behaviors and perceptions about life, the world and God, and is tied to a corresponding attractor field of varying strength that exists beyond our three-dimensional reality.[1]

The numerical scale ranges from 1 (bacteria), representing the weakest form of life on the planet, to 1,000, the level of the great historic Avatars (Buddha, Jesus Christ, Krishna). The numbers on the scale represent exponential calibrations (measurable vibratory frequencies on a scale where each successive level increases exponentially) of the levels of human consciousness and its corresponding level of reality. The numbers themselves are arbitrary; the significance lies in the relationship of one number (or level) to another—and all the levels, like the Perennial Philosophy itself, are relative to the Absolute. In this case, Enlightenment at level

1,000 represents the Absolute, the highest vibrational energy field realizable within the physical domain.

The levels within the Map of Consciousness are not understood as one being "better than" another, which denotes a judgment; rather, each represents various stages of the evolution of consciousness. (Consistent with the Perennial Philosophy, the lesser is contained within the greater but not vice versa.) Similar to evolution observed within the animal kingdom, the evolution of consciousness as expressed in the human domain proceeds through various hierarchical levels. If someone calibrates in the 400s (level of Reason), for example, that person has already transcended the levels of consciousness below 400. For this individual, he must now transcend the 400s to emerge into the field of Love (the 500s).

What Hawkins has offered us through the Map of Consciousness is a tool to contextualize all things (including emotions, people, events, places, and concepts) on both the physical and spiritual plane: a true theory of everything that can be validated (but not proven[2]) using the physiological technique.[3] From Hawkins:

> The sought-for commonality to all realms of subjective experience and investigation turns out to be the omnipresent energy field traditionally denoted as "consciousness," the very substrate and core of all existence and of intelligence itself. Consciousness alone has all the qualities by which to compare and unite these seemingly disparate realms into a comprehensive unity with stratified expressions. Consciousness itself is the key to the sought-for "unified field theory of everything." Beyond the field of consciousness, nothing exists

because it is universal and independent of time or location. Curiously, at the same time, it is knowable, able to be experienced, and its levels are discernable and identifiable.[4]

Although the Map of Consciousness is new (this pioneering work was first published in 1995), increasing numbers of inquisitive souls are becoming attracted to this new framework. Consequently, society as a whole has the opportunity to see a rapid advance in human understanding as all life experiences are contextualized, helping us choose that which affirms, rather than that which denigrates life. The Sages as well as great ancient philosophers like Socrates acknowledged the mind's inability to discern truth from falsehood, essence from appearance. With greater awareness of the levels of consciousness, a person is better-equipped to discern truth. News broadcasters, newspaper editorial writers, and communicators in general can be held to a greater degree of accountability when we become more astute at discerning factual statements from fallacious distortions.

Debates and arguments arise because different individuals perceive the world from different levels of consciousness. Without identifying the context of a given situation, which is facilitated by an understanding of the various levels of consciousness, conflict prevails. The levels provide us with functional degrees of context, which when honestly evaluated, tend to dissolve any and all conflict. (See *Transcending Conflict* in chapter 7 for further discussion.)

Two Great Barriers Within Consciousness

The two barriers of particular importance are consciousness level 200 (Courage) and level 500 (Love). Two hundred, the level of Courage, represents a profound shift from destructive and harmful behavior to life-promoting and integrity-supporting lifestyles.[5] Currently, approximately 85 percent of the world's population is below this significant level.[6] The destructive capacity of this majority would annihilate mankind without the counterbalancing effect of the 15 percent above 200. Because the Map of Consciousness is exponential, each incremental point represents a giant leap in power. As such, one person calibrated at level 600, for example, counterbalances the negativity of 10 million people below level 200.[7]

The second great barrier is level 500—Love. Love as a level of consciousness is a way of being in the world (lovingness)—not an emotional state that we *do* from time to time (romanticized love), as most of us perceive it. At this level, one's inner, subjective reality becomes dominant instead of the mind's abstract "thinkingness" which rules the 400s (Reason). The life view of individuals in the 500s is benign, having general reverence for all life. Divinity is viewed as loving and information is processed through nonlinear revelation instead of intellectual abstraction. According to Hawkins, the level of Love is difficult to realize because the ego is so rooted in the physical domain (the linear, provable domain of classical physics), which is a different experience of reality than the spiritual domain (the nonlinear, formless, spiritual realm) that emerges at level 500.

The 400s represent the level of Reason, guided by the linear, mechanistic world of form—the Old-World paradigm we discussed in chapter 2. Interestingly, the top echelon of intellectual geniuses, including Einstein, Freud, Newton, and physicist Stephen Hawking (currently), all calibrated at level 499. Other brilliant minds like William James, Aristotle, and Plato calibrated in the 490s as well. The 500s, or the level of Love, represents a difficult hurdle, with only four percent of the world's population ever reaching this level.[8] Brilliant minds that transcended the linear domain and learned to acknowledge the relevance of subjective experience include physicist David Bohm at level 505, Carl Jung at level 525, and Socrates at level 540.

Again, it is important to understand that one level is not "better" or "worse" than another. The Levels represent a gradation of consciousness—degrees of the experience of Reality, the realization of the existence of God, and the level of understanding God as Love. The 500s (Love) are not "better" than the 400s (Reason); they simply represent different gradations relative to the Absolute, denoted by 1,000 representing the highest vibrational field possible in the human domain.

Creativity and the Levels of Consciousness

If you've read this far, you may be wondering how the levels of consciousness relate directly to creativity, which is an interesting area for further research.

In reviewing the Map, one might be tempted to peg creativity as a particular level; however, creativity represents a leap from a lower attractor field to a higher one.[9] As such, creative inspiration can occur at virtually any level of consciousness, although it is less likely to occur at levels below 200. A powerful attractor field is present by the time consciousness evolves into the 400s (Reason). Those with greater levels of humility are more likely to experience the creative impulse, assuming they are able to align to the archetypes discussed in chapter 5.

From the perspective of "Big C" creativity which garners a larger degree of public recognition, the creative individual is likely to operate from an attractor beyond the scope of their occupational field. For example, Sigmund Freud in his development of psycho-analysis (level 460) was met by continuous criticism and ostracism by the medical community and the psychological community (level 420) he was helping to create.[10] Even over a hundred years later, Freud's (and Jung's) psychoanalytical perspectives are not even taught in many psychology departments of major universities despite the profound impact psychoanalysis continues to have on our culture (as well as its paramount contributions it has made to our understanding of the human psyche).[11]

Jung astutely noted that we must separate the artist from the creative work he produces.[12] Current consciousness research is confirming this notion as the calibrated level of consciousness of various works of art can vary greatly from the calibrated level of the artist himself.[13] The intention of the individual is a major determinant of the work's calibrated level. For example, a great painter has the choice of creating a "work of art" out of his love for God and his gratitude for existence versus the drive of simply earning a quick dollar.[14] The result of this intention will, in large part, define the attractor field from which the final product will emanate. An intention aligned to something greater than one's self increases the potentiality of the emergence of a creative moment.

In observing the levels of consciousness of numerous "creative geniuses" and / or their respective work, we note that "Big C" creativity generally emerges in the 400s (Reason / Intellect) and flourishes into the 500s (Love). Creative works that tend to have the most significant impact on one's state of being, whether it be in the form of a beautiful piece of music or a magnificent cathedral, are aligned with Spirit denoted by the levels of Love and beyond (500 and up). As Brenda Ueland, author of *If You Want To*

Write, intuited, "For I know that the energy of the creative impulse comes from love and all its manifestations—admiration, compassion, glowing respect, gratitude, praise, tenderness, adoration, enthusiasm."[15]

Victor E. Frankl in his perennial *Man's Search for Meaning*, came to the same conclusion: "A thought transfixed me: for the first time in my life I saw the truth as it is set into song by so many poets, proclaimed as the final wisdom by so many thinkers. The truth—that love is the ultimate and the highest goal to which man can aspire. Then I grasped the meaning of the greatest secret that human poetry and human thought and belief have to impart: *the salvation of man is through love and in love.*"[16]

Consciousness Calibrations of Selected Creative Geniuses[17]

Aristotle	498	Heisenberg, Werner	485
Bell, Alexander Graham	450	Mandela, Nelson	505
Bohm, David	505	Newton, Isaac	499
Bohr, Niels	450	Pasteur, Louis	485
Carnegie, Andrew	490	Pauling, Linus	450
Churchill, Winston	510	Plato	490
Darwin, Charles	450	Rockwell, Norman	500
Edison, Thomas	470	Roosevelt, Eleanor	500
Einstein, Albert	499	Socrates	540
Franklin, Benjamin	480	Tesla, Nicola	460
Freud, Sigmund	499	Washington, Booker T.	460
Galilei, Galileo	455	Washington, George	455
Gorbachev, Mikhail	500		

Consciousness Calibrations of
Selected Creative Works[18]

Armstrong, Louis (music of)	510
Bach, Johann Sebastian (music of)	530
Bacon, Francis ("Great Books of the Western World")	485
Beatles, The (music of)	460
Beethoven, Ludwig van (music of)	510
Bocelli, Andrea (music of)	550
Brahms, Johannes (music of)	495
Browning, Elizabeth (literary works of)	460
Carson, Johnny (program of)	480
Cezanne, Paul (works of)	510
Charles, Ray (music of)	485
Dali, Salvador (works of)	455
da Vinci, Leonardo (works of)	565
Dickens, Charles (literary works of)	540
Emerson, Ralph Waldo (literary works of)	475
Frost, Robert (literary works of)	440
Handel, George Frideric (music of)	510
Haydn, Franz Joseph (music of)	490
Hope, Bob (program of)	465
James, William ("Great Books of the Western World")	490
Longfellow, Henry Wadsworth (literary works of)	465
Matisse, Henri (works of)	525
Michelangelo (works of)	590
Mozart, Wolfgang Amadeus (music of)	540
Picasso, Pablo (works of)	365
Puccini, Giacomo (music of)	550
Rembrandt (works of)	700
Shakespeare, William (literary works of)	500
Tolstoy, Leo (literary works of)	400
Tchaikovsky, Peter Ilyich (music of)	550
Twain, Mark (literary works of)	465
Van Gogh, Vincent (works of)	480
Wagner, Roger (music of)	500
Wilde, Oscar (literary works of)	440

Glossary

Attractors: The study of chaos arose out of the discovery of *Strange Attractors*, or attractor fields. Attractors exist in what physicists call phase space, an abstract reality beyond our three-dimensional experience. Attractor fields are highly organized energy fields that "magnetically" pull everything in a given system toward them. In essence, behind the appearance of randomness is a world of organizing patterns, or order.

MIT meteorologist Edward Lorenz is credited as "accidentally" discovering the existence of Attractors with the now-famous "Lorenz Butterfly." Attractor fields can have high or low energy and, according to consciousness research, they don't only occur in nature. Attractor fields of varying strength exist behind every behavior, belief, and thought. Essentially, our thoughts and intentions have varying degrees of power, governed by these attractors. (For further discussion, see *Patterns of Attraction* in chapter 3.)

Beliefs: Beliefs are a type of mental programming aligned with a specific level of energy (denoted by an attractor field). Most beliefs fall below the radar of our conscious experience and are programmed by society at large. Some beliefs are destructive while others are benign (or even helpful, depending on the individual's level of consciousness). A set of beliefs comprises a "paradigm," which is fortified when a mass of people become entrained to a range of concepts. Such is the case with the Newtonian paradigm, where numerous layers of beliefs are so deeply rooted that they are presumed to be facts, and therefore, not questioned. (A collection of these beliefs is explored in chapter 2.)

Cartesian Thinking: See *Newtonian Paradigm*.

Causality: A core tenet from classical physics (which permeates most of contemporary thought), the law of cause and effect is believed to be a basic law of the universe. Event A *causes* Event B. The notion of causality is an outgrowth of perception, which is linear in nature. When we see a linear progression of events through time—A → B → C—the assumption is that the preceding event is causing the subsequent event. From a more accurate, nonlinear viewpoint, all that can be observed is *emergence*: Event A emerges. Event B emerges. Event C emerges. In Reality, any causal connections made between events are abstract intellectualizations. Instead of crediting "causes," it is more accurate to note that when the right conditions are present, an event manifests. When the sidewalk is icy, you're in a rush, and you aren't paying attention, you may slip and fall. The icy walkway can't *cause* the fall. When the right conditions are present, the falling manifests. (For further discussion, see *Beyond Causality* in chapter 2.)

Consciousness: Westerners often use the term "consciousness" synonymously with "mind," which is erroneous. Consciousness is not thoughts, but our capacity to be aware of them. Consciousness is what gives us sentience—our sense of presence. Consciousness can be equated with awareness or *beingness*. It is the sense that you *are*, that you exist, without words or emotions. That sense of beingness is a complete subjective experience; you know you are without anyone needing to tell you that you exist. Consciousness is not limited to human beings either—all sentient life represents various forms of consciousness. (For further discussion, see chapter 3.)

Context: Context represents the overall field of information that gives content its meaning. *Content* is the details of a particular situation. *Context* is the overall field from which the details arise. Context sets the meaning for content. Without context, content has no meaning. Because the mind generally processes information through abstraction, it often mistakes the symbol for what the symbol represents. The mind tries to interpret *content* without understanding the larger *context*. An understanding of the Perennial Philosophy (appendix B) and Hawkins' Map of Consciousness (chapter 3) illuminate the various levels or hierarchies that exist in Reality. These levels represent the various larger-field contexts that must be understood before information in those categories can be accurately interpreted. (For further discussion, see *Transcending Conflict* in chapter 7.)

Creativity: Creativity is the act of creation, bringing the unmanifest into the manifest. Although commonly mistaken as originating from a person or individual phenomenon, creativity is a nonlocal event that occurs within consciousness. The creative impulse itself is an aspect of Divinity that radiates *through* the individual (not *from* him). Since creativity is an aspect of consciousness, it is therefore available to all mankind. By understanding the internal conditions necessary for creative inspiration, one can increase the potentiality for creative manifestation. (For further discussion, see chapter 5.)

Duality: Here's the dilemma: to activate cognition (the processing of information via thought), there needs to be something (an object) to cognize. Without an "other"—in the form of a person, place, or thing—what would the mind objectify? If you are always the subject, there must (from the mind's perspective) be an object. This dualistic dilemma is intrinsic to the very structure of the mind, which is limited to perceiving dualities—me-and-you, this-and-that, mine-and-yours, subject-and-object. In contrast, the Mystic transcends the mind's dualistic proclivities and apperceives a nondual, nonlocal, infinite reality. (For further discussion on duality, see *Transcending the Opposites* in chapter 2.)

Ego: In spiritual parlance, the ego is equated with what can be called the "survival self," contrasted with the higher Self (with a capital "S"). The ego represents the sense of identification with the body-mind organism. When we say, "I went to the store" or "I'm upset," what is the "I" that is being referred to? This "me" concept—that you exist as an autonomous, separate being—is at the root of the illusion of separation and represents the barrier to true spiritual awakening.

Hawkins terms the ego as "a collection of thoughts that are presumed to represent one's personal reality and identity, with a shading of implication that the grouping of thoughts and beliefs is purposeful. The purpose is to maintain the illusion of the personal self as the inner 'cause' of one's existence and activities, including thoughts and feelings."[1] The more evolved one becomes, the more one's identification with the ego weakens until eventually there is no personal identification as a "me." In this condition, generally termed "enlightenment," the identification now abides in the infinite field of consciousness itself. (For further discussion, see chapter 6.)

Enlightenment: Enlightenment is the state of realization or awakening where the identification is with awareness or consciousness itself rather than the body-mind organism. In fact, in the state of enlightenment, no "personhood" exists. This advanced state or condition has been realized by very few souls—past or present.

Entrainment: Entrainment is a phenomenon found throughout nature where seemingly separate entities are drawn together by hidden attractor fields. Operating in phase space beyond the measurable, physical world, these attractor fields align groups of people to specific rites, rituals, customs and beliefs. Entrainment also helps explain the synchronistic movements of schools of fish and flocks of birds. (For further discussion, see *Entrainment* in chapter 1.)

Heisenberg Uncertainty Principle: One of the founders of quantum physics Werner Heisenberg discovered that at the subatomic level, you cannot simultaneously determine both the momentum (or speed) of a particle and the location; you can determine one or the other. If you measure the particle's speed, you can't know its exact location. If you pinpoint a particle's location, you can't determine its momentum. This leads to a language of probabilities instead of actualities and challenges deterministic classical physics where all elements of nature should be accurately measurable and knowable. The Heisenberg Uncertainty Principle acknowledges that human observation (in the form of observer's consciousness) affects that which it is observing, an assertion impossible by the rules of classical physics. (For further discussion, see *The New World and Beyond* in chapter 3.)

Material Reductionism: Material reductionism (a dominant belief in the world of science and academia), says that if you can't see it or measure it, it isn't real. This highly limiting viewpoint originates from the Newtonian paradigm and Cartesian thinking, which view the world as a giant machine. For example, this paradigm asserts that if the human body is viewed as a machine, then by dissecting every component (part), we'll be able to understand the whole. Reductionism can lead people to believe that our consciousness is nothing more than a chemical reaction in the brain, negating the possibility of divinity or true inner subjective realization. Reductionism presents a barrier to under-standing advanced theoretical sciences and the subjective, spiritual domain. (For further discussion, see chapter 2.)

Morphic Fields: Theoretical biologist Rupert Sheldrake uses his Hypothesis of Formative Causation to demonstrate that hidden energy fields called *morphogenetic fields* (form-changing fields) help explain the evolution and "memory" of various species of animals where habits are formed by the same species in various locations around the world. The hypothesis also demonstrates how morphic fields possess a kind of collective memory aligned to specific thoughts, beliefs, and rituals. (For further discussion, see *Collective Memory* in chapter 1.)

Mystic (and Sage): A Mystic is a Self-Realized sage that has transcended the ego. Technically speaking, within the context of the Map of Consciousness, the Mystic emerges at 600, the beginning level of Enlightenment. Having transcended the dual-istic, linear experience of the body-mind, the Mystic's subjective Realization is nondual and nonlinear, where the personal "I" has dissolved into the Universal I of Absolute Truth. The Mystics of all the great traditions experience the same spiritual truth; however, each uses language and descriptors indicative of their respective time period, location, and group affiliation.

The Sage, in contrast, is Self-Realized, but somehow stays in the world as a Teacher that inspires others. Examples of Sages at various levels of Realization include the Buddha, Jesus Christ, Krishna, Zoroaster, Meister Eckhart, Saint John of the Cross, Sri Aurobindo, Mother Teresa, Ramana Maharshi, Patanjali, Huang Po, Ramakrishna, and Saint Theresa of Avila.

New World (or New Science): The New-World paradigm transcends the belief in a completely definable universe, knowable by the human mind. The New-World understanding puts stock in the reality of subjective awareness as the core of our existence. From the perspective of the scientific community, this New-World viewpoint began emerging with the discovery of quantum mechanics where human consciousness began taking an important role in mankind's understanding of nature. The Old-World (linear, Newtonian, mechanistic and deterministic) beliefs about the nature of reality, however, are still deeply-rooted in the scientific community and the belief system of the general population.

Newtonian Paradigm: The Newtonian paradigm is the linear, dualistic way of viewing the world as established by Sir Isaac Newton's classical physics. This paradigm perceives all events as cause-and-effect relationships in the material world. In fact, the Newtonian perspective negates everything but what can be measured and observed, leaving no space for subjective experience or the spiritual domain. As such, this deep-rooted, old paradigm is seen as limiting and represents a block to higher levels of under-standing.

Other terms used synonymously with "Newtonian paradigm" are "Cartesian thinking" (named after René Descartes), "atomistic thinking" (the atom representing the smallest building block of reality), "scientific determinism" (everything in the universe can be determined and known), or "mechanistic thinking" (thinking in terms of everything as being machine-like). (For further dis-cussion, see *The Dynamic Duo of the Old World* in chapter 2.)

Nonduality: The pathway of Advaita Vedanta in the Hindu tradition is the path of No Mind or nonduality. The pathway of nonduality is arguably the most direct path to enlightenment as it goes straight to the source of consciousness itself. Since the mind's basic structure is linear and dualistic, the nondual teachings instruct the student on transcending the limitations of the mind. At the level of nonduality, there is observing, but there is no individual observer. The duality of subject and object (the polarity of opposites) is transcended and only the Absolute remains. At this level, there is no longer an individual entity or a fixed locus of perception, as there is no longer an ego-identification with the body-mind organism (the false identification of the body as "I"). Everything is seen at an aspect of consciousness—part of the One, Universal Self.

Nonlinear: The mind processes events linearly, in a sequential order. Nonlinearity is difficult to comprehend since the mind generally thinks in terms of cause and effect, which presumes a beginning, middle, and end to any event. The development of chaos theory and the mathematics of nonlinear dynamics have given rise to a language that holds little meaning within the Newtonian paradigm. Nonlinear means chaotic or diffuse with no beginning or end; it is unsolvable by differential calculus. Terms like "now" and "then" have no meaning in relation to that which is nonlinear. The nonlinear nature of reality is expounded on by the Mystics and acknowledged by advanced theoretical science.

Old World: The Old World is a concept used to denote the material reductionist who believes that only what can be measured is "real." The "Old World" doesn't identify a time period; it is a mechanistic way of thinking about the physical universe where everything is provable, measurable, and knowable. (Please see "Newtonian Paradigm" and "Material Reductionist" above for further clarification.)

Opposites: See *Duality*.

Paradigm: A paradigm is comprised of programs, practices, and commonly held beliefs by a group or society in a particular time period. A paradigm represents a field of context or a range of perception or dimension. This programming is so foundational to the thinking of the time that it is generally not questioned, leading to "paradigm blindness" and the inability to see things as they truly are. (For further discussion, see *Old Paradigms* in chapter 2.)

Perception: Perception is the process by which the ego-mind interprets reality. Perception is the brain's way of interpreting the outside world (Descartes' *res cognitas*); it does NOT represent Reality itself. Processing information through the five senses and combining this data with prior experiences, memory, emotions, and associations, we experience a filtered form of reality through our perceptional lens. By understanding the unreliable nature of perception, we gain humility for our true ignorance. With spiritual advancement, perception is replaced by spiritual vision, where accurate discernment becomes available. (For further information, see *Bonds of Perception* in chapter 1.)

Perennial Philosophy: The Perennial Philosophy represents an ordered hierarchy of understanding relative to Absolute Truth, which is the infinite, nonlinear, nonlocal field. An examination of the Perennial Philosophy helps us contextualize the meanings behind the levels of human consciousness and provides a way of interpreting a complete stratum of human experience—both worldly and internal. Within the Absolute, "appearances" unfold at various gradients / degrees / levels / hierarchies where the "lesser" is contained within the "greater," but not vice versa. So we find that the linear, Old-World paradigm is contained within the nonlinear, spiritual domain of subjective experience. (For further information, see appendix B.)

Reductionist: See *Material Reductionist.*

Relativism: Relativism is a philosophic ideology that negates the existence of Absolute Truth and in doing so eliminates the foundation for basic morals and ethics. The relativist may say, *This is true for me, it doesn't have to be true for you.* Under the guise of relativism, any belief system or political position can be justified. Truth is subverted by relativistic principles that undermine the universal truths that have built modern society.

Sage: See *Mystic.*

Subjectivity: From the moment you awake in the morning, you know you are—that you exist. You don't need words to know this, nor do you need someone else to verify it for you. This experience of awareness without words is the very substrate of your existence. A person who denies the validity of subjectivity or claims that only an objective truth exists does so through his subjective experience—there's simply no way around this obvious fact. (For further discussion, see chapter 3.)

Notes

Introduction

[1] Mikkelsen, et al. "Initial sequence of the chimpanzee genome and comparison with the human genome."

[2] Scientists have localized intelligence to the prefrontal cortex and part of that less-than-two-percent difference is because the human brain produces more neurons (brain cells) in the cortex to allow signals to be transported at higher speeds, which seems to correlate with man's higher intelligence. (See Roth, Gerhard, "Evolution of the brain and intelligence.")

[3] Maslow, *The Farther Reaches of Human Nature*, 55-59; Rogers, *On Becoming a Person*, 348; Bohm, *On Creativity*, 23.

[4] Maslow, *The Farther Reaches of Human Nature*, 88.

[5] Pilzer, *Unlimited Wealth*.

[6] Google.com provides one such example.

[7] Wheatley, *Leadership and the New Science*.

[8] Goleman, "The Art of Creativity."

[9] http://www.foodnetwork.com/food/about_us/

[10] "More Americans Telecommute, use flextime," MSNBC/Reuters, May 4, 2006: http://www.msnbc.msn.com/id/12632385/

[11] Anderson and Ray, *Cultural Creatives*.

Chapter 1: Collective Mind

[1] Mathew, *The True Path*, 59.

[2] The Dalai Lama explains the Buddhist concept of emptiness, which highlights the error of human perception: "According to the theory of emptiness, any belief in an objective reality grounded in the assumption of intrinsic, independent existence is untenable." (*The Universe in a Single Atom*, 46)

[3] Wells, et al. "From lab to the police station: A successful application of eyewitness research."

[4] Mathew, *The True Path*, 56.

[5] See quote on page 73-74.

[6] Plato, *Republic*, 186.

[7] Edwin Abbott's classic, *Flatlands: A Romance of Many Dimensions*, originally published in 1880, explores this concept in an entertaining and insightful manner.

[8] The creator of this image was believed to be British cartoonist W. E. Hill in a 1915 publication called *Puck*, however, earlier forms of the illusion can be found in an anonymous German postcard from 1888 and and an 1890 advertisement by Anchor Buggy Company. (Weisstein, Eric W. "Young Girl-Old Woman Illusion." From *MathWorld*—A Wolfram Web Resource. http://mathworld.wolfram.com/YoungGirl-OldWomanIllusion.html)

[9] Plato, *Meno*, 77d-77e. The actual quote is, "Those who are ignorant of the bad do not desire it; they desire what they believe to be good, whereas it is really bad. In other words, they do not know what is bad and yet desire it, believing the bad to be good; so they really desire the good."

[10] Blake, *The Marriage of Heaven and Hell*, Plate 14.

[11] Shakespeare, *Hamlet*, 2.2.268-270.

[12] Aurelius, *Meditations*, 4.3.

[13] Dhammapada, 1:1-2.

[14] Proverbs 23:7 (King James Version)

[15] Kandel, *In Search of Memory*, xii.

[16] Koestler, *The Act of Creation*, 131-144.

[17] Wilber, *The Holographic Paradigm*. Bohm noted that he was working on the holographic metaphor of the universe when he read a paper by Pribram. For an entertaining and educational account of both Bohm and Pribram's work with the "holographic paradigm," see Michael Talbot's *The Holographic Universe*.

[18] Jung, *Synchronicity*.

[19] Campbell, *A Hero with a Thousand Faces*. Also see Campbell's *The Power of Myth* (available in print or DVD).

[20] For an enlightening look at rites, rituals and comparative mythology, see Joseph Campbell's DVD series *The Power of Myth* and *Mythos*.

[21] Sheldrake, *New Science of Life* and *Presence of the Past*. You can also visit www.sheldrake.org and read a set of three research papers on Morphic Resonance.

[22] Hawkins, *Power vs. Force*, 112.

[23] Another example of collective thought is often termed "memes," which is a cultural idea transmitted from one mind to another like a trend, style or catch phrase.

[24] Potts, "The chorus-line hypothesis of manoeuvre coordination in avian flocks."

[25] Bennett, et al., "Huygens's Clocks."

[26] Strogatz, *Sync*, 272-273.

[27] Buck, "Mechanism of Rhythmic Synchronous Flashing of Fireflies."

[28] Strogatz, *Sync*, 14.

[29] The report of the Japanese scientists originally came from Lyall Watson's book, *Lifetide* (1979), which was comprised of anecdotal evidence. In 1985, Ron Amundson wrote a critique of the 100th Monkey Phenomenon. In 1986, Watson responded by

clarifying that all his data was from off the record conversations with people familiar with the occurrence. When one of the senior researchers Masao Kawai was contacted, he claimed not to be aware of any propagation of the washing of sweet potatoes that would not normally be expected, and he didn't observe any of the widespread trends in other places that Watson claimed. According to Hawkins' calibration research, the 100th Monkey Phenomenon is a reality (calibrates around 205); however, this particular illustration may best be viewed metaphorically.

[30] Nelson, "Correlation of Global Events with REG Date: An Internet-Based, Nonlocal Anomalies Experiment."

Visit http://noosphere.princeton.edu/ for a detailed look at this experiment and the current results.

[31] See Lynne McTaggart's experiments on collective human intention at http://www.theintentionexperiment.com.

Chapter 2: Concepts of the Old World

[1] If you question the parallels and commonalities between various traditions and mystical teachings, see Campbell's 10-hour DVD series, *Mythos*.

[2] Kuhn, *The Structure of Scientific Revolution*, 175.

[3] Lehrer, "The Reinvention of the Self."

[4] Hawkins, *Transcending the Levels of Consciousness*, 311. Also, see Hawkins, "Paradigm Blindness: Academic vs. Clinical Medicine."

[5] Harmon and Rheingold, *Higher Creativity*, 67.

[6] Koestler, *The Act of Creation*, 108.

[7] In the model of classical physics, there are four objective realities: bodies, forces, space and time—all of which are objectively measurable and discernable.

[8] Radin, *The Conscious Universe*.

[9] Jung, *Synchronicity*.

[10] Dorsey, *Reinventing Medicine*; Cousins, *Anatomy of an Illness as Perceived by the Patient*; Weil, *Spontaneous Healing*.

[11] Eadie, *Embraced by the Light*.

[12] As Kuhn noted, "Normal science often suppresses fundamental novelties because they are necessarily subversive of its basic commitments." (*The Structure of Scientific Revolutions*, 5)

[13] Dalai Lama, *The Universe in a Single Atom*, 39.

[14] James, *The Varieties of Religious Experience*; Deikman, "Functional Approach to Mysticism." Generally speaking, the Eastern philosophies called this cosmic consciousness Atman while Christianity called it the Holy Spirit.

[15] James, *Psychology: Briefer Course*.

[16] This mechanistic worldview can be traced back to ancient philosophers Plato (Platonic), Aristotle (Aristotelian) and Pythagoras (Pythagorean). Also, leading thinkers like Galileo Galilei, Johannes Kepler, Nicolaus Copernicus, and Francis Bacon further solidified mechanistic thinking.

[17] Descartes, *Discourse on Method*.

[18] Hawkins, *Truth vs. Falsehood*, 12.

[19] Capra, *The Turning Point*.

[20] Hawkins describes this core dilemma: "The mind cannot know the world itself but only its selective, abstract mentalization about it, just as a photo is not the object photographed." (*Truth vs. Falsehood*, 11)

[21] Bohm, "A New Theory of Mind Matter" (quoting Cottingham, J. 1986. *Descartes*. Oxford, Basil Blackwell.)

[22] Ibid.

[23] Harokopos, "Power as the Cause of Motion and a New Foundation of Classical Mechanics."

[24] *Memoirs of Newton*, v. II, ch. 27, ed. Brewster (1855).

[25] Bohm, *On Dialogue*.

[26] In the insightful DVD series *Mythos*, Joseph Campbell clearly illustrates how man, throughout history, has mistaken symbols for what those symbols represent.

[27] Hawkins, *Discovery of the Presence of God*, 225.

[28] Hawkins, *The Eye of the I*, 277.

[29] "Subjective Perception of Time and a Progressive Present Moment: The Neurobiological Key to Unlocking Consciousness." (See also Lynds, "Time and Classical and Quantum Mechanics: Indeterminacy vs. Discontinuity.")

[30] Foundation of Inner Peace, *A Course in Miracles*, 298 (Lesson 158 in the workbook portion).

[31] Erdman, From Blake's Notebook, 480.

[32] Of course, some concepts are more valuable than others. Different concepts define varying levels of beauty, utility, and truth (as determined by the concept's level of consciousness). As one might imagine, the concept of abortion calibrates differently than the concept of super string theory; the concept of prayer calibrates differently than the concept of stem cell research. The mind is incapable of discerning the calibrated level of consciousness of a concept. A concept's calibration can be derived at using the physiologic technique outlined in *Truth vs. Falsehood*, appendix C.

[33] Harokopos's paper, "Power as the Cause of Motion and a New Foundation of Classical Mechanics," revised Newton's theory that forces are causing counter-forces in the universe. It identifies a power beyond the physical domain that influences motion in the material, three-dimensional reality. This discovery is consistent with Bohm's notion of the Implicate Order. See Bohm's *Wholeness and the Implicate Order*.

[34] The Big Bang theory is a limited interpretation from a linear viewpoint. What preceded the Big Bang approximately thirteen billion years ago? The mind thinks in a linear sequence—from a

starting point to a finish line. Beyond the notion of this linear reality is the nonlinear, nonlocal understanding of nonlinear dynamics and quantum mechanics. From the Hindu perspective, the creation and destruction of universes are eternal occurrences, represented by the dance of Shiva.

[35] Maslow examines the limits of causal thinking regarding creativity in *The Farther Reaches of Human Nature*, 71.

[36] Even the academic "systemic approaches" to creativity like those by Csikszentmihalyi are looking for the external "causes" for creative genius.

[37] As psychologist Carl Jung notes, "Any reaction to stimulus may be causally explained; but the creative act, which is the absolute antithesis of mere reaction, will forever elude the human understanding." (Ghiselin, *The Creative Process*, 218)

[38] Libet, "Reflections on the interaction of the mind and brain."

[39] Briggs and Peat, *Turbulent Mirror*, 110.

[40] Hawkins, *The Eye of the I*, 113.

[41] The Dalai Lama notes: "This principle is very ancient in Buddhism—the Buddha himself argued that if one wishes to avoid certain types of results, one needs to change the conditions that give rise to them." (*The Universe in a Single Atom*, 146)

[42] For a detailed description of the error of causality, see Hawkins' *The Eye of the I*, 110-113.

[43] Bell, "On the Einstein Podolsky Rosen paradox."

[44] Einstein didn't agree with the concept behind quantum mechanics because of his firm belief in an independent, objective external reality aligned with classical determinism where perfect order was achieved. To refute the principles of quantum mechanics, Einstein developed a thought experiment known as the Einstein-Podolsky-Rosen (EPR) experiment. Bell's Theorem,

which came three decades later, dramatically weakened the position Einstein long held.

[45] As Hawkins explains, "In Quantum Mechanics, therefore, it is importantly noted that the discoveries of Quantum Theory led to a breakdown of the causality principle. This clarifies that 'causality' is a mentation and an operative theory and explanation rather than a provable reality." (*I: Reality and Subjectivity*, 434)

[46] To quote brand expert, Bolivar J. Bueno.

[47] Hawkins, *I: Reality and Subjectivity*, 46-47.

[48] Ibid., 169.

[49] Capra, *The Tao of Physics*, 145.

[50] From the perspective of the mind, the obstacle of dualism is insurmountable. Transcending this intellectual limitation requires the letting go of linear thinking for the realization of subjective experience. In the context of the Map of Consciousness, this represents the critical barrier between the high 400s (Intellect / Reason) and the 500s (Love) and the emergence of spiritual reality.

[51] Amazingly, the Flat Earth Society even has a website: http://www.alaska.net/~clund/e_djublonskopf/Flatearthsociety.htm

Chapter 3: The New World and Beyond

[1] Lindley, *Uncertainty*, 22.

[2] Goswami, *The Self-Aware Universe*, 51.

[3] University of Michigan professor, Ed Sarath, does a terrific job highlighting the discrepancies of definitions of consciousness in "Meditation, Creativity, and Consciousness: Charting Future Terrain With Higher Education."

[4] *What the #$*! Do We Know?*

[5] The Standard Model of particle physics represents the most comprehensive and successful theory of nature, and yet, there

remains a number of unexplained phenomena. (See Kane, "The Dawn of Physics Beyond the Standard Model.")

[6] Maharshi, *The Spiritual Teachings of Ramana Maharshi*, foreword. Interestingly, Jung's theories have been considered taboo in the traditional field of psychology, which is aligned with the Newtonian, mechanistic paradigm.

[7] Wilber, *The Holographic Paradigm*; Krishnamurti, *The Awakening of Intelligence*.

[8] Dalai Lama, *The Universe in a Single Atom*, 29.

[9] Maslow, *Toward a Psychology of Being*.

[10] Hawkins, *Truth vs. Falsehood*, 12.

[11] Muktananda, *Play of Consciousness*, 216.

[12] *Bhagavad-Gita*, 2:71-72. The Beatles song "I Me Mine," written and performed by George Harrison, was inspired by this quote.

[13] Maharaj, *I Am That*, 186.

[14] Ken Wilber and proponents of the Integral Model would argue that an understanding of consciousness requires both a subjective and objective interpretation, giving both the linear and nonlinear domain *equal* validity. Although this integral approach may seem the most holistic and functional approach to an understanding of consciousness, as Hawkins' Map of Consciousness and the perennial philosophy demonstrate (see appendices B and C), there is an overall hierarchy of truth. In fact, the subjective gives rise to the objective, not vice versa. As the perennial philosophy dictates: the lesser is contained in the greater, but not vice versa. From the context of the Map of Consciousness, the objective models or theories of consciousness calibrate in the 400s (Reason) as mental constructs. The subjective understanding of Consciousness begins to emerge as an inner realization at consciousness level 500 (Love) and becomes self-evident with the

emergence of nonduality at 600. So although Wilber's Integral Model seems comprehensive, it is a conceptualization restricted to the linear level of 400s and will not help one understand the nonlinear, subjective domain of consciousness itself.

[15] Mathew, *The True Path*, 104.

[16] *The Upanishads*, 69-70.

[17] Wilber sees this relativistic perspective and the resulting "Culture of Narcissism" as an enormous block to our collective evolutionary development, labeling it as a phenomenon called "Boomeritis." (*A Theory of Everything*, 16)

[18] Macdonald, "Moral Relativism."

[19] The American Civil Liberties Union calibrates at 190 (Pride) and the concept of secularism calibrates at 165.

[20] Hawkins, *Truth vs. Falsehood*, 220-225.

[21] Plato, *Theaetetus*, 30 (152a).

[22] It is worth noting that Marxism and the overall socialistic movement are also guided by this relativistic ideology.

[23] Wilber calls this phenomenon "Boomeritis" and offers a concise analysis of how it arose in his book *A Theory of Everything*. David Hawkins also spends a great deal of time explaining the downsides of moralistic relativism in *Truth vs. Falsehood*, 220-225.

[24] James, *The Varieties of Religious Experience*, 419.

[25] Hegel, *Hegel's Phenomenology of Spirit*, 4.

[26] Maharshi, *I Am That*, 257.

[27] Hawkins, "Realizing the Root of Consciousness: Meditative and Contemplative Techniques."

[28] A third state different from deep sleep and waking is dreaming. In the dream state, you once again have a sense of presence. This sense of awareness departs when consciousness transitions from dreaming back to deep sleep.

[29] Maharaj, *I Am That*.

[30] Deikman, "I = Awareness." (Deikman offers numerous enlightening papers on mysticism, meditation and consciousness on his personal website: www.deikman.com.)

[31] A thorough explanation of the progressive fields of realization can be found in Hawkins' *I: Reality and Subjectivity*, 292-294.

[32] Schroedinger's *What is Life* as quoted in Gowan's "Some New Thoughts on the Development of Creativity."

[33] Wilber, *The Holographic Paradigm*, 20. (original source unknown)

[34] Huxley, *The Perennial Philosophy*, 11.

[35] Maharshi, *The Spiritual Teachings of Ramana Maharshi*, 3.

[36] Powell, *The Ultimate Medicine*, 2-3.

[37] Powell, *Nectar of Immortality*, 11-13.

[38] Huxley, *The Perennial Philosophy*, 12.

[39] Po, *The Zen Teaching of Huang Po*, 29.

[40] Ibid., 31.

[41] As quoted in Gowan, *Trance, Art & Creativity*, 1. Available here: http://www.csun.edu/edpsy/Gowan/content.html

[42] Hawkins, *Truth vs. Falsehood*, 14-16.

[43] The exponential function is expressed as $f(x) = a^x$, where *a* must be a real number. So level 500 (10^{500}) is not twice the amplitude as 250 (10^{500})—it's amplitude is far greater.

[44] Hawkins, "Qualitative and Quantitative Analysis and Calibration of the Level of Human Consciousness," 81.

[45] Hawkins, *Power vs. Force*.

[46] Currently, approximately 85 percent of the world's population is below this significant level and 49 percent of America falls below the critical level of integrity—200, Courage (Hawkins, *Truth vs. Falsehood*). The destructive capacity of this majority would annihilate mankind without the counterbalancing effect of the 15 percent above 200. Because the scale of consciousness is expon-

ential, each incremental point represents a giant leap in power. As such, one person calibrated at 600, for example, counter-balances the negativity of 10 million people below 200 (Hawkins, *Power vs. Force*, 234).

[47] Hawkins, *I: Reality and Subjectivity*, 152-153.

Chapter 4: The Anatomy of Thought

[1] Hawkins, *Power vs. Force*, 235.

[2] *Atomic Physics* (1948) by the J. Arthur Rank Organization, Ltd as quoted in Wikiquote.

[3] Another important aspect of Einstein's theory of relativity is the implication that space, time, and mass cannot be seen as self-existent, unchanging realities to be viewed in isolation—they can only be observed relative to one another. This notion flies in the face of classical physics which requires a measurable, objective reality to be studied.

[4] Jung, *The Structure and Dynamics of the Psyche*, 215.

[5] Hawkins, *Power vs. Force*, 235.

[6] For a good primer on chaos theory, see James Gleick's *Chaos* or Briggs and Peat's *Turbulent Mirror*.

[7] Hawkins, *Power vs. Force*, 59.

[8] According to Hawkins' research, the average person progresses about five points in their calibratable level of consciousness within his lifetime. (*Power vs. Force*, 237)

[9] Hawkins, *Power vs. Force*, 234.

[10] Hawkins, *The Eye of the I*, 79.

[11] Nobelist John Eccles believed that we have a nonmaterial mind which acts upon our material brains—that the mental world (which Karl Popper called World 2) was distinguishable from the physical world (World 1). (See Eccles, *The Wonder of Being Human*, 27-33.) In esoteric philosophies, there are numerous "bodies" concomitant with

the physical body; these subtle energy fields include the etheric, astral, psychic, and causal body. It is possible that thought first arises through these bodies before transmitting to the brain. Of course, this is not verifiable under modern testing procedures. Eccles believed that "experiences in the mind (World 2) need not have a neuronal counterpart in brain activity (World 1)," which seems logical if thoughts are not arising in the physical brain first. (118)

[12] Bohm, "New Theory of Mind and Matter."

[13] Thomas, *Walt Disney: An American Original*, 11.

[14] Mathew, *The True Path*, 172.

[15] Gowan, "Incubation, Imagery, and Creativity."

[16] "If we explore the relationship between mentalization and the brain using consciousness research ... thoughts exist independently of the brain. The brain is activated by thoughts is their correlate within the physical domain of form ... Like a radio that converts unseen energy waves into intelligible sound, the brain is a receiver instrument of the energies of thought forms." (Hawkins, *I: Reality and Subjectivity*, 215)

[17] Hawkins, *I: Reality and Subjectivity*, 101 and 307.

[18] Weber, "The Enfolding-Unfolding Universe," 72.

[19] Hawkins, "Realizing the Root of Consciousness: Meditative and Contemplative Techniques."

[20] From the context of the Map of Consciousness, the desire for peace begins to emerge at level 200 (Courage), where consciousness is no longer dominated by the energies of the lower emotions. (See appendix C for further discussion.)

Chapter 5: The Creative Condition

[1] Intelligence Quotient equals mental age divided by chronological age times 100 (IQ = MA/CA * 100).

[2] Andreasen, *The Creating Brain*, 11-13; Vernon, *Creativity*, 25-42.

[3] Kim, "Can only intelligent people be creative?: A meta-analysis."

[4] Gardner, *Multiple Intelligences*.

[5] *Creativity*, 25.

[6] Goswami, *The Self-Aware Universe*, 225.

[7] Rogers, *On Becoming a Person*, 350.

[8] Maslow, *Farther Reaches of Human Nature*, 58.

[9] de Bono, *Six Thinking Hats*, 89.

[10] Sheldrake, *Presence of the Past*, 308.

[11] Ghiselin, *The Creative Process*, 232.

[12] Vernon, *Creativity*, 91-97.

[13] Jung, *Archetypes and the Collective Unconscious*, 5.

[14] Ibid., 4.

[15] As Hawkins explains, "Consciousness is a universal quality, like the quality of physicality. Because genius is a characteristic of consciousness, genius also is universal. That which is universal is available to every man." (*Power vs. Force*, 165)

[16] Goleman, "The Art of Creativity."

[17] As Hawkins explains, "What characterizes this type [genius] is the capacity to utilize exhaustively what experience they have and to capitalize on it by the dedication necessary to reach a high degree of mastery." (*Power vs. Force*, 167)

[18] Einstein, Albert. 1991. *The Enlightened Mind*, ed. Stephen Mitchell, New York: Harper Collins, as quoted in Deikman, "A Functional Approach to Mysticism."

[19] Rilke, *Letters from a Young Poet*, 27.

[20] Gardner, *Creative Minds*, 32.

[21] Gruber and Davis, "Inching Our Way Up Mount Olympus," 265, as quoted in Lavery, "Creative Work: On the Method of Howard Gruber."

[22] Moore, "About Half of Americans Reading a Book."

[23] Robison, "Does Reading Still Stack Up?"

[24] Wilber, *Speaking of Everything.*

[25] Ghiselin, *The Creative Process*, 25.

[26] Hawkins, *Power vs. Force*, 164.

[27] An often-cited characteristic of creative genius is the approval of peers in the particular field of study. While this may be a useful characteristic in defining what one labels "creative genius," from the perspective of the genius, their cause is internally motivated. The person who is predominantly concerned with what everyone else thinks will likely be operating from fear—a mechanism of the ego—and will have difficulty aligning to true creative inspiration.

[28] Bohm, *On Creativity*, 4

[29] Creativity researcher Gowan, writes, "Incubation is the mental analog of physical gestation in which an ovum is developed into a baby. Incubation is the process of metamorphosis, and right-hemisphere imagery is the vehicle through which incubation produces creativity." ("Incubation, Imagery, and Creativity," 30)

[30] The Wanderer is "nonattached," which affords him the grace of enjoying his surroundings without needing (or wanting) to "own" anything in the surroundings in order to be happy.

[31] Hawkins: "The basis of this non-materiality, this seeming naiveté, is a radical understanding of the nature of the universe itself: that which supports life is supported by life; survival is thus effortless, and giving and receiving are one and the same thing." (*Power vs. Force*, 167)

[32] Vernon, *Creativity*, 55.

[33] Ghiselin, *The Creative Process*, 162.

[34] Ibid., 186.

[35] Jung noted, "The creative process has a feminine quality, and the creative work arises from unconsciousness depths—we might say, from the realm of the mothers." (Ghiselin, *The Creative Process*, 230)

[36] Ibid., 208.

[37] As the Terman study revealed, this dynamic is prevalent since the majority of people with unusually high IQs do NOT demonstrate creative genius.

[38] Zukav, *Dancing Wu Li Masters*, 9-10.

[39] Csikszentmihalyi, *Flow: The Psychology of Optimal Experience*.

[40] Whitney, "Matter of Heart."

[41] Abell, *Talks with Great Composers*, 19-21.

[42] Gowan, "Incubation, Imagery, and Creativity."

[43] Andreasen, *The Creating Brain*, 37.

[44] Ghiselin, *The Creative Process*, 51.

[45] Andreasen, *The Creating Brain*, 78. But remember that these neural processes are concomitant with creativity and NOT its *cause*. It's simply a *condition* that can be observed when the creative impulse is present.

[46] James, *The Varieties of Religious Experience*, 380-381.

[47] Maharshi, *I Am That*, 395.

[48] Dunn, *Seeds of Consciousness*, 62.

[49] Jung, *Modern Man in Search of the Soul*, 226; Ghiselin, *The Creative Process*, 220.

[50] Explained in numerous Hawkins' lectures in Sedona, Arizona.

[51] Sheldrake, *Presence of the Past*, 308.

[52] Erdman, *The Complete Poetry & Prose of William Blake*, 1.

[53] Abell, *Talks with Great Composers*, 117.

54 Ibid., 3.

55 Ghiselin, *The Creative Process*, 161.

56 Vernon, *Creativity*, 55.

57 Abell, *Talks with Great Composers*, 86.

58 Campbell, *Hero with a Thousand Faces*, 40.

59 This inner realization of Divinity is often termed "God Immanent" in the Eastern traditions as opposed to "God Transcendent" in Judeo-Christian religion that views God as something "out there" and beyond experiential reality.

60 Powell, *The Ultimate Medicine*, 177.

61 Ghiselin, *The Creative Process*, 34.

62 Ibid., 84.

63 Ibid., 80.

64 Ibid., 209-210.

65 Ibid., 52.

66 Andreasen, *The Creating Brain*, 37.

67 As Hawkins explains, "The capacity to finesse genius can be learned, though often through painful surrender, when the phoenix of genius arises out of the ashes of despair after a fruitless struggle with the unsolvable. Out of defeat comes victory, out of failure, success, and out of humbling, true self-esteem." (*Power vs. Force*, 166)

68 Ghiselin, *The Creative Process*, 47.

69 B. M. Kedrov, "On the Question of Scientific Creativity," Voprosy Psikologii, vol. 3, (1957): 91-113, as quoted in Harmon, *Higher Creativity*, 30-31.

70 Wilber, *A Theory of Everything*.

71 As Hawkins explains, "The universal characteristic of genius is humility. The genius has always attributed his insights to some higher influence." (*Power vs. Force*, 163)

72 Ghiselin, *The Creative Process*, 229.

[73] Erdman, *The Complete Poetry & Prose of William Blake*, 2. (From "All Religions are ONE")

[74] Andreasen, *The Creating Brain*, 6.

[75] Maslow, *The Farther Reaches of Human Nature*, 61.

[76] Similar to the state of "Flow" described by Csikszentmihalyi.

[77] Ibid., 353.

[78] Criticalness calibrates at 120.

[79] Ghiselin, *The Creative Process*, 185.

[80] Bohm, *On Creativity*, 20-24.

[81] Maslow, *The Farther Reaches of Human Nature*, 66.

[82] Ghiselin, *The Creative Process*, 229.

[83] Andreasen's research on random episodic silent thought (REST) using PET scans noted that when the person was unconsciously free associating, almost all of the brain activity was in the association cortex—the frontal, parietal and temporal lobes—the most sophisticated brain region, larger in humans than in other higher primates. The association cortex gathers information from the senses and other areas in the brain and links them together in potentially unique ways. (*The Creating Brain*, 72-73)

[84] See Maslow's Hierarchy of Human Needs in appendix B.

[85] Hawkins, *The Eye of the I*, 117.

[86] Rogers, *On Becoming a Person*, 353.

[87] See Maslow's Hierarchy of Human Needs in appendix B.

[88] Csikszentmihalyi, *Creativity*, 6.

[89] Andreasen, *The Creating Brain*, 110-120.

[90] Ibid., 129-132.

Chapter 6: The Guard to Creative Genius

[1] "Lizard brain," "leopard brain," and "learning brain" are terms found in Howard's *The Owner's Manual for the Brain*, 37-38.

[2] Cannon, *Bodily Changes in Pain, Hunger, Fear and Rage.*

[3] Selye, *Stress of Life.*

[4] This description of brain evolution is found in Pierce Howard's *The Owner's Manual for the Brain.* A similar explanation was given by neurophysiologist Paul D. MacLean where the brain consists of three separate but closely-interconnected layers representing our animal ancestry: Reptilian, Paleomammalian (Limbic System), and Neomammalian (see Mathew, *The True Path*, 164).

[5] Contrast the PC to Apple Computers, which were initially designed with a graphic user interface (GUI). Apples are known for their superior stability and functioning; they don't have a primitive architecture lurking in the background like the PC. (Yes, I'm a Mac user.)

[6] Howard, *The Owner's Manual for the Brain*, 39.

[7] Hawkins, *The Eye of the I*, 125.

[8] According to Hawkins' research, approximately 15% of the world's population calibrates above the critical level of Integrity (200). See appendix C for further explanation.

[9] Hawkins, *Truth vs. Falsehood*, 65.

[10] Ibid., 64-71.

[11] Andreasen, *The Creating Brain*, 146.

[12] Begley, "Scans of Monks Brains."

[13] Lazar, "Meditation experience is associated with increased cortical thickness."

[14] Mathew, *The True Path*, 224-234; Aftanas and Semen, "Impact of regular meditation practice on EEG activity at rest and during evoked negative emotions."

[15] Ibid.

[16] Ibid, 163-211.

[17] Freud, *The Ego and the Mechanisms of Defense.*

[18] Deikman, "A Functional Approach to Mysticism."

[19] As Jung inquired, "Do we delude ourselves in thinking that we possess and command our souls?" (Ghiselin, *The Creative Process*, 225)

[20] Hawkins, *I: Reality and Subjectivity*, 38.

[21] Abraham Maslow's Hierarchy of Human Needs demonstrates how certain base-level needs must be met before we move onto higher-level needs. The person who "needs" a Rolex to impress his friends is driven by outward Esteem Needs. Once this need is transcended, this individual's self-worth will no longer be derived from external validation. See appendix B for further discussion.

[22] Hill, *Think and Grow Rich*, 33-47.

[23] Robbins, *Live with Passion*.

[24] Hawkins, *Power vs. Force*, 64.

[25] Maslow, *A Theory of Human Motivation*.

[26] Foundation of Inner Peace, *A Course in Miracles*, 121. (Lesson 71)

[27] As Hawkins explains, "Positionality then automatically creates a duality of seeming opposites. At this point, the mind is creating the world of perception, which is like a lens that distorts, enlarges, or diminishes meaning and significance. The perception is the product of belief systems and presumptions and thus becomes a distracting filter. Therefore, essence cannot be perceived from a dualistic positionality." (*I: Reality and Subjectivity*, 119)

[28] Faherty, "Disproving Einstein harder than it looks."

[29] Hawkins, *The Eye of the I*, 84.

[30] Hawkins, *I: Reality and Subjectivity*, 39.

[31] Hawkins, *The Eye of the I*, 110.

[32] Maharshi, *I Am That*, 392.

[33] Hawkins, *Eye of the I*, 181.

[34] A phrase borrowed from Anthony Robbins.

[35] As Hawkins clearly explains, "Every mind has endless opinions on everything, even if it knows nothing at all about the subject. All opinions are vanities with no intrinsic value and are actually the result of ignorance. Opinions are dangerous to their owners because they are emotionally charged triggers for dissent, strife, argument, and positionality." (*Eye of the I*, 104-105)

[36] Hawkins explains, "The undoing of opinion is facilitated by humility; when the mind penetrates through its own self-infatuation, it discerns that it is not actually capable of knowing anything in the true sense of what knowing actually means. The mind has only information and imaginations *about* anything; it cannot actually 'know' because to know is to be that which is known. All else is only speculation and supposition." (Ibid., 105)

[37] An additional distinction should be drawn here between the spiritually advanced and the creative genius. Just because a person is aligned to high levels of creative achievement doesn't necessarily mean he is spiritually advanced to the point where he has transcended all his opinions, positions, and judgments. In fact, this is unlikely. Even from the perspective of the creative genius, they are still likely to hold varying degrees of positions. For example, Einstein, who reached the pinnacle of intellectual genius at calibration level 499, balked at the principles underlying quantum mechanics. After years of lively discussions with his contemporary Neil Bohr, another genius and one of the founders of quantum mechanics, Einstein was unable to surrender his position of an objective universe that existed beyond human consciousness, ultimately preventing him from embracing quantum mechanics. (See David Lindley's *Uncertainty*.)

[38] Plato, *The Nicomachean Ethics*, 12.

[39] Judge, *Bhagavad-Gita*, Chapter 3, 19.

[40] Merton, *The Way of Chuang Tzu*, 107.

[41] Brickman, "Lottery Winners and Accident Victims: Is Happiness Relative?"

[42] Their level of consciousness is such that their experiences are simply joyful. See appendix C for further discussion on levels of consciousness.

[43] Hawkins, *The Eye of the I*, 145; *I: Reality and Subjectivity*, 349-354.

[44] Hawkins, *Transcending the Levels*, 95.

[45] Hawkins, *The Eye of the I*, 100-105.

[46] Erdman, *The Complete Poetry & Prose of William Blake,* 470.

[47] Hawkins, *Transcending the Levels*, 158.

[48] Three *gunas* or attributes in Hindu philosophy are *tamas* (doership, inertia), *rajas* (activity, turmoil), and *sattva* (beingness, harmony).

Chapter 7: Finding Higher Ground

[1] Bohm, *On Creativity*, 32. (Italics are my emphasis.)

[2] In the case of the Mystic, the ego-mind is completely vanquished and the state of Oneness prevails eternally.

[3] Based on a book with the same title by Steven Pressfield.

[4] Suzuki, *The Zen Doctrine of No-Mind.*

[5] Rodes, *A Dictionary of Environmental Quotations*, 53.

[6] Maslow, *Farther Reaches of Human Nature*, 66.

[7] Philosopher Arthur Koestler believed the connection of two ideas from different contexts, what he called "bisociation," was the key behind an understanding of the creative act. He puts forth a compelling dissertation in his book, *The Act of Creation.*

[8] Bohm's little book *On Dialogue* showcases his essays on the subject and offers valuable insight and direction on how to facilitate these open dialogues. His book, *Thought as a System*, is essentially the transcript of such a dialogue.

[9] Bohm, *On Creativity*, 32.

[10] Heisenberg, *Physics and Philosophy*, 46.

[11] Hawkins, *Power vs. Force*, 164.

[12] Gruber, "The Emergence of a Sense of Purpose," 6, as quoted in Lavery, "Creative Work: On the Method of Howard Gruber."

[13] Lindley, *Uncertainty*, 111.

[14] Sullivan, "The Einstein Papers: A Man of Many Parts."

[15] Hawkins spends a great deal of time clarifying this difference in *The Eye of the I* and *I: Reality and Subjectivity* as well as his lectures held in Sedona, Arizona.

[16] Hawkins, *Truth vs. Falsehood*, 266.

[17] Countries with calibrated levels below 200 are not interested in resolution; in fact, calibrated levels below 200 represent purely primitive drives and self-interest.

[18] Robbins reminds his audience of this mantra repeatedly at his public events like "Unleash the Power Within."

[19] Wilber, *A Theory of Everything* and *Integral Operating System*.

[20] de Bono, *Six Thinking Hats*.

[21] Bohm, *On Dialogue*.

[22] Hawkins, *Transcending the Levels of Consciousness*.

[23] Hawkins, *I: Reality and Subjectivity*. 152-153.

[24] Hawkins, *Truth vs. Falsehood*, 210.

[25] Using the kinesiologic response, anything below 200 is represented by a non-response whereas everything above 200, from the quantum perspective, demonstrates a collapse of the wave function signifying existence in Reality.

[26] Hawkins, *Truth vs. Falsehood*, 131. (Wal-Mart's founder, Sam Walton calibrated at 380, as did his company.)

[27] Ibid.

[28] Often called the "etheric body" in metaphysical literature.

[29] Emerson, "Spiritual Laws," 32.

[30] Edison, *The Diary and Sundry Observations of Thomas Alva Edison*, 56.

Epilogue

[1] Hawkins, *The Eye of the I*, 177.

[2] See Huxley's *The Perennial Philosophy*, chapter 1.

[3] Additionally, the spiritual domain is only understandable and attractive to those who have a natural propensity or drive for understanding it.

[4] Maharshi, *The Spiritual Teaching of Ramana Maharshi*, 48.

[5] Williams, "Too much e-mail! A new IABC survey suggests who is to blame and what we can do about it."

Appendix A: A Brief History of Quantum Theory

[1] The following explanation is derived mainly from University of California, Berkeley, physicist Henry Stapp's quantum approach to consciousness (also discussed in appendix D of Hawkins' book *I: Reality and Subjectivity*).

[2] Zukav, *The Dancing Wu Li Masters*, 73.

[3] Ibid., 112.

[4] Stapp, Lucerne Lecture.

[5] Ibid.

[6] Stapp, "Attention, Intention, and Will in Quantum Physics."

[7] From Stapp: "Von Newmann capitalized upon the key Copenhagen move of bringing human knowings into the theory of physical reality." (*The Mindful Universe*, 57)

[8] Stapp, "Quantum Theory of the Human Person."

[9] As Stapp explains: "Given a well posed question about the world to which one's attention is directed, quantum theory says that nature either gives the affirmative answer, in which case there

occurs an experience describable as "Yes, I perceive it!" or, alternatively, no experience occurs in connection with that question." ("Attention, Intention and Will in Quantum Physics")

[10] From the perspective of Hawkins' Map of Consciousness, anything above the level of Courage (200) collapses the wave function, whereas anything below 200 does not.

[11] Goswami, *The Self-Aware Universe*, 60.

Appendix B: The Perennial Philosophy Revisited

[1] Wilber, *The Atman Project*.

[2] Huxley, *The Perennial Philosophy*, 1-21.

[3] Wilber, *Holographic Paradigm*.

[4] Balsekar, *Pointers from Nisargadatta Maharaj*, 221.

[5] Campbell, *Mythos*, Disc 9.

[6] John 10:30.

[7] *The Upanishads*, 60.

[8] Ibid., 61.

[9] Maslow, *A Theory of Human Motivation*, 370.

[10] Maslow, *Religions, Values, and Peak-Experiences*.

Appendix C: A Theory of Everything

[1] Hawkins, *Power vs. Force*, 54.

[2] Proof is restricted to the linear domain of the 400s; only that which is clearly measurable and definable can be provable.

[3] See Hawkins' "Qualitative and Quantitative Analysis and Calibrations of the Level of Human Consciousness," *Power vs. Force*, and *Truth vs. Falsehood*.

[4] Hawkins, *Truth vs. Falsehood*, 6-7.

[5] Using the physiologic response, anything below 200 is represented by a non-response whereas everything above 200, from the quantum perspective, demonstrates a collapse of the wave function signifying existence in Reality.

[6] Hawkins, *Truth vs. Falsehood*, 35. (It was 78% below 200, but at press the percentage had risen to 85%.)

[7] Hawkins, *Power vs. Force*, 234.

[8] Hawkins, *Truth vs. Falsehood*, 23.

[9] Hawkins, *Power vs. Force*, 163.

[10] Gardner, *Creating Minds*, 50-86. Interestingly, both Freud and Jung's psychoanalytical approach calibrate at 460, according to Hawkins, while the overall field of psychology calibrates at 420. This disparity translates to a psychological community that is still unable to comprehend the genius of the psychoanalytical approach.

[11] Cohen, "Freud Is Widely Taught at Universities, Except in the Psychology Department."

[12] Ghiselin, *The Creative Process*, 232.

[13] Personal research.

[14] Private conversation with Dr. Hawkins.

[15] Ueland, *If You Want To Write*, 172.

[16] Frankl, *Man's Search for Meaning*, 57.

[17] These calibrations can be found in Hawkins' *Truth vs. Falsehood* (Axial Publishing 2005).

[18] Ibid.

Appendix D: Glossary

[1] Hawkins, *I: Reality and Subjectivity*, 38.

Bibliography

Abbott, Edwin A. 1992. *Flatland: A Romance of Many Dimensions*. New York: Dover Publications.

Abell, Arthur. 1994. *Talks with the Great Composers*. New York: Citadel Press.

Aftanas, Ljubomir, and Semen Golosheykin. 2005. Impact of Regular Meditation Practice on EEG Activity at Rest and During Evoked Negative Emotions. *International Journal of Neuroscience* 115 (6): 893-909.

Andreasen, Nancy C. 2005. *The Creating Brain: The Neuroscience of Genius*. New York: Dana Press.

Aristotle. 1996. *The Nicomachean Ethics*. Edited by Martin Ostwald. Ware, Hertfordshire: Wordsworth Editions.

Arntz, William, and Betsy Chassy (dir). 2005. *What the #$*! Do We Know!?* DVD. Los Angeles: 20th Century Fox.

Aurelius, Marcus. 2002. *Meditations*. Trans. by Gregory Hays. New York: The Modern Library.

Bacon, John U. 2006. *Cirque du Soleil: The Spark*. With Lyn Heward. New York: Currency Doubleday.

Balsekar, Ramesh S. 1982. *Pointers from Nisargadatta Maharaj*. Durham, NC: The Acorn Press.

_____. 1989. *A Duet of One: The Ashtavakra Gita Dialogue*. Los Angeles: Advaita Press.

Begley, Sharon. 2004. Scans of Monks' Brains Show Meditation Alters Structure and Functioning. *Wall Street Journal* (Science Journal), November 5: B1.

Bell, John S. 1964. On the Einstein Podolsky Rosen paradox. *Physics* 1 (3): 195-200.

Bennett, Matthew, et al. 2002. Huygens's Clocks. *Proceedings: Mathematical, Physical and Engineering Sciences* 458 (2019): 563-79.

Bentov, Itzhak. 1988. *Stalking the Wild Pendulum: On the Mechanics of Consciousness*. Rochester, VT: Destiny Books.

Bohm, David. 1980. *Wholeness and the Implicate Order*. London: Routledge Classics.

————. 1990. A New Theory of the Relationship of Mind and Matter. *Philosophical Psychology* 3 (2): 271-86.

————. 1994. *Thought as a System*. London: Routledge Classics.

————. 1996. *On Creativity*. London: Routledge Classics.

Brewster, David, ed. 2001. *Memoirs of the Life, Writings, and Discoveries of Sir Isaac Newton*. Boston: Elibron Classics.

Brickman, Philip, Dan Coates, and Ronnie Janoff-Bulman. 1978. Lottery Winners and Accident Victims: Is Happiness Relative? *Journal of Personality and Social Psychology* 36 (8): 917-27.

Briggs, John. 1992. *Fractals: The Patterns of Chaos*. New York: Simon & Schuster.

Briggs, John, and F. David Peat. 1990. *Turbulent Mirror: An Illustrate Guide to Chaos Theory and the Science of Wholeness*. New York: Harper & Row.

Buck, John. 1988. Synchronous Rhythmic Flashing of Fireflies. *The Quarterly Review of Biology* 63 (3): 265-89.

Campbell, Joseph. 1973. *The Hero with a Thousand Faces*. Princeton, NJ: Princeton University Press.

————. 1988. *The Power of Myth*. With Bill Moyers. New York: Doubleday.

————. 1997. *Mythos: The Shaping of Our Mythic Tradition*, DVD Series. New York: Wellspring Media.

Cannon, W.B. 1929. *Bodily Changes in Pain, Hunger, Fear and Rage*. New York: Appleton.

———. 1932. *Wisdom of the Body*. New York: W. W. Norton.

Capra, Fritjof. 1984. *The Turning Point: Science, Society, and the Rising Culture*. New York: Bantam.

———. 2000. *The Tao of Physics*. Boston: Shambhala.

Cohen, Patricia. 2007. Freud Is Widely Taught at Universities, Except in the Psychology Department. *The New York Times*. November 25.

Cousins, Norman. 2005. *Anatomy of an Illness as Perceived by the Patient*. New York: W.W. Norton & Company.

Covey, Stephen R. 1989. *The Seven Habits of Highly Effective People*. New York: Simon & Schuster.

Csikszentmihalyi, Mihaly. 1997. *Creativity: Flow and the Psychology of Discovery and Invention*. New York: Harper Perennial.

———. 2005. Flow, *Handbook of Competence and Motivation*, New York: Gilford Press, April.

de Bono, Edward. 1999. *Six Thinking Hats*. New York: Back Bay Books.

Deikman, Arthur. 1996. I = Awareness. *Journal of Consciousness Studies* 3 (40): 350-6.

———. 2000. A Functional Approach to Mysticism. *Journal of Consciousness Studies* 7 (11-12): November/December.

Descartes, René. 1999. *Discourse on Method and Related Writings*. Trans. by Desmond M. Clarke. New York: Penguin Classics.

Dorsey, Larry. 2000. *Reinventing Medicine: Beyond Mind-Body to a New Era of Healing*. San Francisco: HarperSanFrancisco.

Dunn, Jean, ed. 1982. *Seeds of Consciousness: The Wisdom of Sri Nisargadatta Maharaj*. Durham, NC: The Acorn Press.

———. 1985. *Prior to Consciousness: Talks with Sri Nisargadatta Maharaj*. Durham, NC: The Acorn Press.

_____. 1994. *Consciousness and the Absolute: The Final Talks of Sri Nisargadatta Maharaj.* Durham, NC: The Acorn Press.

Eadie, Betty J. 1994. *Embraced by the Light.* New York: Bantam.

Easwaran, Eknath, trans. 1985. *The Dhammapada.* Tomales, CA: Nilgiri Press.

_____. 1985. *Bhagadvad Gita.* Tomales, CA: Nilgiri Press.

_____. 1997. *The Upanishads.* Tomales, CA: Nilgiri Press.

Eccles, John and Daniel N. Robinson. 1984. *The Wonder of Being Human: Our Brain and Our Mind.* New York: The Free Press.

Edison, Thomas Alva. 1948. *The Diary and Sundry Observations of Thomas Alva Edison.* Ed. by Dagobert D. Runes. New York: Philosophical Library.

Emerson, Ralph Waldo. 1883. "Spiritual Laws." In *Works of Ralph Waldo Emerson*, 30-8. New York: George Routledge and Sons.

Erdman, David V., ed. 1988. *The Complete Poetry & Prose of William Blake.* New York: Anchor Books.

Faherty, John. 2006. Disproving Einstein harder than it looks. *The Arizona Republic*, November 16.

Feinstein, David. 1998. At Play in the Fields of the Mind: Personal Myths as Fields of Information. *Journal of Humanistic Psychology* 38 (3): 71-109.

Foundation for Inner Peace. 1996. *A Course in Miracles.* New York: Viking Press.

Frankl, Victor. 1984. *Man's Search for Meaning.* New York: Pocket Books.

Freud, Anna. 2000. *The Ego and the Mechanisms of Defense.* Madison, CT: International Universities Press, Inc.

Gardner, Howard. 1993. *Creating Minds.* New York: Basic Books.

_____. 2006. *Multiple Intelligences.* New York: Basic Books.

Gerber, Michael E. 1995. *The E-Myth Revisited.* New York: HarperCollins.

Ghiselin, Brewster, ed. 1985. *The Creative Process*. Berkeley, CA: University of California Press.

Gleick, James. 1987. *Chaos: Making a New Science*. New York: Penguin Books.

Godman, David, ed. 1985. *Be As You Are: The Teachings of Sri Ramana Maharshi*. London: Penguin Arkana.

Goleman, David. 1992. The Art of Creativity. *Psychology Today*, 40-47, March.

Goswami, Amit. 1993. *The Self-Aware Universe: How Consciousness Creates the Material World*. New York: Tarcher/Putnam.

Gowan, John C. 1975. *Trance, Art, and Creativity*. Buffalo, NY: Creative Education Foundation.

http://www.csun.edu/edpsy/Gowan/content.html

_____. 1976. Some New Thoughts on the Development of Creativity. *The Journal of Creative Behavior* 11 (2).

_____. 1978. Incubation, Imagery and Creativity. *Journal of Mental Imagery*, 2.

Gyatso, Tenzin, H.H. the Dalai Lama. 2005. *The Universe in a Single Atom: The Convergence of Science and Spirituality*. New York: Morgan Road Books.

Harokopos, Efthimios. 2005. "Power as the Cause of Motion and a New Foundation of Classical Mechanics," *Progress in Physics*, 2, July.

Hawkins, David R. 1995. *Qualitative and Quantitative Analysis and Calibrations of the Level of Human Consciousness*. Sedona, AZ: Veritas Publishing.

_____. 1995. *Power vs. Force: An Anatomy of Consciousness*. Sedona, AZ: Veritas Publishing.

_____. 2001. *The Eye of the I*. Sedona, AZ: Veritas Publishing.

_____. 2002. "Ego and Causality." Lecture 1, January. Sedona, AZ: Veritas Publishing.

_____. 2002. "Realizing the Root of Consciousness: Meditative and Contemplative Techniques." Lecture 6, June. Sedona, AZ: Veritas Publishing.

_____. 2003. *I: Reality and Subjectivity*. Sedona, AZ: Veritas Publishing.

_____. 2005. *Truth vs. Falsehood*. Toronto: Axial Publishing Company.

_____. 2006. *Transcending the Levels of Consciousness*. Sedona, AZ: Veritas Publishing.

_____. 2006. *Discovery of the Presence of God*. Sedona, AZ: Veritas Publishing.

_____. 2006. Paradigm Blindness: Academic vs. Clinical Medicine. *Journal of Orthomolecular Medicine* 21 (4): 1997-9.

Heisenberg, Werner. 1958. *Physics and Philosophy: The Revolution in Modern Science*. New York: Harper.

Hill, Napoleon. 1987. *Think and Grow Rich*. New York: Ballantine Books.

Howard, Pierce. 2000. *The Owner's Manual for the Brain*. Atlanta: Bard Press.

Hunt, Valerie. 1996. *Infinite Mind: Science of the Human Vibrations of Consciousness*. Malibu, CA: Malibu Press.

Huxley, Aldous. 2004. *The Perennial Philosophy*. New York: Perennial Classics.

James, William. 1985. *Psychology: Briefer Course*. Boston: Harvard University Press.

_____. 1985. *The Varieties of Religious Experience*. New York: Penguin Books.

Judge, William Q. 1978. *Bhagavad-Gita / Essays on the Gita*. Pasadena, CA: Theosophical University Press.

Jung, Carl. 1933. *Modern Man in Search of a Soul*. New York: Harcourt, Brace & World, Inc.

_____. 1969. *Archetypes and the Collective Unconscious*. New York: Bollingen Foundation.

———. 1969. *The Structure and Dynamics of the Psyche.* 2nd ed. Trans. by R. F. C. Hull. Collected Works 8. Princeton, NJ: Princeton University Press.

———. 1973. *Synchronicity: An Acausal Connecting Principle.* Princeton, NJ: Princeton University Press.

———. 1993. *The Basic Writings of C. G. Jung.* New York: The Modern Library.

Kandel, Eric R. 2006. *In Search of Memory: The Emergence of a New Science of Mind.* New York: W.W. Norton.

Kane, Gordon. 2006. The Dawn of Physics Beyond the Standard Model. *Scientific American* (February 20): 4-11.

Kim, Kyung Hee. 2005. Can Only Intelligent People be Creative?: A Meta-Analysis. *The Journal of Secondary Gifted Education* 16 (2/3): 57-66.

Koestler, Arthur. 1989. *The Act of Creation.* London: Arkana.

Krauss, Andreas. 2006. False Memory. Interview with Elizabeth Loftus. *Scientific American Mind* (February 6): 14-15.

Krishnamurti, J. 1987. *The Awakening of Intelligence.* San Francisco: HarperSanFrancisco.

Kuhn, Thomas. 1996. *The Structure of Scientific Revolutions.* Chicago: The University of Chicago Press.

Lavery, David. 1993. Creative Work: On the Method of Howard Gruber. *The Journal of Humanistic Psychology* 33 (2): 101-21.

Lazar, Sarah W., et al. 2005. Meditation Experience is Associated With Increased Cortical Thickness. *NeuroReport*, 16: 1893-7.

Lehrer, Jonah. 2005. The Reinvention of the Self. *Seed.* February/March.

Libet, Benjamin. 2004. *Mind Time: The Temporal Factor in Consciousness.* Cambridge, MA: Harvard University Press.

———. 2006. Reflections on the Interaction of the Mind and Brain. *Progress in Neurobiology.* 78: 322-6.

Lindley, David. 2007. *Uncertainty*. New York: Doubleday.

Lynds, Peter. 2003. Time and Classical and Quantum Mechanics: Indeterminacy vs. Discontinuity. *Foundations of Physics Letters.* 16 (4).

––––––. 2003. Subjective Perception of Time and a Progressive Present Moment: The Neurobiological Key to Unlocking Consciousness. http://cogprints.org/3125/

Macdonald, Brad. 2005. Moral Relativism. *Philadelphia Trumpet*, July.

Mackay, Charles. 1980. *Extraordinary Popular Delusions & the Madness of the Crowds*. New York: Three Rivers Press.

Maharaj, Sri Nisargadatta. 1973. *I Am That*. Trans. By Maurice Frydman. Durham, NC: The Acorn Press.

Maharshi, Ramana. 1998. *The Spiritual Teachings of Ramana Maharshi*. Boston: Shambhala.

Maslow, Abraham H. 1943. A Theory of Human Motivation. *Psychological Review* 50 (4): 370-96.

––––––. 1968. *Toward of Psychology of Being*. New York: Van Nostrand Reinhold.

––––––. 1970. *Religions, Values, and Peak-Experiences*. New York: Penguin Compass.

––––––. 1971. *The Farther Reaches of Human Nature*. New York: Penguin Compass.

Mathew, Roy. 2001. *The True Path: Western Science and the Quest for Yoga*. Cambridge, MA: Perseus Publishing.

Merton, Thomas, trans. 1965. *The Way of Chuang Tzu*. New York: New Directions Publishing.

Mikkelsen, Tarjei S., et al. 2005. Initial Sequence of the Chimpanzee Genome and Comparison with the Human Genome. *Nature* 437 (7055): 69-87.

Miller, A.V. 1977. *Hegel's Phenomenology of Spirit*. Oxford: Oxford University Press.

Moore, David W. 2005. About Half of Americans Reading a Book. *Gallup*, June 3.

Muktananda. 2000. *Play of Consciousness*. South Fallsburg, NY: Syda Foundation.

Nelson, Roger. 2001. Correlation of Global Events with REG Date: An Internet-Based, Nonlocal Anomalies Experiment. *The Journal of Parapsychology*. 65 (September): 247-71.

Pilzer, Paul Zane. 1991. *Unlimited Wealth*. New York: Crown.

Plato. 1987. *Theaetetus*. Trans. by Robin A.H. Waterfield. London: Penguin Classics.

_____. 1989. *Meno*. Translated by W.K.C. Guthrie. In *The Collected Dialogues of Plato—Including the Letters*. Edited by Edith Hamilton and Huntington Cairns. Princeton, NJ: Princeton University Press.

_____. 1992. *Republic*. Translated by G.M.A. Grube. Indianapolis, MN: Hackett Publishing Company.

Potts, Wayne K. 1984. The Chorus Line Hypothesis of Maneuver Coordination in Avian Flocks. *Nature* 309 (5966): 344-5.

Powell, Robert, ed. 2001. *The Ultimate Medicine: As Prescribed by Sri Nisargadatta Ma*haraj. San Diego, CA: Blue Dove Press.

_____. 2001. *The Nectar of Immortality: Sri Nisargadatta Maharaj's Discourses on the Eternal*. San Diego, CA: Blue Dove Press.

Pratt, David. 1997. Consciousness, Causality, and Quantum Physics. *Journal of Scientific Exploration* 11 (1) Spring.

Radin, Dean. 1997. *The Conscious Universe: Scientific Truth of Psychic Phenomena*. San Francisco: HarperEdge.

Ragas, Matthew W., and Bolivar J. Bueno. 2002. *The Power of Cult Branding*. New York: Prima Venture.

Ray, Paul, and Sherry R. Anderson. 2001. *The Cultural Creatives: How 50 Million People Are Changing the World*. New York: Three Rivers Press.

Rilke, Rainer Maria. 2004. *Letters to a Young Poet.* New York: W. W. Norton & Company.

Rodes, Barbara K., and Rice Odell. 1992. *A Dictionary of Environmental Quotations.* New York: Simon & Schuster.

Robbins, Anthony. 1998. *The Time of Your Life: More Time for What Really Matters to You.* Audio Series. San Diego, CA: Robbins Research International.

_____. 2002. *Live with Passion: Strategies for Creating a Compelling Future.* Audio Series. Chicago: Nightingale-Conant.

Robison, Jennifer. 2002. Does Reading Still Stack Up? *Gallup,* September 3.

Rogers, Carl R. 1989. *On Becoming a Person.* Boston: Houghton Mifflin Company.

Roth, Gerhard, and Ursula Dicke. 2005. Evolution of the Brain and Intelligence. *Trends in Cognitive Sciences* 9 (5): 250-7.

Sarath, Ed. 2006. Meditation, Creativity, and Consciousness: Charting Future Terrain With Higher Education. *Teachers College Record,* 108 (9): 1819.

Selye, H. 1952. *The Story of the Adaptation Syndrome.* Montreal: Acta.

_____. 1978. *Stress of Life.* New York: McGraw-Hill.

Shakespeare, William. 1992. *Hamlet.* Folger Shakespearean Library edition. Edited by Barbara A. Mowat and Paul Werstine. New York: Washington Square Press.

Sheldrake, Rupert. 1981. *A New Science of Life: The Hypothesis of Morphic Resonance.* Rochester, VT: Park Street Press.

_____. 1987. Mind, Memory, and Archetype: Morphic Resonance and the Collective Unconscious. *Psychological Perspective.* 18 (1): 9-25.

_____. 1988. *The Presence of the Past: Morphic Resonance & the Habits of Nature.* Rochester, VT: Park Street Press.

_____. 2002. *Seven Experiments that Could Change the World.* Rochester, VT: Park Street Press.

Stapp, Henry P. 1999. Attention, Intention, and Will in Quantum Physics. *Journal of Consciousness Studies* 6 (May 24).

———. 2001. Quantum Mechanics and the Role of Mind in Nature. *Foundations of Physics* 31: 1465-99.

———. 2003. Lucerne Lecture: Quantum Theory of the Human Person. January 19. http://www-physics.lbl.gov/~stapp/stappfiles.html.

———. 2007. *Mindful Universe*. New York: Springer.

Stewart, Ian. 2002. *Does God Play Dice? The New Mathematics of Chaos*. Malden, MA: Blackwell Publishing.

Strogatz, Steven. 2003. *Sync: How Order Emerges from Chaos in the Universe, Nature, and Daily Life*. New York: Theia.

Sullivan, Walter. 1972. The Einstein Papers: A Man of Many Parts. *The New York Times*, March 29.

Suzuki, D.T. 1991. *The Zen Doctrine of No-Mind: The Significance of the Sutra of Hui-Neng*. York Beach, ME: Weiser Books.

Talbot, Michael. 1992. *The Holographic Universe*. New York: Harper Perennial.

Terman, L. W. 1959. *Genetic Studies of Genius*. Stanford, CA: Stanford University Press.

Thomas, Bob. 1976. *Walt Disney: An American Original*. New York: Simon & Schuster.

Ueland, Brenda. 1987. *If You Want to Write: A Book About Art, Independence and Spirit*. Saint Paul, MN: Graywolf Press.

Vernon, P. E., ed. 1970. *Creativity: Selected Readings*. Middlesex, England: Penguin Books.

Wada, Stephanie. 2002. *The Oxherder: A Zen Parable Illustrated*. New York: George Braziller.

Wallas, Graham. 1926. *The Art of Thought*. New York: Harcourt Brace.

Weil, Andrew. 2000. *Spontaneous Healing*. New York: Ballantine Books.

Wells, Gary L., et al. 2000. From Lab to the Police Station: A Successful Application of Eyewitness Research. *American Psychologist* 55 (6): 581-98.

Wheatley, Margaret J. 1999. *Leadership and the New Science.* San Francisco: Berrett-Koehler Publishers.

Whitney, Mark, dir. 1985. *Matter of Heart: The Extraordinary Journey of C.G. Jung.* DVD. New York: Kino Video.

Wilber, Ken, ed. 1982. *The Holographic Paradigm and Other Paradoxes.* Boulder, CO: Shambhala.

———. 1996. *The Atman Project: A Transpersonal View of Human Development.* Wheatlon, IL: Quest Books.

———. 2001. *A Theory of Everything.* Boston: Shambhala.

———. 2001. *Speaking of Everything.* Audio program. Menlo Park, CA: Enlightenment.com.

Williams, Ryan and Tudor Williams. 2006. Too Much E-mail! A New IABC Survey Suggests Who Is To Blame And What We Can Do About It."(IABC = International Association of Business Communicators). *Communication World*, November 1.

Young, James Webb. 2003. *A Technique for Producing an Idea.* New York: McGraw-Hill.

Zukav, Gary. 1979. *The Dancing Wu Li Masters.* New York: Bantam Books.

Acknowledgements

A work such as this involves a great many talented folks aligned to various aspects of the creative impulse. Quite honestly, very little of this work can be said to be "original," outside perhaps the presentation and contextualization of the assembled information.

First and foremost, my deepest gratitude, love, and appreciation to Dr. David R. Hawkins whose work provided both the impetus and continued inspiration and guidance for this project. Other notable inspiration was provided by brilliant minds like David Bohm, Carl Jung, Albert Einstein, Joseph Campbell, Nisargadatta Maharaj, Ramana Maharshi, Plato, and Socrates.

To Aaron Shields, for his unsurpassed research skills and ability to find even the most elusive references.

To Misty Williams, for her incredibly thorough editing skills and caring dedication to improving the readability and comprehensibility of the manuscript.

To Jared McDaniel, for his graphic design gifts of translating an idea for the book cover into a work of art.

To the advanced readers of the manuscript, Robert D. Smith, Charles Shanok, Ozzie Coto, Steve Flood, Patricia Leonard, Tova Kaplan, and Andrew Colyer for their encouragement and comments to help improve readability. A special thank you to Matt Laughlin who provided insightful suggestions to improve the overall quality of the work.

To my parents, Carrie and Steve, for their continuous unconditional loving support.

To Jenny Lee, for whose continuous encouragement, thoughtful comments, inquisitive nature, and love helped create a better book.

To my brother and partner-in-arms, Bolivar J. Bueno, for his insights, creativity, and uniquely-gifted mind. You are a constant source of inspiration and a true friend.

Gloria in Excelsis Deo

About the Author

Scott Jeffrey is a writer, executive coach, and life-long student of Truth. He is a managing partner of Nonbox Consulting, a consumer insight think tank that lends its signature ingenuity to clients like Kohl's Department Stores, Scheels, LA Lakers and Turner Classic Movies. Scott is also the author of *Journey to the Impossible: Designing an Extraordinary Life,* a Benjamin Franklin award finalist.

Creativity Revealed is a project Scott researched and developed for nearly five years. He received his Bachelor of Arts from the University of Michigan. Scott lives in the foothills of the Catskill Mountains in Upstate New York, which allows him to sift through the chaos from the rivers of his own creativity.

Visit Scott's Web site:
www.scottjeffrey.com

Index